Protesting on Bended Knee

Race, Dissent, and Patriotism in
21st Century America

All works in this book are licensed under a

Creative Commons
By Attribution 4.0 International License
unless otherwise indicated.

Book Design: William Caraher
Cover Design: Chris Olsen

Library of Congress Control Number: 2018911511
Digital Press at The University of North Dakota, The, Grand Forks, NORTH DAKOTA

ISBN-13: 978-1-7328410-0-0
ISBN-10: 1-7328410-0-4

Protesting on Bended Knee

Race, Dissent, and Patriotism in 21st Century America

Edited by
Eric Burin

The Digital Press at the University of North Dakota
Grand Forks, ND

*A first draft of history for
Max and Zoey*

Table of Contents

OPENING CEREMONIES

A Regent of Justice
D. M. Kingsford i

PREFACE

Praesens Historicum (The Historic Present)
Eric Burin iii

INTRODUCTION

Race, Dissent, and Patriotism in 21st Century America
Eric Burin 1

SECTION ONE: THE UNITED STATES AND ITS ANTHEM

"Oh Say, Can You See?": The National Anthem
Jon Foreman 87

Mild Protest
Clay S. Jenkinson 93

SECTION TWO: THE LAW

Bearing Witness for Civil Liberties
Shawn Peters 101

Trump's National Anthem Outrage
Ignores Decades of Supreme Court Rulings
Emma Long 105

Anthem Protests in High School Athletics
Mark Rerick 111

Celebrity Voices are Powerful,
But Does the First Amendment
Let Them Say Anything They Want?
Shontavia Johnson 115

The Surprising Connection between
'Take a Knee' Protests and Citizen United
Elizabeth C. Tippett 123

Section Three: Athlete-Activists

#PlayingWhileWhite: The Colin Kaepernick Saga and the (A)political White Athlete
David J. Leonard 133

Black Women Athletes, Protest, and Politics:
An Interview with Amira Rose Davis
Ashley D. Farmer 141

Voices Beneath the Helmets:
Athletes as Political Outsiders
Joseph Kalka 149

The Oppressive Seeds of the Colin Kaepernick Backlash
J. Corey Williams 157

A Former NFL Players Explains
Why We Need More Colin Kaepernicks
[An Interview with Chris Kluwe]
Matt Connolly 165

What Does It Mean to be Important?
Jack Russell Weinstein 171

Section Four: Tactics

Allen's Knee
Richard Newman 177

Colin Kaepernick and the Power of Black Silent Protest
Ameer Hasan Loggins 179

African American Patriotism during the World War I Era
David Krugler 187

We Interrupt This Program
Sharon Carson 195

E Kaepernick Unum: How Our Changing Media Habits
Have Left Sports Our Place for Diverse Debate
Sarah Cavanah 201

Section Five: Counter-Tactics

"They Will Use This Against You":
The Context and Legacy of the 2001 France vs. Algeria Protests
Andrew N. Wegmann 207

Unite the Right, Colin Kaepernick, and Social Media
Azmar K. Williams 215

Endgames
Mark Stephen Jendrysik 221

Reparations as Fantasy:
Remembering the Black-Fisted Silent Protest at the
1968 Mexico City Games
Jamal Ratchford 225

Section Six: Others in the Arena

Why Sports Journalists Shouldn't Just "Stick to Sports"
Brad Elliott Schlossman 233

Coaches, Athletes, and Colin Kaepernick
Gelaine Orvik 235

Learning Extends Beyond the Practice Field
Mike Berg 239

If You're Explaining, You're Losing:
Questioning Kaepernick's Tactics, Not Cause
Mac Schneider and David Butler 243

How Social Activism Can Clash with Military Core Values
Randy Nedegaard 247

The Veteran View of Colin Kaepernick
Matt Eidson 253

The Difference Between
Black Football Fans and White Football Fans
Tamir Sorek and Robert G. White 257

A Regent of Justice

D. M. Kingsford

Then kneel before your
        queen, knee capped
    by hands up still shot,
       brought to bear
         the weight of your men and
            women and sexless
                children who
             didn't even
       have time to
      beg for their lives,

       kneel, then, before justice
           who blindly
         sways with a wind
           which isn't
      meant to billow your sails, for
     you were never afforded
       them,
athleticism and good looks,
      brains and charm, but for
    all that, as much a target
down range as anyone.

        kneel, and while you do, pray
          for change.

Praesens Historicum (The Historic Present)

Eric Burin

"Believe in something. Even if it means sacrificing everything," urges an advertisement featuring Colin Kaepernick. The passage is inscribed across an undoctored, black-and-white close-up of Kaepernick's face, a nine-word label affixed right below his eyes, which stare directly and forever forward. The ad is for NIKE, the corporate colossus that generates two-and-half times as much revenue as the National Football League (NFL), and it was unveiled to hyperbolic praise and condemnation in early September 2018, just as this volume was going to press. That a marketing campaign showcasing Kaepernick could roil emotions and dominate headlines testifies to the electrifying nature of his historic crusade against inequality generally and police brutality particularly. Kaepernick began protesting these matters on the field of play in August 2016, when he was a San Francisco 49ers' quarterback, doing so initially by sitting and later by kneeling during the national anthem. Others followed suit. These gestures incited a national furor, and several of this volume's essays were originally published during that tumultuous period. A little over a year later, in September 2017, Kaepernick was out of the NFL, a free agent unable to secure employment despite the fact that many of the league's thirty-two teams needed a good quarterback and that Kaepernick's statistics indicated that he merited a shot. But Kaepernick remained sidelined and only about a dozen NFL players were still demonstrating during the anthem. Then President Donald Trump, while attending a rally in Alabama, addressed the issue using derogatory language, exhorting team owners to fire protesters and encouraging fans to quit watching games if they witnessed a demonstration. Trump's harangue landed like a lit match in a tinderbox, and amid the ensuing conflagration were written most of this volume's essays. All of the essays offer perceptive insights about the protests; collectively, they provide a panoramic view of them; most importantly, they show, as does the Introduction, that this tale, with its vast cast and varied scenes, with its knotty conundrums that could not be undone perhaps by any means, was but the latest chapter in a still-grander saga, that of black Americans' fight for freedom, an epic struggle that has necessitated many sacrificing some and some sacrificing everything.

Section One, "The United States and Its Anthem," situates the Kaepernick-inspired protests within the larger story of Americans' quest to secure the rights of "life, liberty, and the pursuit of happiness" and to form "a more perfect union." National anthem singer **Jon Foreman** reminds us that the Star-Spangled Banner's lyrics pose a question, a critical one for country that will always be "in process"—yes, the flag yet waves, but is it over "the land of the free and the home of the brave?" Humanities scholar **Clay S. Jenkinson** hits a similar note, remarking that the "mild protest" of Kaepernick and others comports with the image of the U.S. envisioned by Thomas Jefferson, a revolutionary who wrote the Declaration of Independence and who welcomed "a little rebellion now and then" as a means of protecting humankind's rights against overbearing rulers. Challenges to the status quo are as American as apple pie.

Section Two, "The Law," surveys dissent's legal landscape. Historian **Shawn Peters** explores whether government entities can force residents to perform patriotic exercises, using as a case study World War II-era Jehovah's Witnesses who broke state law by refusing to salute the American flag (an act they deemed idolatrous). The U.S. Supreme Court initially ruled against the group, leading to their frenzied persecution; however, the court soon reversed itself, a civil liberties triumph that has benefitted all Americans but which is also scuffed by the "characteristically virulent" response to Kaepernick's protest. Historian **Emma Long** likewise examines how the Supreme Court has safeguarded an individual's right to engage in what others deem contemptuous expressions (such as burning the flag), noting, as the court once did, that allowing such demonstrations does not "threaten the nation's future, strength, or unity," while disallowing them—or, worse still, mandating patriotic rituals—hardly makes a flattering case for the principles represented by the flag, anthem, and other symbols. Even so, the protester's path is strewn with legal obstacles. As **Mark Rerick**, a public school athletic director, writes, participation in school sports is a voluntary endeavor, and while school administrators hopefully would approach a demonstration as a "teachable moment regarding civic duty and peaceful protest," they are ultimately empowered to remove from a team any athlete who engages in what they adjudge inappropriate behavior. Attorney **Shontavia Johnson** adds that businesses are generally free to dismiss employees for expressions deemed harmful by company officials, a fact that must be taken into account when considering the long history of celebrities influencing public opinion generally and protesting in particular. While the boundaries of expression for students and employees remain circumscribed, those of corporations have been expanding. Law professor **Elizabeth C. Tippett** considers the manner in which the Supreme Court's *Citizens United* ruling in 2010 augmented corporate "speech," a power that can be deployed to advance protesters' causes—or thwart them. For these reasons and more, the law itself is contested terrain between crusaders for change and their opponents.

Section Three, "Athlete-Activists," focuses on sports figures' advocacy. Interdisciplinary scholar **David J. Leonard** analyzes how white privilege (i.e., racial assumptions and customs that advantage white Americans) shapes perceptions of activists and non-activists among athletes, concluding that "it matters for those who remain silent; [and] it matters for those [who] speak out." Gender also influences athlete advocacy, observes **Amira Rose Davis** in her interview with fellow historian **Ashley D. Farmer**, from the unique challenges faced by black female athletes who take a stand individually or collectively, to the manner in which their activism, pioneering and enduring though it may be, is nevertheless usually eclipsed in the popular mind by that of their male counterparts. History M.A. student **Joseph Kalka** emphasizes the importance of contextualizing athlete activism, noting, on one hand, that the protests associated with Kaepernick occurred within an unusual political milieu that elevated "outsiders" who claimed to give voice to those who felt unheard by traditional figures, yet, on the other hand, those demonstrations elicited a disdainful backlash that was all-too-familiar. Physician **J. Corey Williams** suggests that the outrage over the Kaepernick-style protests should not have been surprising, for there is an extensive history of white people trying to circumscribe, sometimes by savage means, the activities and expressions of black people, and especially black male athletes, whom they believed threatened the racial order. Even so, a warning is offered by former NFL punter **Chris Kluwe**, who believes that his public support for same-sex marriage played a role in his ouster from the league. In an exchange with interviewer **Matt Connolly**, Kluwe asserts that given all that they risk, athlete-activists probably aren't lying when they say a problem exists, and that, morality aside, sports executives would be wise to take their pleas seriously, because the protesters are urging the repair of a societal framework upon which their businesses rest. Philosopher **Jack Russell Weinstein**, reflecting on the enormous physical, psychological, and emotional toll professional football players endure to earn a precarious paycheck for themselves and riches for team owners, league officials, and corporate partners, opines that the NFL ought to celebrate the Kaepernick-connected demonstrations to honor "the humanity of its players, the citizenship of its viewers, and its role in educating a global audience," and only then can the league have "moral worth," only then can it be justified. Athletes are thus distinctive activists, crusaders that (to borrow Theodore Roosevelt's metaphor) are literally "in the arena."

If strategy is why one protests, and operations are where one protests, "tactics"—the subject of Section Four—concerns how one protests. Historian **Richard Newman** illuminates the issue by spotlighting the original kneeler, Richard Allen, a devout black Christian from Philadelphia who in 1787 knelt in prayer in the "white section" of his biracial but newly segregated church; manhandled by his white coreligionists, Allen walked out of the church and established the African Methodist Episcopal Church, which has played such an outsized role in the black freedom struggle that Newman calls it "perhaps the most important institution in African-American life." History Ph.D. candidate **Ameer Hasan Loggins** describes the power of protesting, as Kaepernick and many of his predecessors have done, silently. During the World War I era, explains historian **David Krugler**, African Americans wielded their love of country as a protest weapon, proudly pointing to their service at home and abroad while they demanded equality, a tactic that so threatened the racial order and the popular association of patriotism with whiteness that it triggered a ferocious, widespread, and deadly response. Professor of English **Sharon Carson** notes that activists do not always agree on tactics, as was the case with those who demonstrated at the 1964 World's Fair in New York City (some organized a "stall in" to paralyze traffic while others protested at the event's opening ceremonies); yet both factions aimed to use this extravaganza of commercialized leisure "to shake people's complacency and turn their attention to serious and persisting racial injustice." Communications professor **Sarah Cavanah** observes that the NFL is a unique platform upon which to demonstrate, for in an age of self-selecting media fragmentation, the league commands an exceptionally large and diverse audience. While the different groups that watch the NFL don't debate each other about the protests, they discuss the episodes among themselves and are aware that their counterparts are doing likewise. Kaepernick thus initiated a far-reaching conversation perhaps only "a professional athlete—and probably a professional football player—would be able to achieve." Although the Kaepernick-inspired protests are about the flag and anthem in that they use the acme of Americana to dramatize injustice, in truth proponents of change have nearly countless tactical options, an arsenal of protest forged in the fires of history.

Section Five, "Counter-Tactics," investigates how opponents subvert protesters. Historian **Andrew N. Wegmann** considers the issue by examining a 2001 soccer match in Paris between France and its former colony of Algeria, an event that was supposed to represent a reconciliation between the two countries and the advent of a welcoming, tolerant "New France." However, the game was disrupted by Algerian immigrants who stormed the field, prompting France's star player Lilian Thuram, himself a black immigrant from Martinique, to lash out at them, not because, as some naysayers carped, they had unpatriotically betrayed the nation, but rather on account of what Thuram deemed their immature, counterproductive protest methods. History Ph.D. candidate **Azmar K. Williams** advises those who champion racial equality to pause before relying too heavily on the market as a tool for change, for it "has proven to be a poor and unreliable moral arbiter." Political scientist **Mark Stephen Jendrysik** identifies another counter-tactic—the way opponents demand that dissenters articulate a final goal, even though there can be no such "endgame" in a nation where the fight over rights will continue as long as the republic exists. Historian **Jamal Ratchford** inspects another powerful impediment to dissent—the effacing of historical role models, for activists who once boldly challenged the status quo are by subsequent generations often stripped of their radicalism and re-packaged as benign do-gooders instead of courageous crusaders for justice. In light of these and other stumbling blocks to change, Frederick Douglass had good reason to declare, "Power concedes nothing without a demand. It never did and it never will."

Section Six presents the perspectives of "others in the arena." Sports journalist **Brad Elliott Schlossman** contends that reporters are supposed to hold a mirror to society, so if they "stick to sports" only, as some critics demand, they wouldn't be doing their job. Former teacher and coach **Gelaine Orvik** wishes Kaepernick had chosen a more "positive" method of protest, adding that his players were told that there would be "repercussions" for any act that jeopardized the "integrity of the game," caused "embarrassment, complication, [or] conflict," or necessitated an "apology for yourself, your teammates, your family, your coaches, [or] your community." Fellow educator and coach **Mike Berg** likewise acknowledges that players must abide by team rules, including, were he still coaching, standing respectfully for the national anthem. However, he also insists that coaches have responsibilities that transcend sports, so, if he still headed a team, he would establish a mandatory forum for addressing phenomenon like the Kaepernick protests in a well-informed and non-judgmental way, even if doing so cut into practice time, a sacrifice that would illustrate the matter's importance. Former players on the University of North Dakota's 2001 Division II championship-winning football team, **Mac Schneider** and **David Butler**, do not take issue with Kaepernick and others' crusade for equality, but they have doubts about their tactics, opining, "if you're explaining why it's patriotic to take a knee during the national anthem, in many ways you've already lost." Veteran **Randy Nedegaard** remarks that the flag has a special place in the military, for rituals that involve it are designed to inculcate members with certain institutional values. But what really makes protests alien to the nation's armed forces is that they are designed to cause discomfort, and thus they run counter to a military culture that demands discipline, conformity, and obedience. Another veteran, **Matt Eidson**, smiles when he sees Kaepernick and others protesting against injustice, because he served in the military for the same reason—"to make the country a better place." Finally, sociologists **Tamir Sorek** and **Robert G. White** take note of the fans, pointing out that for white NFL fans, there's a positive relationship between their passion for football and their pride in America. The opposite is true for black fans, who feel ever-more alienated when comparing their lives to the onslaught of NFL marketing that depicts the league (and, by extension, the U.S.) as a racially collaborative, patriotic meritocracy. The chasm between their reality and the league's branding was so great that the Kaepernick protests maybe were "only a matter of time." If true, if the world inhabited by black Americans is so utterly foreign to their white counterparts, it suggests that fifty years after Tommie Smith and John Carlos raised their fists in protest during the anthem at the 1968 Summer Olympics, the nation largely remains, as the famed Kerner Report had described it earlier that year, "two societies, one black, one white—separate and unequal."

Race, Dissent, and Patriotism in 21st Century America

Eric Burin

Black people have fought for freedom throughout American history. They fought for freedom during the Revolutionary era, when the United States was born. They fought for freedom during the Early National period, when the country emerged from its infancy. And they were still fighting in 1814, when a nighttime battle between U.S. and British forces at Fort McHenry in Maryland inspired Francis Scott Key to pen the words that became the lyrics to the national anthem.[1] Key, a white, thirty-five-year-old lawyer who owned a few slaves himself, knew that black people longed for freedom and that the chaos of war presented them with opportunities to seize it. But when the smoke cleared the following morning, Key, whose opinions on slavery were moderate by his day's standards, boasted that those who had struck for freedom had done so in vain. They had been captured or killed, having found, as Key put it, "no refuge...from the terror of flight or the gloom of the grave." And thus "in triumph," crowed Key, did the "star-spangled banner...wave." Undeterred, black people continued to fight for freedom.

When Key scrawled his now-famous poem, the U.S. was a modest-sized nation of seven million people (one million of whom were enslaved African Americans),[2] with most living east of the Appalachian Mountains. As Key attested, the U.S. prevailed at Fort McHenry, and soon thereafter the war ended. During the peace negotiations, the British largely abandoned their Native Americans allies, who had suffered several military losses in what is now dubbed the Midwest and Deep South. Defeated and forsaken, Native Americans were displaced by onrushing white settlers during the postwar period. In the Deep South, the newcomers brought with them enslaved African Americans, and after their arrival, they purchased still more from interstate traders.[3] The result was that as the decades passed, over one million black people were forcibly taken from their families and communities in the Upper South to perform the backbreaking labor of draining the swamps, felling the forests, clearing the fields, and cultivating the crops of the Deep South. By these means, the world's largest slave society took root in Key's "land of the free."

Slavery collapsed during the Civil War, but new forms of racial control were erected in its place. This didn't happen instantaneously. The flickering light of interracial democracy during the Reconstruction era wasn't extinguished until 1877, and even then, in the estimation of some scholars, there lingered "forgotten alternatives" to white supremacy.[4] By 1900, however, lynching, disfranchisement, sharecropping, segregation, compulsory prison labor, and other forms of exploitation brutalized black people. And when these practices were outlawed or fell into disrepute, others emerged to replace them. The downfall of de jure segregation, for example, was followed by the ascendance of mass incarceration.[5]

Like the systems of racial control that preceded it, mass incarceration arose over time, a process fueled by the cultural, legal, political, and economic dynamics of the era. The tumult of the 1960s, along with rising crime rates in the latter part of the decade,[6] made anxious Americans yearn for, as Republican presidential candidate Richard Nixon termed it in 1968, "law and order."[7] So as the years passed, law enforcement units became more militarized,[8] eventually acquiring equipment and weapons that previously had been reserved for the nation's armed forces.[9] They also adopted more aggressive tactics, as evidenced by the advent of "broken windows"[10] and "stop-and-frisk"[11] policing methods (which to those subjected to them constituted harassment for "living while black");[12] the proliferation of SWAT teams (which were deployed in racially disparate ways);[13] and the use of asset forfeiture and other "for-profit" policing practices (which sometimes siphoned money from poor black communities into government coffers).[14] As a result, more Americans—and especially black ones—ended up in court. There, they encountered prosecutors who brandished an expanding array of "tough on crime" laws,[15] some of which seemed racially discriminatory and nearly all of which aimed to ensure that the guilty would serve long sentences.[16] Emboldened, from the mid-1990s onward prosecutors sought felony convictions against more defendants,[17] often piling on charges to achieve their goal. Consequently, the number of defendants released on their own recognizance decreased and the price of bail increased. Those who could afford it resorted to the burgeoning and ravenous bail bond industry while others remained behind bars, charged but not convicted.[18] Thus situated, well over ninety percent of defendants (including some innocent ones) opted for a plea bargain.[19] For these reasons, between 1984 and 2005 a new prison was opened in the U.S. every 8.5 days.[20] In federal facilities, approximately half of the inmates were doing time for a drug crime; by contrast, in state facilities the majority had been convicted of violent offenses such as robbery and assault. The latter group's long-term imprisonment became a critical feature of mass incarceration, simply because state prisons held over ten times as many people as federal ones.[21] Whether housed in a state or federal institution, or in one of the for-profit private prisons that were multiplying in number by the early 2000s,[22] convicts were economically exploited as captive laborers and captive consumers.[23] None of this made the nation much safer—crime rates had been plummeting since the mid-1990s, and many of those locked up were, if released, unlikely to commit more violent acts, partly because there were only so many hardcore criminals and partly because long-time inmates had grown older and thus less crime-prone. While the criminal justice practices that undergirded mass incarceration offered diminishing returns in regard to public safety,[24] they undercut democracy and circumscribed opportunity, for even after they left prison, ex-felons faced legalized discrimination in voting, education, housing, and public assistance.[25] All totaled, by 2008 the nation's prison population,[26] which numbered 200,000 when Nixon called for "law and order," had increased to nearly 2.4 million, with another 4.2 million on probation and 826,000 on parole. All of this cost taxpayers $75 billion per year.[27] And it cost black Americans, and especially black males (who had a thirty-three percent chance of being imprisoned in their lifetimes), still more.[28] The fight for black freedom, a struggle as old as America itself, was unfinished, for the nation that had once maintained the world's largest slave system had erected the world's largest carceral system.[29]

Before Kaepernick

Colin Kaepernick's protest against these and other inequities occurred within a political context that was profoundly shaped by Barack Obama's successful bid for the presidency in 2008. Although Obama had not intended to make race a campaign issue, it became one. It was inherent in the "birther movement,"[30] which questioned his citizenship, and in the controversy over the Rev. Jeremiah Wright, which prompted Obama's "A More Perfect Union" speech.[31] Obama won the election (a remarkable feat, given how few African Americans had ever won statewide elections, much less twenty-nine of them in one fell swoop, as Obama did), but his triumph did not signal the dawning of a "post-racial" America, as many had hoped.

The Obama presidency witnessed historic levels of partisan polarization, and divergent racial attitudes played a significant role in dividing the nation. Previously, many Americans had held a mixture of liberal and conservative views, depending on the topic at hand. During the Obama years, individuals became more idealogically consistent,[32] adopting conservative or liberal positions across the board, a trend first witnessed among conservatives in the aftermath of Obama's election and then later among liberals. The widening divisions were especially evident in regard to race relations: Republican attitudes toward African Americans, when measured by a "feeling thermometer" (which asks respondents to rate on a scale of 0-100 how warm they feel about a subject) took a historic plunge after 2008.[33] This may have been one reason why an unprecedented number of Democrats (sixty-four percent in 2017, up from twenty-eight percent in 2009) came to see racial discrimination as the main reason why black Americans struggled to "get ahead."[34] This ideological and partisan tribalism, especially regarding race, would affect Americans' responses to the Kaepernick-inspired protests.

So, too, would political extremism among the nation's lawmakers.[35] Continuing a trend that stretched back decades, the "average" Congressional Republican was becoming more conservative and the "average" Congressional Democrat was becoming more liberal. By the time Kaepernick took a knee in 2016, House Democrats were, as a group, the most liberal they had been since 1905. And House Republicans were even further to the right than their Democratic counterparts were to the left. In 2016, Republicans in the House were, collectively, the most conservative in the nation's history. It wasn't just that the center was collapsing; it was growing wider, producing a political chasm of unequaled breadth.

Obama's initial years in office were also marked by intense, highly visible forms of civic engagement. To cite two prominent examples from the right and the left, the Tea Party movement staged hundreds of rallies across the nation, and soon thereafter, the Occupy Wall Street movement commenced its own dramatic protests. For many participants, it was their first venture into public advocacy. Great numbers, having taken that initial step, remained engaged with their causes,[36] especially when such tactics proved effective in pressuring policymakers.[37] For these reasons, politicized public performances became increasingly prevalent during the early years of Obama's presidency.

The NFL joined in. Prior to 2009, teams usually remained in their locker rooms during the national anthem. But that changed once the NFL contracted with the U.S. Department of Defense to showcase on game days nationalistic displays of the flag,[38] military flyovers, soldier reunions, and comparable acts which Republican senators John McCain and Jeff Flake, after realizing that millions of taxpayer dollars had been spent on such activities, dismissed as "paid patriotism."[39] At the same time, the NFL grew more invested in "corporate social responsibility,"[40] championing causes such as breast cancer awareness and youth fitness. Simply put, in the early 2010s, the NFL was substantially engaged in endeavors that had nothing to do with "X's and O's."

Then players got in on the act. In some ways, this was a continuation of a phenomenon that appeared during Obama's presidential campaign. Up until that time, many of the outspoken sports figures of the civil rights era—Muhammad Ali, John Carlos, Tommie Smith, Curt Flood, and a host of others—either had been forgotten or mythologized in ways that made them acceptable to contemporary sensibilities, and most of their successors had shied away from politics. This was the case not just for liberal athletes, but for conservative ones, too. Although fairly conservative organizations like the Fellowship of Christian Athletes had made extensive inroads into the nation's locker rooms, its members generally had remained tight-lipped about issues that were overtly political or partisan.[41] In short, in the early 2000s, few athletes had been willing to jeopardize their livelihoods or endorsement opportunities for the sake of politics. But Obama's campaign changed that.[42] An unusual number of sports figures weighed in on the election, and insofar as NFL players were concerned, there were racial patterns in terms of those who supported Obama (most were black) and those who supported John McCain (most were white).[43] Obama's candidacy, in other words, marked a watershed moment in the revival of the athlete-activist, and the demonstrative, racialized, and polarized political climate that arose following his election countenanced continued advocacy on their part.

At the time, the NFL was immensely popular, and no player capitalized more on its enormous audience than Denver

Broncos' quarterback Tim Tebow, who in 2011 began kneeling in prayer after on-field successes. "Tebowing," as the act became known, was the subject of controversy—praised by some, mocked by others. But in either case, the brouhaha gave Tebow numerous opportunities to bear witness to his understanding of Christianity.[44] Although Tebow is often presented as a conservative foil to the Kaepernick-inspired NFL protesters, in truth, both have used the league as a platform to promote non-sports causes, and many of the latter are, like Tebow, devout individuals. Although they may differ on what it means to do the Lord's work, they are two sides of the same "sports ministry" coin.[45]

By 2012, then, America had become more polarized,[46] especially concerning racial matters, and athletes, whether on the field or campaign trail, were increasingly revealing their personal views in public spaces. But if there was one episode that accelerated the resurgence of athlete activism, it was the February 2012 killing of an unarmed black teenager, Trayvon Martin, by George Zimmerman, who initially wasn't arrested by police because they believed he had had a right to defend himself with lethal force on account of Florida's "Stand Your Ground" law. Former basketball star Chris Webber was the first National Basketball Association (NBA) figure to speak publicly about the matter, making his radio show on March 20, 2012, which he devoted to Martin and Emmett Till, an often-overlooked milestone in athlete advocacy.[47] Two days later, LeBron James and his Miami Heat teammates took a photo in which they wore hoodies to commemorate the slain Martin.[48] That photo was also something of a milestone, in part because of how it was distributed: James posted it on Twitter, which proved instrumental in the revival of the athlete-activist.

This wasn't the first time activists had capitalized on a revolution in communications technology. During the antebellum period, the newly invented steam-powered press advanced the abolitionists' crusade; during the 1950s and 1960s, television's proliferation helped win over viewers to the civil rights cause; and in the age of mass incarceration, communications breakthroughs are showing previously unaware Americans examples of black people's fraught and sometimes lethal encounters with police officers and, in addition, they are allowing advocates of change, including athletes, to bypass traditional news outlets, create communities of support, and shape public opinion. In short, technological advances have traditionally bolstered protest movements.

James and other athletes may have decried the Trayvon Martin episode because they were distressingly familiar with such tragedies.[49] As young children in the late 1980s and early 1990s, they may have witnessed the crack cocaine epidemic that eviscerated many black communities and which was seen,[50] even exploited, as a moral and criminal matter, rather than a public health issue.[51] As time progressed, they would have watched the rollback of many civil rights era achievements, especially regarding residential and educational segregation, voting rights, and public assistance. As they grew older still, they would have observed police departments becoming increasingly militarized. In addition, the individuals potentially wielding the materiel may have been a cause for concern, for following Obama's election, the FBI and Homeland Security reported that right-wing extremist groups were proliferating and attempting to infiltrate law enforcement agencies (an ironic development, given that these groups pose such a deadly threat to law enforcement personnel).[52] In short, James' generation grew up with a front-row view of the forces that led to Martin's demise.

Among professional athletes, the initial outcry over Martin was mostly confined to basketball players. Why? Perhaps it was partly due to the racial composition of the different sports leagues.[53] Over three-fourths of NBA players were black, compared to less than ten percent of Major League Baseball (MLB) players. Yet the NFL had a large percentage of African-American players (about two-thirds). They hailed from the same generation and had the same communication devices as their NBA counterparts. Why didn't they speak out more? There were many reasons, but most importantly, public protests would have entailed greater risks for football players. At the time, all but one NFL team was owned by a white person (most of whom were men), and there was a particularly conservative bent among them—seven would contribute $1 million each to Republican Donald Trump's inauguration committee;[54] they had developed an archly nationalistic identity for their league (especially compared to the NBA's global brand); and the culture of conformity they had established was so strong that some called the NFL the "No Fun League."[55] In addition, the players' union (the NFL Players Association [NFLPA]) was comparatively weak: there were fifty-three active players, plus ten practice squad players, on the league's thirty-two teams, and it was difficult to get 1,500-2,000 individuals to act in concert. Moreover, most NFL players had a very narrow window to make money playing football: they did not have guaranteed contracts,[56] the typical career lasted less than three years,[57] and the league's salary structure was top-heavy, with the top twelve percent of players taking home approximately half the league's pay.[58] However one felt about Martin, under such circumstances, prudence suggested keeping quiet about this and other hot-button issues.

Nevertheless, some NFL players refused to "stick to sports." In fall 2012, Baltimore Ravens' linebacker Brendon Ayanbadejo caused a stir by voicing his support for same-sex marriage,[59] which was on the ballot in Maryland. State lawmaker Emmett

C. Burns, Jr. responded to Ayanbadejo's advocacy by sending a note on official government letterhead to Ravens' owner Steve Bisciotti, urging him to "inhibit such expressions" by his employee. Soon others entered the fray. Among them were Minnesota Vikings' punter Chris Kluwe, who published an open letter blasting Burns,[60] and Ayanbadejo's teammate Matt Birk, who wrote an Op-Ed opposing same-sex marriage. "I am speaking out on this issue," explained Birk in language that would be echoed by those who would later protest during the anthem, "because it is far too important to remain silent."[61]

If Birk, Kluwe, and Ayanbadejo represented small leaks in the dam of reticence among NFL players, the acquittal of George Zimmerman in July 2013 blew apart that structure. As had been the case with NBA players' outcry over the initial handling of the Trayvon Martin case the previous year, Twitter was the medium of choice for the scores of black NFL players who expressed disbelief, anger, and condolences. At the time, only thirty percent of white Americans disagreed with the verdict,[62] and many objected to the players' tweets on the subject. The players, in turn, responded with an argument that would be deployed often during the Kaepernick-inspired protests—that the First Amendment protected their right to free speech. But some, including Minnesota Vikings' linebacker Desmond Bishop, went further, identifying the contradictory expectations that bedeviled sports figures. On the one hand, fans wanted players to be role models, tweeted Bishop, but, on the other hand, they looked "down upon...athletes...who speak out politically."[63]

If voicing one's opinions could engender outrage, so could remaining silent. NFL players were contractually required to be available to the media after games and practices. Most complied, even when they disliked the policy. But some bristled. For example, in 2014, after a reporter confronted Houston Texans' running back Arian Foster at a private residence over a personal matter,[64] he became distrustful of the media and merely paid lip service to the NFL policy by repeating, in at least one of his mandatory interviews, the same nondescript answer.[65] Later that year, Seattle Seahawks' running back Marshawn Lynch, who had long balked at compulsory interviews, was fined $100,000 for violating the league's media rules; he, too, subsequently adopted the tactic of minimal compliance, answering every question, for example, with "Thank you for asking."[66] During this period, Colin Kaepernick also gave nearly monosyllabic replies during required interviews.[67] He was chided by some reporters and fans, described with a term that would become in some quarters virtually synonymous with his given name: "disrespectful."

On the surface, these episodes had nothing to do with race. But it was there, for this friction between the black laborers who played the game and answered the questions and the white professionals who owned nearly all the teams and usually wrote the stories was set against the long historical backdrop of white Americans policing their black counterparts' speech and movement. That the players were well-compensated for their work was beside the point—if anything, it illustrated the difference between wealth and power. In any case, reporters took umbrage at the laconic athletes. The Pro Football Writers of America inveighed against what it perceived to be a mockery of the league's media policy. Individual journalists also vented, as when one reprovingly told Foster that he was being "a distraction when you act like this."[68] As for the league, it insisted that players do the interviews, but it defined "participation" loosely. Most of all, NFL executives expected that these would be isolated affairs, not "the start of a defiant trend among players."[69]

Yet "defiance" among NFL players only escalated in the aftermath of still more high-profile episodes in which white police officers killed unarmed African Americans. On November 30, 2014, during pregame introductions, five St. Louis Rams' players raised their hands in "don't shoot" poses, a gesture of support to those in Ferguson, Missouri, who were protesting a grand jury's decision not to indict police officer Darren Wilson, who had fatally shot Michael Brown, an unarmed black teenager.[70] Two weeks later, Cleveland Browns' receiver Andrew Hawkins engaged in a solitary demonstration.[71] The demonsration was perhaps inspired by the "I Can't Breathe" t-shirt that LeBron James had recently donned to honor Eric Garner (a black man who had died after being taken down with a chokehold by a Staten Island police officer),[72] Hawkins wore a t-shirt during pre-game warmups with the words, "Justice for Tamir Rice and John Crawford" (the former a twelve-year old black child who was playing with a toy gun when he was killed by a Cleveland police officer less than two seconds after his arrival on the scene, and the latter a twenty-two year old black man who was fatally shot by police while holding a fake rifle inside a Beaverton, Ohio Walmart). "[A] call for justice," reasoned Hawkins, "shouldn't offend or disrespect anyone."[73]

The response to these episodes was telling. Law enforcement groups denounced them. The St. Louis Police Officer's Association demanded that the Rams' players be disciplined and that the team and NFL issue an apology.[74] The Cleveland police union president called Hawkins' t-shirt "pathetic" and disrespectful and said that Hawkins should "stick to playing football."[75] The team owners tried to strike a balance by articulating their respect for law enforcement, supporting their employees' First Amendment rights, and trying to win football games by keeping their best players on the field. Finally, from the perspective of would-be activists, it was clear that any demonstration—tweeting an opinion, wearing a t-shirt, making hand gestures, remaining silent—could breed vitriol, and that the protest's original point was likely to be lost in rancorous debates over one's methods. If that was the case—if vilification and obfuscation were inevitable—would it make sense to go "all in" and demonstrate in the most symbolically powerful way possible?

After all, the protests seemed to be working, for policymakers were re-examining police practices. For years, Center for Disease Control (CDC), the Federal Bureau of Investigation (FBI), and the Bureau of Justice Statistics (BJS) had struggled to gather accurate information about officer-involved deaths,[76] thanks in part to "unstandardized data collection" among the states, some of which simply did not send federal agencies materials on the subject. But with police shootings in the national spotlight, Congress passed and President Obama signed the Death in Custody Reporting Act, which required states to submit to the Justice Department quarterly reports concerning "the death of any person who is detained, under arrest, or is the process of being arrested, is en route to be incarcerated, or is incarcerated." States that failed to comply risked losing up to ten percent of their federal "Byrne grant" funds for law enforcement (the authority to mete out punishment rested with the U.S. Attorney General).[77] In addition, Obama created a "Task Force on 21st Century Policing."[78] Six months later, in May 2015, that group released its final report, which recommended, among many other things, that law enforcement agencies be "require[d]...to collect, maintain, and report data to the Federal Government on all officer-involved shootings, whether fatal or nonfatal, as well as any in-custody death." The following month, the BJS began experimenting with a new system of data collection, one that supplemented media reports of arrest-related deaths with surveys of state and local law enforcement units, medical examiners, and coroners. The federal government, with its manifestly inadequate data, was under pressure to provide better responses to questions that had been raised by protesters about police work.

Others were already supplying answers. Investigative teams at the Washington Post,[79] the Guardian,[80] and other entities were using open-source records, tips from the public, and inquiries of police departments to assemble robust databases on arrest-related deaths.[81] Preliminary results released in early June by the Guardian indicated that the federal government's statistics were off-the-mark by fifty percent or more.[82] Thus did number-crunchers become prime figures in the debates over police brutality.

Of course, the data illuminated only so much. They did not show, for example, the socio-psychological effects of a shooting episode. Indeed, while some police shootings gained national attention, the vast majority did not. Instead, they were felt most at the local level, where, regardless of whether the shooting ended in death, they sent shock waves of grief, anxiety, fear, and anger reverberating through the community, waves of trauma that, as one scholar put it, literally contributed to the "slow death" of its members.[83]

Statistics may have had their limitations, but, by this juncture, nearly all observers agreed that the federal government needed better data. The problem was that they disagreed on what to collect and how to collect it. Those differences of opinion, particularly regarding whether the federal government should replace a largely voluntary reporting system with a mandatory one, had important political ramifications. For example, in early June 2015, Democratic senators Barbara Boxer and Corey Booker proposed legislation that would have required reports on all incidents that had involved the use of force by or against law enforcement personnel and had resulted in serious bodily injury or death,[84] but their bill died in the Republican-controlled Judiciary Committee.[85] Obama's recently confirmed Attorney General, Loretta Lynch, wanted better data, too, but she opposed compulsory reporting because it was not her top priority in terms of improving law enforcement's relations with the public and also because she did not want Washington dictating "the minutia of record-keeping" to every local police department.[86] FBI Director James Comey held similar views: he said it was "embarrassing" and "ridiculous" that the *Washington Post* and the *Guardian* had better data than his agency, but he did not favor mandatory reporting, and insisted that, even if he thought otherwise, he did not have the authority to force the hand of the nation's 18,000 law enforcement units.[87] Laurie Robinson, who had co-chaired Obama's Task Force on policing, said Comey was right, noting, "We're still at the mercy of having embraced this very, very decentralized state and local law enforcement system." As some frustrated individuals pointed out, it was easier to learn how many Americans caught the flu or attended a movie each year than how many and under what circumstances they were killed by police.[88]

Pressing that argument still stirred controversy, and a couple of seemingly minor incidents in 2015 left little doubt about what could happen to NFL players who voiced unpopular opinions. A year after being admonished for not earnestly engaging reporters, Arian Foster said during an interview that he was an atheist. Noting that the Texans' owner Bob McNair was a vocal Christian, one commentator noted that Foster was getting "beat up bad by people in Houston," adding, "I just think the timing of it is really stupid. He should have waited until his career is over."[89] Around the same time, Pittsburgh Steelers' running back DeAngelo Williams spoke freely about the media, and he was advised to refrain from doing so because fans, reporters, and marketers would turn on him.[90] "That pink nail polish on your toes and the career you've had make you a most interesting character the press would love to engage," Williams was told. As for the other stuff? "You can't win...Stop it." Was this a no-win situation—condemned for being reticent and chided when forthright? "[W]hen you don't give them what they want or expect," reflected Foster, "they chastise you."[91] Nevertheless, the new era of athlete activism churned on. In fall 2015, the University of Missouri, which lay a little over one hundred miles from Ferguson and had a checkered history of race relations of its own, was beset by several incendiary racial incidents (e.g., slurs hurled at the student body president and other black students; a swastika drawn in feces on a residence hall bathroom wall). Student protesters held rallies and urged the administration to adopt measures that would improve the campus climate, such as hiring more minority faculty. When university president Tim Wolfe appeared unresponsive, activists called for his resignation, staged walkouts, and, in the case of graduate student Jonathan Butler, engaged in a hunger strike. In support, over thirty of the university's football players announced they would not participate in team functions until Wolfe resigned or was removed from office. Their coach supported the boycotting players, and team activities were suspended. Within days, Wolfe resigned, saying he took full responsibility for the "frustration" and "inaction."[92] While college athletes had occasionally decried various matters, such as NCAA image-use, compensation, and unsafe facilities,[93] the Missouri episode was a rare instance of players leveraging their economic clout—if the university had canceled an upcoming game, it would have forfeited $1 million— to achieve a specific political goal. "It takes these drastic measures for us to be taken seriously," remarked Butler, "for us to actually be considered humans."⁹⁴

By mid-2016, professional female basketball players were among the movement's leaders. In some ways, this was unexpected. Compared to their male counterparts, they had smaller platforms, inferior salaries, and fewer endorsement opportunities, so public advocacy came with acute risks. In other ways, their leadership was foreseeable. One commentator compared the Women's National Basketball Association (WNBA) to baseball's former Negro Leagues, remarking, "In both cases, the mere existence of the institutions was an act of protest."⁹⁵ Viewed in this light, it wasn't entirely surprising that in July 2016, in the wake of two more unarmed black men (Alton Sterling and Philando Castile) dying at the hands of police officers, four members of the Minnesota Lynx held a pre-game press conference wearing t-shirts that read, "Change Starts With Us: Justice & Accountability." That demonstration inspired comparable ones—New York Liberty star Tina Charles even donned a symbol of protest (a plain black t-shirt) while accepting the July 2016 Player of the Month Award. Despite pushback from WNBA officials, police organizations, and some fans, female basketball players remained resolute and in fact challenged team owners and league executives to practice what they preached, to truly show that the WNBA wasn't merely a business but was instead something bigger and nobler.⁹⁶ As Phoenix Mercury forward Mistie Bass tweeted, "Don't say we have a voice and then fine us because we use it."⁹⁷ Bass' teammate Kelsey Bone expressed similar sentiments. "In a time where our league is searching for relevance," wrote Bone, "why not take a stand and support your players on issues that effect [sic] the majority of them[?]"⁹⁸

Female athletes' activism in mid-2016 was all the more striking because it occurred amid a resurgence in confidence in the police. Back in December 2014, in the aftermath of the Ferguson protests and the on-duty deaths of two New York City police officers, a group of law enforcement officials formed "Blues Lives Matter NYC" to solicit aid for police officers' needs and to provide "comfort and support" for their families "as they go through hard times."[99] Insofar as popular attitudes were concerned, the group's labors did not yield immediate results: six months after the organization's creation, the number of Americans who expressed confidence in police, while high compared to most institutions, had dipped to fifty-two percent, which was down five points from 2013 and on par with the historically low polling figures that had been taken on the subject in 1993, when four Los Angeles police officers were being tried in federal court for the 1991 beating of Rodney King. The decline had been especially evident among Democrats, but fiscal conservatives (who occasionally questioned the costs associated with police militarization) and libertarians (who sometimes resisted aggressive police tactics with an "Am I Being Detained?" campaign) also expressed dissatisfaction with law enforcement.[100] Even so, thanks in part to Blue Lives Matter's social media campaign, which showcased tragic "fallen heroes" tales and evocative crime stories, attitudes toward the police began to rebound.[101] By June 2016, public confidence in the police had returned to its previous levels.[102]

Among the ways Americans mythologize protest movements is they extract them from their historical contexts and they simplify their origins, lionizing individuals who supposedly took a stand first, like Rosa Parks in Montgomery and college students in Greensboro. In truth, large-scale forces of the day invariably shape crusades. Moreover, there almost always were actions, individual and organizational, that preceded the famed "firsts"—and those efforts usually ended in disappointment. As historian Glenda Elizabeth Gilmore has noted, most protests "fail, time and time again. When they succeed, they win only partial victories."[103] Such had been the case for those who protested long before Kaepernick took a knee.

Why Kaepernick?

By the summer of 2016, Colin Kaepernick had been in the public spotlight for many years. Yet the "real" Kaepernick was difficult to see. Since childhood, others had affixed labels to him, revealing, along the way, more about themselves than Kaepernick. Indeed, the practice obscured the fact that the twenty-eight-year old had evolved into the kind of person who would endure slings and arrows for a cause he thought righteous.

"Black" was among the first labels slapped on Kaepernick. Biracial, Kaepernick was adopted when he was just a few weeks old by a white Wisconsin couple, who had had four biological children of their own, two of whom had died at a young age due to congenital heart defects. The family moved from the Midwest to the mostly white community of Turlock, California, and as time passed, Kaepernick realized that he would be treated differently because of his race.[104] During family vacations, he explained, "Every year, in the lobby of every motel, the same thing always happened, and it only got worse as I got older and taller. It didn't matter how close I stood to my family, somebody would walk up to me, a real nervous manager, and say, 'Excuse me, is there something I can help you with?'" The uninvited dawning of racial consciousness had come to Kaepernick; "the shadow," as W.E.B. Du Bois described the experience, had "swept across" the youngster.[105]

As Kaepernick aged, he was, in the estimation of local townspeople, a good kid. He was disciplined (as the high school's varsity quarterback, despite being faster than everyone else, he averaged zero rushing yards, because his coach insisted that he avoid the risk of leaving the pocket and scrambling downfield.)[106] He was smart and sedulous (he earned straight "A's," and, as his pre-calculus teacher said, he was "obsessed with problem-solving...[H]e was in that class to learn.")[107] And he was well-mannered ("My dad, being a businessman," recalled Kaepernick, "constantly talked to me about carrying myself in a certain way and treating people with respect.")[108] Turlock's residents' esteem for Kaepernick was no doubt sincere, but it remained to be seen the extent to which their admiration was contingent upon him not causing them discomfort, especially regarding racial matters.

Still more labels were engrafted onto Kaepernick once he enrolled at the University of Nevada. To many, he was a marvel. The school's associate athletic director, recalling that Kaepernick bought a season ticket for an elderly woman who could no longer afford to go to games on account of being recently widowed, joked that it was the first time he had had to inquire about the legality of an athlete giving rather than receiving benefits.[109] In addition, already shouldering the burden of being a Division I athlete and a full-time student with superlative grades, during his junior year Kaepernick sought to join Kappa Alpha Psi, a predominantly black fraternity that demands much of its pledges. Skeptics suspected that Kaepernick would stumble. "The process is not easy," remarked Olumide Ogundimu, one of the organization's members. "It's definitely something that will shine a light on your weaknesses and shine a light on your strengths."[110] Kaepernick, the naysayers soon learned, "was all strength." Kaepernick also proved something of a wonder on the gridiron. Although Nevada was the only school to offer him a scholarship, he became a record-setting, nationally renowned quarterback. For this reason, in April 2011, Kaepernick, who had created further buzz with an eye-grabbing performance in the Senior Bowl and an impressive score of thirty-seven on the Wonderlic "intelligence" test, was selected by the San Francisco 49ers with the thirty-sixth pick in the NFL draft.[111]

After less than two years in the league, Kaepernick had achieved stardom. But the price of fame was that he became, in effect, "public property," a one-of-a-kind object upon which still more individuals affixed still more labels, a sui generis canvass upon which others, consciously or not, painted their own thoughts about race, masculinity, religion, and more. For example, to some he was the "anti-[Peyton] Manning," the famed white quarterback who came from a storied football family, played a brilliant if conventional game, and whose wry humor and folksy demeanor made him a marketer's dream.[112] Kaepernick, by contrast, was often viewed as an otherworldly athlete who might render Manning's traditional style of play obsolete; an inconsiderate adoptee who ought to reconcile with his birth mother;[113] and maybe, on account of all his tattoos (though some were Biblical passages), a public relations problem. One sportswriter, who likened a quarterback to the head of a company, said of the extensively inked Kaepernick, "You don't want your CEO to look like he just got paroled."[114]

These journalistic observations frequently bore a racial subtext (e.g., was "raw athleticism" code for "black"?) Nevertheless, one well-known columnist justified such commentary, maintaining that the media "is as intensely interested in the people who play the game as it is in the game itself."[115] That may have been true, but players were required to talk with reporters, and even when the former did so willingly, the question remained whether the latter profiled them accurately. One essayist (who wasn't a sportswriter) sensed that some articles of this sort were off the mark, insisting, "Kaepernick is a guy who's earned the right to be taken at face value."[116] And what did Kaepernick make of it all? When asked what had changed most since his arrival in the NFL, he replied, "people's perception of me." The public scrutiny heightened Kaepernick's self-awareness, and fashion became a means by which he projected his evolving identity. As he explained in September 2015, "[A]ll this stuff made me ask myself in a really focused way: 'What do I represent?'"[117] At the time, the nation was embroiled over shootings in Charleston and elsewhere, and while Kaepernick had said little about these matters, race was on his mind. "My racial heritage is something I want people to be well aware of," he professed. Employing revealing language, Kaepernick said he wanted to represent "the African community."[118] And he would do so unapologetically: "I want black kids to see me and think: 'Ok, he's carrying himself as a black man, and that's how a black man should carry himself.'" In Kaepernick's mind, that meant embracing a "clean" look occasionally accentuated with tokens of contumacy (e.g., socks with police officers depicted as cartoon pigs). Yet even as he asserted himself sartorially off the field, Kaepernick faltered on it, and the phenom who only two years earlier had led a star-studded team deep into the playoffs was struggling with less talented teammates, ultimately losing his starting job in November 2015.[119]

Kaepernick would regain the starting position the following year, and in the interim he reflected even more deeply on race relations. His interest in black history had been whetted during his Kappa Alpha Psi days, and now he asked Ameer Hasan Loggins, a University of California, Berkeley doctoral student in African Diaspora Studies, for reading recommendations on the subject. Soon thereafter, Kaepernick audited Loggins' summer class on representations of black people in popular culture. "Colin came in aware, focused, well-read, and eager to learn," recalled Loggins. "He was a sponge."[120] That was the summer of 2016, right before Kaepernick took a knee.

In retrospect, if one could see past the labels, Kaepernick exhibited many of the hallmarks of a human rights crusader. He was an assiduous, disciplined, and confident individual who had experienced both acclaim and "infamy"; he was learned yet intellectually evolving; and he was an introspective and self-aware person who was civil but not obsequious. Perhaps most importantly, Kaepernick, while reveling in the camaraderie of teammates and fellow travelers, may have had what sociologist Mark Granovetter calls a "low social threshold"—the willingness to go it alone, to forgo the security and comfort of public favor to endure scorn and worse.[121] Indeed, as Kaepernick averred when first asked about his protest, "I am not looking for approval. I have to stand up for people that are oppressed."[122]

Taking a Knee

As Kaepernick prepared for the 2016 NFL season, he remained attuned to the times. On social media, he discussed human rights issues, black history, and the deaths of Charles Kinsey, Freddie Gray, and others at the hands of police. But he was not ready to join the protests. "I felt that I needed to understand the situation better," he explained.[123]

Then, on August 14, 2016, before a preseason game, Kaepernick, who was injured and therefore not in uniform, sat during the national anthem. Was this permissible?[124] Like all NFL players, Kaepernick had signed a contract that obliged him to eschew activities that diminished "public respect" for the game or could be "reasonably judged" by his team to "adversely affect or reflect" on the franchise. Likewise, he was bound by the Collective Bargaining Agreement (CBA), which had been negotiated by the NFLPA and which mandated that league personnel refrain from "conduct detrimental to the integrity of and public confidence" in the NFL.[125] In addition, the league's Personal Conduct Policy discountenanced behavior that undercut "public respect and support for the NFL."[126] At the same time, the NFL's game operations manual, which was not subject to NFLPA approval, required players to be on the sidelines during the anthem but merely stated that they "should" stand during the song.[127] So was Kaepernick's gesture punishable? "Probably," wrote a legal scholar, but it was "by no means a sure thing."[128]

Kaepernick was hardly the first to use the flag, anthem, or a comparable symbol as a means of protest. Indeed, it may not have been coincidental that later, when associates of his compiled a "Kaepernick reading list,"[129] they included Frederick Douglass's famous 1852 speech, "What to the Slave is the Fourth of July?," a meditation on African Americans' relationship to the nation that Douglass delivered, in a symbolic act that foreshadowed Kaepernick's, on July 5.[130] At times, Douglass portrayed black Americans as aliens in a foreign land, captives in a star-spangled Babylon, and at other times, he depicted them as the true heirs of the founding generation, the redeemers that would save the U.S. from itself. Over 160 years later, Kaepernick may have been pondering those same issues.

Kaepernick described sitting during the anthem as a personal decision.[131] After the game, he did not issue a press release, discuss the act with sports journalists, or mention the episode on social media. The following week, Kaepernick again sat with no fanfare. But one reporter, Mike Garafolo, had noticed.[132] So prior to the 49ers' third preseason game on August 26, the New York-based Garafolo alerted his colleague Steve Wyche, who was in California to cover the game, about the matter.[133] Sure enough, Kaepernick, this time in uniform, sat once more.[134] He did so between two water coolers, an unobtrusive spot, he reckoned, that would not infringe on others' right to stand during the anthem. As Wyche looked down from the press box, he saw a big story.

Wyche later said in a personal communication that he merely "served the message in a moment." But he was not delivering ordinary news. History beckoned, and Wyche was ready. He was a veteran reporter who had broken major stories before, so he knew what steps to take, like getting a statement from the 49ers' media relations department and telling the NFL Media desk to prepare for a potential firestorm.[135] He was also an African American, the only black reporter at the game in fact, and thus he understood the issues that he soon learned vexed Kaepernick. (Wyche subsequently reflected, "I've got three sons close to his age who I fear for every time they leave the house at night, so there's a lot of things he talked about that are...rooted [in] concerns that I have.") Finally, Wyche had a strong rapport with Kaepernick, having long covered his exploits on the field and having watched his growing social awareness off it. Kaepernick appreciated what Wyche brought to this moment, later telling him, "I am kind of glad that you wrote that [article] because you were able to put some historical context to it." Good thing, too, because the story hit America like a meteorite.[136]

"I am not going to stand up to show pride in a flag for a country that oppresses black people and people of color," Kaepernick told Wyche, an utterance that became his most-quoted remark. Alluding to instances of police officers shooting unarmed black Americans, Kaepernick continued, "There are bodies in the street and people getting paid leave and getting away with murder." Wyche knew that other sports figures had protested such matters, and he situated Kaepernick's actions within the contemporary revival of the athlete-activist. But Kaepernick's gesture seemed different—it appeared momentous and transcendent—and Wyche immediately compared him to Mahmoud Abdul-Rauf, the young, black Muslim star on the NBA's Denver Nuggets who caused a national uproar in 1996 by engaging in a similar protest and who was soon, as he later put it, "weed[ed]" out of the league.[137] And if a comparable backlash awaited Kaepernick? "If they take football away, my endorsements from me," contended Kaepernick, "I know that I stood up for what is right."

After practice two days later, on August 28, Kaepernick fielded more questions from reporters.[138] When asked what he hoped to accomplish, Kaepernick replied that the U.S. "stands for freedom, liberty, [and] justice for all. And it's not happening for all right now." Many things needed to be addressed, elaborated Kaepernick, including police brutality, for which "people aren't being held accountable." Thus he was protesting to draw attention to "what's really going on in this country."

Kaepernick's assertion that he was protesting to raise awareness about un-American injustices echoed statements made by his activist predecessors. As W.E.B. Du Bois explained in 1910, just as a toothache tells the body that a disease exists, demonstrations tell society that something is amiss.[139] The discomfort caused by both warns of a larger problem that requires resolution. Over fifty years later, Martin Luther King, Jr. likewise maintained that nonviolent, direct action protests don't create tension.[140] The tension already exists—and when it is denied or smothered, the frustrated will choose destructive methods for dealing with it. So demonstrations bring that pre-existing, suppressed tension to the surface, where it can be constructively addressed. They "dramatize the issue [so] that it can no longer be ignored," observed King. By these means, "A community which has constantly refused to negotiate is forced to confront the issue." Yet, as scholar Ta-Nehisi Coates has suggested, it's debatable how much black Americans should labor to awaken their white counterparts. On one hand, Coates told his teenaged son, "The terrible truth is that we cannot will ourselves to an escape on our own." On the other hand, "You cannot arrange your life around...the small chance of [white Americans] coming into consciousness."[141] For now, at least, Kaepernick vowed to protest until the flag "represents what it's supposed to represent."[142]

Already the subject of intense debate, Kaepernick was soon embroiled in another controversy, this one concerning socks that he had previously worn that depicted police officers as cartoon pigs. A verbal hailstorm descended on Kaepernick, who quickly issued a statement on Instagram. "I wore these socks in the past," he explained, because "rogue cops" didn't just endanger the communities they serve.[143] By "creating an environment of tension and mistrust," they also imperiled officers "with the right intentions," including two uncles and friends of his who worked in law enforcement "to protect and serve ALL people." With that clarification, Kaepernick hoped that his former footwear wouldn't be "used to distract from the real issues."

In less than a week, Kaepernick had sparked a national—and often vitriolic—debate. Among those who weighed in was Nate Boyer, a thirty-five-year-old ex–Green Beret who in 2015 had tried and failed to make the NFL as a long snapper. On August 30, Boyer penned a thoughtful and earnest open letter to Kaepernick,[144] who subsequently invited Boyer to the 49ers' final preseason game in San Diego on September 1, which happened to be when the host Chargers held their annual "Salute to the Military" festivities.[145] Hours before kickoff, the two, along with Eric Reid (Kaepernick's teammate who wanted to join the protest but was wary of sitting during the anthem), talked at the team hotel.[146] A few days earlier, while conversing with reporters, Kaepernick had professed that he intended no disrespect to the military. Even so, Boyer showed him text messages that he had received from veterans who were hurt by his protest. As the conversation continued, Boyer mentioned that twenty-two veterans a day were committing suicide. The nation, reflected Kaepernick, would send those people to war yet offered insufficient aid upon their return home. "That's another issue," insisted Kaepernick, "and these issues need to be addressed." Indeed, as Reid acknowledged, many problems demanded solutions. There were "too many to name," he lamented, which was unfortunate and, insofar as it made it difficult to clarify one's message, potentially problematic.

The trio devised a compromise on the national anthem issue. During the pregame ceremonies, Kaepernick and Reid, with Boyer standing by their side, knelt during the Star-Spangled Banner.[147] Echoing scholars who study the psychology of kneeling,[148] Boyer explained, "Soldiers take a knee in front of a fallen brother's grave...to show respect."[149] Later in the game, Kaepernick stood and clapped for the singing of "God Bless America."[150] "I'm not anti-American," he said afterwards. "I love America. I love people. That's why I'm doing this."

In Kaepernick's mind, the exchange between Boyer, Reid, and himself was a model for effecting change. Protests heightened awareness; awareness countenanced dialogue; dialogue promoted mutual understanding; and mutual understanding provided the foundation for progress. "I've had more conversations about human rights and oppression...in the last week than I've had in my entire life," gushed Kaepernick during a postgame interview, adding that those conversations were "a start."[151] Of course, it wouldn't work always work that way. As Reid foresaw, "People are going to look at the initial headline and form an opinion without even digging deeper to see what it's about."[152] But the switch to kneeling, it was hoped, would appease those who thought sitting was disrespectful and thereby help the national conversation get "back on track."

The conversation may not have gotten back on track, but other athletes got on board. During the first week of the NFL's regular season, thirteen more players knelt or raised a fist either during or after the anthem.[153] "Freedom," asserted kneeler Arian Foster, is supposed to run in Americans' bloodlines, so if "somebody is telling you they don't feel like they're free, why wouldn't you listen to them?"[154] Many did, but many others never got the message.

Critics had at their disposal an immense and diverse arsenal of opposition. The protesters were pressed to explain themselves and specify their end goal, and they replied while fearing that long, nuanced answers could be clipped into provocative sound bites.[155] Detractors belittled them, and said they were entitled,[156] ungrateful,[157] and "out of line."[158] Self-styled patriots claimed they insulted veterans while Islamophobes depicted them as Muslims.[159] One demonstrator, Denver Broncos' linebacker Brandon Marshall, who had been Kaepernick's teammate in college, lost two endorsement deals (though music mogul Russell Simmons, who called Marshall a "great American hero," signed him to another).[160] Kaepernick himself was hounded by death threats.[161] Indeed, by September 22, according to one poll, Kaepernick's popularity among African Americans had skyrocketed, but he was nevertheless the most disliked player in the league, thanks to the white backlash against him.[162]

Kaepernick remained steadfast. In fact, he branched out, extending and diversifying his activism. After the game on September 1 when he first took a knee, Kaepernick pledged to donate the proceeds from the sale of his jersey, which, despite the outcry over his protests had quickly become the top seller in the league.[163] "That support," he said, "is something that I have to give back to the communities."[164] He further vowed to contribute $1 million (of his $11 million salary) to social justice organizations. One week later, the 49ers made a matching donation to the Silicon Valley Community Foundation and the San Francisco Foundation.[165] Team officials selected these two organizations because of their track record and wide reach. The former, boasted 49ers' owner Jed York, was "the largest community foundation in the world, managing $7.3 billion in assets and more than 1,800 philanthropic funds globally." By contrast, Kaepernick bypassed such institutional behemoths when making donations.

Kaepernick often expressed his love for "the people," and those affections guided his charitable contributions.[166] He didn't give to mammoth entities with lots of overhead, far removed from those they served. Rather, he usually donated relatively modest sums—typically $25,000—to grassroots organizations toiling in the trenches. The nonprofits to which he made contributions were a diverse lot. Anti-police brutality organizations received only seventeen percent of his donations. Youth initiatives (twenty-three percent), community reform and minority empowerment enterprises (twenty-six percent), and healthcare and nourishment programs (thirty-one percent) received greater sums. Among the enterprises he supported were 100 Suits for 100 Men (which provides business attire to underprivileged individuals seeking employment),[167] Appetite for Change (which uses food to strengthen families, create economic prosperity, and encourage healthy living),[168] and Life After Hate (an organization comprised of former violent white extremists devoted to combatting discrimination).[169] This broad range of causes reflected an expansive understanding of freedom and justice, and the connection between seemingly disparate issues—that systemic racism, for example, is not just a "social" or "economic" matter, but a public health concern, too. Moreover, Kaepernick's strategy was to play the long game, to see contributions as investments, as seed money that would produce more activists. As Loggins quipped, Kaepernick was "helping the people, that help the people, so that they can help more people."[170]

The same mindset was evident in Kaepernick's "Know Your Rights" camps,[171] which were modeled on the "freedom schools" established by civil rights crusaders in the mid-1960s and the "Free Breakfast for School Children" program run by the Black Panther Party in the late 1960s and early 1970s.[172] The camps spotlighted ten "rights": the right to be free, healthy, brilliant, safe, loved, courageous, alive, trusted, educated, and the right to know one's rights. The camps also tackled legal issues, providing attendees with lawyers' contact information and reminding them that they had the right to say, "Am I being detained?" and "I do not consent to be searched."[173] In addition, there were conversations about history, nutrition and health, financial literacy, and higher education. Furthermore, participants received resource guides that identified where to find a community garden, how to support black-owned businesses, and much more. However, the highlight of the camps, the thing that made "students explode with joy," was when they learned that they'd get DNA kits, an item, Kaepernick informed them, that would allow them to trace their ancestry, connect with lost relatives, and create a new sense of self.[174] By these means, Kaepernick, who purposefully did not court media attention to these camps, strove to create a leaderful movement, "because," as he declared at one of them, "in oppressed communities no one is going to help them but themselves."

Meanwhile, across America Kaepernick's protest had, for a while, blossomed into a movement. In the two months that had passed since he first took a knee, forty-eight NFL players, nine NBA teams, fourteen WNBA players, one Olympic swimmer, one professional female soccer player, fifty-two high schools, thirty-nine colleges, one middle school, two youth football teams, and three national anthem singers had demonstrated during the Star-Spangled Banner.[175] Yet, by the NFL season's midpoint, only about a dozen players were still doing so. Their increasing isolation was clarifying, even inuring. It was one thing to denounce an online video of a police shooting, posited demonstrator Malcolm Jenkins of the Philadelphia Eagles. But protesting was different. "[W]hen your endorsements and your popularity and your followers and all that stuff start to get threatened, or we move on to different things," said Jenkins, "is this still something that you're passionate about?"[176] Jenkins was. In late October, during a nationally televised game in Dallas, Jenkins stood alone, fist raised as the anthem played, a solitary figure amid 80,000 fans of the Cowboys, a team owned by the disapproving Jerry Jones. "[T]hose who are still standing tall," Jenkins reflected afterwards, "those are the guys that are kind of linking together."

Jenkins' lonesome stand occurred about a week before Election Day, and the demonstrations had long been intertwined with the presidential race. From the start, Kaepernick disparaged the Democratic nominee, Hillary Clinton. Her alleged email scandal, proclaimed Kaepernick, would have landed "any other person...in prison."[177] In addition, Kaepernick accused Clinton of once having referred to "black teens or black kids" as "super predators."[178] As for Trump, Kaepernick adjudged him "openly racist." From Kaepernick's perspective, what distinguished Trump from Clinton was virtually a distinction without difference. "[Y]ou have to pick the lesser of two evils," he opined, "but in the end, it's still evil."[179]

Liberals couldn't believe Kaepernick likened Clinton unto Trump. It was true that in 1996, when mass incarceration was on the rise, Clinton had described certain "gangs of kids" as "super predators," but she had not specified that they were African Americans, as Kaepernick claimed (though this was a "reasonable inference" on his part).[180] In any case, Clinton had disavowed those twenty-year-old comments and embraced criminal justice reform. Indeed, by 2016, many politicians on both sides of the aisle had done so.

These bipartisan efforts were partly a response to reports published by the Washington Post,[181] the *Guardian*, and other entities that continued to assemble ever-expanding databases on police-involved fatalities.[182] Their findings differed in the details, but, overall, they painted a similar picture. For instance, they showed that police shot and killed about three Americans each day, for a total of around one thousand such fatalities per year.[183] This made the U.S. extremely unusual, for other western, industrialized democracies experienced far fewer deaths of this sort.[184] In addition, the statistics suggested that black Americans, and especially black males between the ages of fifteen and thirty-four, were, compared to their white counterparts, more likely to be killed, unarmed at the time of death, and die as a result of a routine pedestrian or traffic stop.[185] Some skeptics insisted that these deaths were the product of other factors, like the fact that African Americans were over-represented in high-crime neighborhoods. Still others contended that, after taking all variables into account, black Americans were less likely to be fired upon by officers than white Americans.[186] Either way, the rich datasets provided grist for debates over police work.

The databases inspired wide-ranging conversations about "best practices" in the field of law enforcement. For example, an analysis of episodes in which officers shot at moving vehicles begged the question of whether it would be wiser if they got out of the way instead of discharging their weapons, given what might happen if their aim was true.[187] Another analysis revealed that approximately twenty-five percent of those gunned down by police were mentally ill or suffering a mental crisis—would enhanced officer training help reduce the number of fatalities among them?[188] And given that local district attorneys work with law enforcement personnel on a daily basis, and that ninety-five percent of them receive campaign contributions from police unions, affiliated political action committees, or individual officers, should, when a cop has killed a community member, the matter be transferred to other authorities, such as the state's law enforcement officials?[189] Constructive, evidence-based dialogue about these and related matters could be advantageous for all, for the data further showed that police departments that recently had instituted reforms, including those recommended by Obama's Task Force,[190] had seen drops in the number of officer-involved shootings.[191]

Skeptics who doubted that police brutality was widespread also turned to the data. For starters, the numbers illustrated the dangers of police work. In over half of the officer-involved fatal shootings, for example, the decedent had had a gun,[192] and twenty percent of them had fired their weapon.[193] In addition, statistics could contextualize well-publicized episodes in which cops felled civilians. For this reason, FBI Director Comey urged police chiefs to submit data to the federal government. "In a nation of almost a million law enforcement officers and tens of millions of police encounters each year," rued Comey, "a small group of videos serve as proof of an epidemic."[194]

The national conversation ranged beyond the police shootings, as different elements of the criminal justice system were reconsidered by Republicans and Democrats alike.[195] Several GOP-controlled states passed reform measures, including Georgia (which revised its criminal code and juvenile justice system), Texas (which overhauled its probation and parole guidelines, and bolstered its mental health and drug addiction programs), and Kentucky (which expanded its pretrial services as part of a larger bail reform movement). Liberals and conservatives didn't always agree on the proper course of action. One commentator remarked that the former tended to promote programs that would keep people out of prison while the latter usually championed measures that would help inmates after their release.[196] But at least both sides were at the table, and as a result, for the first time in a generation, the number of incarcerated Americans had fallen. A Clinton victory in the presidential election presaged further progress on that front while a Trump presidency augured poorly at best, or so held conventional wisdom.

Trump had been a racially divisive figure long before he entered politics and he remained so on the campaign trail.[197] Moreover, his alarmist depictions of rampant lawlessness and his emphasis on the criminal aspects of immigration policy,[198] along with his promise that as a "law and order" president he would "give power back to the police" and end what he subsequently called this "American carnage,"[199] portended the undoing of recent bipartisan criminal justice reforms. The fact that Alabama senator Jeff Sessions, a hardliner who was outside the mainstream of conservative thought on these matters, was an early supporter of Trump's and a likely pick as Attorney General, also gave reformers cause for concern.[200] As one African-American commentator opined, a Trump presidency would endanger the people in his predominantly black and immigrant neighborhood. Surveying what might happen with health care, immigration, marriage equality, and Supreme Court vacancies, he warned, "Our very being would be at risk."[201]

Nonetheless, some defended Kaepernick's views on the candidates. As one of his supporters argued, Kaepernick's goals transcended electoral politics. He aimed to revolutionize society, to truly establish "justice for all," and this necessitated rejecting the "partisan framework that passes for politics."[202] If this flummoxed Democratic politicians, then Kaepernick was "upsetting many of the right people." Such persons needed to understand why even Democratic policies tasted like the "thinnest possible gruel" to those who hungered for "bold changes and some semblance of justice." There were millions of such Americans, and they were especially numerous among the youth. Democrats alienated this group at their peril; without their support, Clinton would lose the election.

As that left-of-center debate roiled, Trump sized up Kaepernick and the protests. Although he later turned the demonstrations into his personal political piñata, in fall 2016, while running for president, Trump's response to them was comparatively restrained. On one hand, many of his supporters were obsessed with the protests (back in Kaepernick's hometown of Turlock, California, white locals wondered what had happened to the good kid they had once known).[203] On the other hand, Trump himself did not make the demonstrations a centerpiece of his campaign, perhaps because he hoped to appeal to racial minorities (or at least discourage them from voting for Clinton, a phenomenon that played a small but important role in the election's outcome).[204] Indeed, Trump's outreach to African Americans led to instances wherein he and Kaepernick seemed to echo one another.[205] For example, Trump made much ado about the email imbroglio and dredged up Clinton's "super predator" comment. In a similar vein, Trump told a largely black audience, "Our government has totally failed our African-American friends [and] our Hispanic friends." To be sure, Trump took shots at Kaepernick. For example, when the story first broke, Trump suggested that the protesting quarterback "maybe...should find a country that works better for him."[206] But when conservative pundit Bill O'Reilly asked Trump, who had once owned a team in the defunct United

States Football League and who had unsuccessfully tried to acquire a NFL franchise in 2014, whether, if he owned a team now, he would fire a player who knelt during the anthem, Trump pulled his punches. "[H]e has the right to protest and that's one of the beautiful things about the country," replied Trump. "He's trying to make a point," he continued, "[b]ut I don't think he's making it the correct way." O'Reilly suggested it was unlike Trump to hold back. Trump responded, "[L]et's keep the headlines down to a minimum."[207]

When he wanted headlines, Trump almost always got them, and due to the additional attention the presidential election became, some claimed, a referendum on him.[208] As a result, Trump, not the protests, were said to have torn apart NFL locker rooms.[209] If that was the case before the election, when Trump wielded no actual governmental power, it was likely to be true after the ballots were cast. Although nearly three million more people voted for Clinton,[210] Trump won the Electoral College,[211] and thus the presidency, with its tremendous powers that could be pushed still further. That night, Kaepernick was a bystander to it all. He didn't vote.

Kaepernick's decision was not unprecedented among activists. Before the Civil War, some abolitionists eschewed voting, office-holding, and the like, partly because they believed that the U.S. Constitution was a proslavery document ("a covenant with death," as the famed white antislavery crusader William Lloyd Garrison put it),[212] and partly because abstaining from formal politics afforded them the independence to raise difficult questions typically avoided by majority-seeking politicians.[213] By these means, such abolitionists, most of whom were devout Christians, hoped to challenge America, to effect a moral awakening, and thereby transform public opinion, that ever-shifting foundation upon which the republic stood. These abolitionist radicals built the path down which later strode moderate antislavery statesmen like Abraham Lincoln, though as trailblazers they were much-despised. As was Kaepernick, who was pilloried by liberals and conservatives for sitting out the election. Even so, he was unapologetic. A few days after the election, he answered questions about the matter, standing before reporters attired in a Black Panther-style leather jacket and a t-shirt that featured the Malcolm X quotation, "If you don't stand for something, you will fall for anything." "I'd said from the beginning I was against...a system of oppression," Kaepernick explained. "I'm not going to show support for that system," he continued. Seen in this light, he reasoned, "it would be hypocritical of me *to* vote."[214] Moreover, there was nothing to be gained by casting a ballot, because "the oppressor isn't going to allow you to vote your way out of your oppression." That's why it "didn't really matter" to him who had won the election.[215] Still, did he feel heightened urgency about his cause with Trump's victory? Kaepernick answered, "[E]verybody should feel urgency...to protect ourselves from what comes in front of us." For Kaepernick, that meant continuing to work in communities and to protest in stadiums.

By the end of the regular season in early January 2017, only thirteen other players were, like Kaepernick, demonstrating during the national anthem.[216] When the final whistle blew, the movement's destiny was unclear, as were Kaepernick's prospects in football. The 49ers told Kaepernick that if he opted into his $14.5 million contract for the next season, they would cut him. In what others would later deem a strategic mistake, Kaepernick did not force the team's hand. Instead, in early March 2017, he opted out of his contract, becoming an unrestricted free agent that could sign with any team.[217] He knew that his activism might be a sticking point for some owners, but he wanted to keep an open mind moving forward. For this reason, as well as for some legal considerations, Kaepernick declined an offer from the NFLPA to prepare for collusion litigation should team owners blacklist him.[218] In addition, he decided that he would not grant interviews concerning the NFL. Would this suffice? Would any offers be forthcoming? Kaepernick had just put up very solid numbers playing for a bad team.[219] It would have been unprecedented for a quarterback of his caliber to remain a free agent for long. Even so, no one knew what would happen next. Although this crusade mirrored its predecessors, the past could reveal only so much of the future.

The Trump Effect

In late summer 2017, as the NFL prepared for its upcoming season, the league was bedeviled by a variety of problems.[220] The previous year, there had been an eight percent decline in television ratings.[221] The dip was partly attributable to temporary phenomenon, like the distracting allure of the 2016 presidential election. Other factors were more worrisome (e.g., domestic violence cases involving players; dissatisfaction with the slow pace of games) and possibly enduring (e.g., unsettling reports concerning football-induced brain injuries; new means of media consumption). And then there was role that the Kaepernick-inspired protests had played. This was going to be a challenging season for the league in any case. That Kaepernick remained unsigned promised to make it even more so.

Some of Kaepernick's supporters vowed to boycott the NFL until he secured employment.[222] Among those who favored this idea was the Rev. Al Sharpton, who believed his National Action Network could mobilize 10,000 people to demonstrate in front of NFL headquarters or elsewhere. The problem, however, was that the league's players appeared ready to start the season without showing a sign of solidarity with Kaepernick. Complicating matters was the fact that Kaepernick himself remained uncommunicative, frustrating and bewildering his would-be allies. As Sharpton confessed, "I don't know what his strategy is. Does he have a strategy?"[223] This uncertainty might help explain why, once games got underway, relatively few players protested during the anthem. Only of handful did so during the first week of the preseason;[224] a few more joined the following week. The clash between white supremacists and their opponents in Charlottesville, Virginia, on August 11–12, 2017, portended an upsurge in demonstrations in a league in which approximately seventy percent of the players were black Americans. Indeed, the following Monday, nearly a dozen Cleveland Browns' players knelt during the anthem (including the first white player to do so, Seth DeValve) while several others made gestures of support.[225] The next day, President Trump shocked many by insisting that at Charlottesville there had been "some very fine people on both sides."[226] In the end, Charlottesville was a turning point, but not in the way one might expect.

Charlottesville proved pivotal because it made wide receiver Anquan Boldin consider retirement. The episode, during which a Nazi enthusiast sped his car into a crowd, injuring nineteen and killing civil rights advocate Heather Heyer,[227] shook the fourteen-year NFL veteran, who had recently signed a one-year contract with the Buffalo Bills. While Boldin had never demonstrated during the anthem, he had been passionate about the issues that prompted the protests, and for this reason he had been a leading figure in the Players Coalition,[228] an interracial group that had worked informally since the earliest days of the Kaepernick-inspired protests and had assumed a more formal structure in February 2017. (Kaepernick appreciated the organization, but he had not officially joined it,[229] preferring, perhaps, to maintain his characteristic independence.) In the aftermath of Charlottesville, Boldin contemplated hanging up his cleats so that he could fully dedicate his time to fighting for racial equality. When speaking with NFL Commissioner Roger Goodell about the matter, Boldin explained that while some league executives and team officials said they "supported" the protests, what they really meant was that they were "permitting" them (and Boldin felt they didn't need anyone's permission to speak out on issues of importance). Goodell had never seen the distinction between mere permission and actual support. "For you," he asked Boldin, "what does support look like?"[230] That question would eventually lead to a multi-year, $89 million commitment by the NFL to social justice causes, and that pledge, in turn, would fracture the protest movement.

Those developments, however, occurred in the future and usually behind closed doors. At the time, in mid-August, Charlottesville didn't seem to change much. Although there were protests outside NFL headquarters decrying Kaepernick's unemployment and confidants like Loggins were sounding upbeat about the movement,[231] by the end of the month, when the NFL wrapped up its preseason, only a dozen players were demonstrating or signaling their support for those who did. The same was true during the first two weeks of the regular season.[232] That was a dozen more than NFL executives and team owners would have preferred—it's easy to forget that even a handful of protesters was highly unusual by historical standards. Still, the demonstrations were not as prevalent as they had been one year earlier, when many more had rallied behind Kaepernick.

Then President Trump entered the picture. In a September 22 speech in Alabama, Trump exclaimed, "Wouldn't you love to see one of these NFL owners, when somebody disrespects our flag, to say, 'Get that son of a bitch off the field right now. Out. He's fired! He's fired!'"²³³ Trump also urged fans to leave the stadium or turn off their televisions if they saw "even...one player" taking a knee. The president's comments set the stage for a weekend like no other in the history of American sports. Every franchise in the league witnessed demonstrations of some sort.²³⁴ Nor was it just the players protesting. Coaches and staff did, too. Even several owners—many of whom had a close relationship with the president—joined in. The gestures were diverse: some individuals remained in their respective locker rooms during the anthem; others came out but knelt before, during, or after the song; still others raised their fists, locked arms, or wore apparel with powerful messages. It was a potpourri of protest. And that was the problem. The message was being lost.

What were these individuals protesting? Trump's threats against the league? The idea that players could be fired for demonstrating? Racial injustice? This confusion infiltrated that weekend's nationally televised Sunday night game, when the NFL ran a commercial it had shown during the previous year's Super Bowl,²³⁵ a one-minute piece called "Inside These Lines" that emphasized "unity."²³⁶ Kaepernick had called for unity. But he also sought accountability, justice, and change.

Complicating matters further was the fact that some insisted that the protests weren't about inequality, justice, unity, or even free speech. Among them was President Trump, who tweeted early the following Monday that the controversy had nothing to do with race;²³⁷ it concerned "respect" for the nation and its symbols. It was a question of patriotism.

The struggle to "control the narrative," contested ever since Kaepernick started protesting, was now being fought with an unrivaled intensity. In a *New York Times* Op-Ed, Eric Reid, the 49ers' safety who had been the first player to kneel with Kaepernick, expressed frustration that the demonstrators' message was being hijacked.[238] Kaepernick was not an un-American villain, Reid insisted. Nor were the protests anti-military. "It is imperative," he wrote, "that we take control of the story behind our movement, which is that we seek equality for all Americans, no matter their race or gender." Yet other commentators wondered if most people, deep down inside, already knew that equality was the real issue at hand. Sanctimonious proclamations about proper flag and anthem etiquette, the argument went, were merely a means of deflecting questions about societal inequities.

After all, Americans seem to violate the U.S. Flag Code on a routine basis. The most striking example of this sort concerned a New York Jets' fan who wore an "I Stand for the National Anthem" t-shirt while sitting on the flag.[239] This episode was distinguished not just by its high irony. It was also noteworthy because a "real" flag was involved, and that arguably was important, because the Flag Code, according to the American Legion, applies to only "actual" flags.[240] Consequently, instances wherein the code was allegedly disregarded—such as when the flag was signed by a politician,[241] used in advertising,[242] or worn as apparel[243]—technically were permissible because they involved non-regulation flags. This reasoning could justify the NFL's own suspect handling of the flag: displaying the Stars and Stripes horizontally is a no-no according to the Flag Code, but the enormous flags that league, team, and military personnel sometimes stretch across football fields during the anthem are slightly too long to qualify as "regulation" flags.[244] Such nit-picking, however, doesn't make for an especially gratifying argument, if for no other reason than it requires explaining why kneeling silently during the anthem is disrespectful but wearing flag-themed Speedo underwear that is sweat-stained and champagne-soaked is unobjectionable.[245]

A better way to approach the issue, one could argue, would be to ask what a "reasonable person" would think about the treatment of the flag, be it a "real" one or otherwise.[246] This standard, which is frequently used in legal circles to assess an individual's conduct, has the advantage of steering clear of the Flag Code's idiosyncrasies. But it also privileges the views of observers over the words of actors. It means that, the protesters' explanations notwithstanding, "respect" ultimately rests in the "eye of the beholder." But everyone sees the world through the lens of their own experiences and preferences, and in America, the lens of race greatly alters outlooks. Indeed, Kaepernick's original point was that racially distorted perceptions had prompted police officers to shoot unarmed black Americans and to otherwise caring people defending such episodes. Outrage, whether over "bodies in the streets" or flag protocol, is selective because the "eye of the beholder" is never color-blind.

Americans' conduct during the anthem provides another case in point. Few watching the game at home or in a bar rise when the song is played. And even when attending an event, a good number go on with their business during the anthem, standing perhaps, but also sipping a beer, taking a photograph, or, in some cases,[247] yelling toward the song's end "Chiefs!,"[248] "O!,"[249] or "Sioux!"[250] Still others buy concessions during the anthem and team owners are happy to keep the cash registers ringing.[251] Green Bay Packers' quarterback Aaron Rodgers tried to address these inconsistencies humorously, posting on Instagram a picture of a camera crew on the ground, filming the players' deportment during the Star-Spangled Banner, commenting, "I can't imagine what kind of social media attacks these cameramen must be enduring after taking a knee during the anthem and wearing a hat."[252] In like manner, columnist John Branch, after surveying a host of dubious behaviors during the anthem, waggishly pointed out that "stadiums and arenas...are rarely sanctuaries of patriotic conformity and decorum."[253]

For these reasons, some observers suggested that race was the real reason why detractors denounced the player-protesters. Commentator Nick Wright,[254] for example, emphatically asked whether the response to the demonstrators would have been different had they kneeled in support of better veterans' services (which was something Kaepernick championed, having donated $25,000 to Black Veterans for Social Justice).[255] Wright's remarks, in turn, illustrated another important aspect about the clamorous debate: that ever since Steve Wyche had broken the Kaepernick story, black journalists, analysts, and reporters had been covering the protests. As sportswriter Robert Klemko noted when discussing a related subject, the "difference now is we have excellent black voices to call out this hypocrisy, whereas years ago the responsibility was left to white newspaper columnists with no interest or incentive to call out the league."[256] African Americans' expanding presence in traditional and social media meant that the protesters' opponents wouldn't be able to completely dictate the terms of the debate.

Indeed, Americans' opinions regarding the demonstrations greatly depended on whether they saw them through the lens of patriotism, free speech, or racial inequality.[257] That viewpoint, in turn, was closely associated with one's race and partisan leanings, with white people and Republicans generally being less supportive of the protests than black people and Democrats. In addition, it mattered whether a respondent was thinking about these issues in the abstract or more concretely—whether they were envisioning nonviolent demonstrations generally or kneeling players specifically, or whether they were contemplating the problem of racism in theory or picturing an organization like Black Lives Matter particularly. Support eroded as comforting, nebulous ideas became real-world actions.

The muddled messages among protestors, alternative narratives by their opponents, and irresoluteness among some of their allies countenanced a backlash that made demonstrating an increasingly risky endeavor, especially for those who lacked the safeguards that protected professional athletes. At a Kennesaw State University football game in late September, for example, five black cheerleaders took a knee during the anthem, with one saying, "It was the scariest thing I've ever done."[258] Likewise, high school players who demonstrated faced threats of violence.[259] Even fans could incur others' ire, as when two black men who did not stand for the anthem at a Los Angeles Lakers preseason game were cursed, had drinks throw at them, and told to "take a kneel [sic] for the land of the slaves."[260] Under such circumstances, resolve required courage, not fearlessness.

The Trump administration, meanwhile, refused to sit idly on the sidelines. On October 8, Vice President Mike Pence flew from Las Vegas to Indianapolis to attend a Colts vs. 49ers game, only to dramatically walk out when members of the latter team, including protest stalwart Eric Reid, took a knee during the anthem. Pence explained via Twitter that he "would not dignify any event that disrespects our soldiers, our Flag, or our National Anthem."[261] Critics impugned the move. Some claimed it was a taxpayer-funded political stunt (it was even noted that Pence included a two-year-old picture in his posts from the stadium that day);[262] others, with a heavy dose of irony, told Pence that they respected his right to protest but insisted that "A football game is an inappropriate place to flaunt your politics."[263] Trump himself seemed to undercut Pence's earnestness by disclosing that he had asked the vice president to leave the stadium.²⁶⁴ Despite the criticism, Pence's gambit signaled to everyone that the administration would continue to use its sizable influence against the player-protesters.

Some team owners were also pushing back. When Dallas Cowboys' owner Jerry Jones, a Trump supporter who had long resented the protests, was asked about the Pence episode, he offered a dramatic answer, announcing that any player on his team who demonstrated during the anthem would be benched.²⁶⁵ This was the first time an owner had openly declared that protesting players would be punished. Once again, observers were quick to point out the irony of the situation.²⁶⁶ One, noting that Jones had repeatedly signed players accused of domestic abuse, wrote, "Imagine Jerry Jones demanding the Cowboys respect women as strongly as he demands respect for [the] flag."²⁶⁷ Even so, it was Jones' team; he could discipline players—probably even fire them—if he wished, for the law was likely on his side.²⁶⁸

Jones' hard-hitting policy illustrates the risks that individuals took when protesting. NFL players had few legal safeguards against recrimination, and amateur sports figures had even fewer. For all practical purposes, universities and colleges could dismiss protesters from their squads, as Albright College's Gyree Durante discovered on October 9.²⁶⁹ High school officials had comparable leeway, and they exercised it, sometimes in humiliating ways, as when a Texas football coach responded to two kneeling players by immediately booting them from the team and making them strip off their uniforms "pads, the pants and all, in front of everyone."²⁷⁰ Even journalists suffered consequences for speaking forthrightly on these matters, thanks to vague but standard contractual prohibitions against bringing their employer's company into disrepute. ESPN, for example, suspended Jemele Hill for two weeks for suggesting—on her personal Twitter account—that fans of the Cowboys could respond to Jones' threat to bench protesting players by boycotting the team's advertisers.[271] Those with power could make the price of protesting quite steep.

By this point, the NFL was anxious to end the demonstrations. The key figure in this regard was Commissioner Roger Goodell, who was in the middle of negotiating his own contract, was perceived to have mishandled other controversies like player brain injuries, and was now being buffeted by numerous groups, including disgruntled owners like Jones, accommodating ones like the 49ers' York, factions within the league office, jittery advertisers, union representatives, and, of course, the players themselves. Moreover, Goodell's thinking about race and sports was evolving. Back in 2006, Harry Edwards, a sociologist who had played a role in Carlos and Smith's famed protests at the 1968 Summer Olympics and who had been recognized as an expert on athlete activism ever since, told Goodell that more African Americans were going to become stars in the NFL—and with stardom came power, and black power would rankle those accustomed to the status quo.[272] Edwards said that Goodell never fully comprehended his advice—until the Kaepernick protests began. Even so, after the demonstrations commenced, Goodell had participated in some player-protesters' outreach activities and thereby had come to a greater appreciation of the problems that plagued their communities.[273] It was within this context that Goodell, being batted in every direction, felt determined to get this issue right.

"The controversy over the Anthem," asserted Goodell in a memo sent to every team just two days after Pence's ploy and Jones' threat, "is a barrier to having honest conversations and making real progress on the underlying issues."[274] So how could the league go from "protest to progress"? On one hand, Goodell unambiguously stated that "We believe that everyone should stand for the National Anthem." On the other hand, he suggested establishing an "in-season platform to promote" the players' work on "core issues." Goodell wasn't envisioning a quid pro quo—the players wouldn't have to stand if a "platform" was created, but he surely hoped they would do so. Within hours of it being made public, Goodell's olive branch was nearly snapped in two. At 4:47 a.m. (EST), Trump essentially claimed victory, tweeting, "It is about time that Roger Goodell...is finally demanding that all players STAND for our great National Anthem—RESPECT OUR COUNTRY."[275] That, of course, was not what Goodell had proposed, so the NFL quickly released a statement indicating that certain "commentary" on Goodell's memo was "not accurate."[276] Even so, some remained fixated on the idea of compulsory standing. Even people who knew otherwise couldn't resist discussing it. Sportswriter Adam Schefter, for example, shared the NFL's statement via Twitter on the morning of October 11, but later that day, while recording a podcast, he asked Tampa Bay Buccaneers' defensive tackle Gerald McCoy, who had not knelt during the anthem, what would happen if the league forced players to stand, to which McCoy replied, "It's going to be an uproar."[277] Just as the protesters had strained to control their story's narrative, Goodell struggled with his, even though it was written in black and white on league letterhead for all to see.

Misunderstandings, distortions, and apprehensions about the nature of his proposal were not the only problems troubling Goodell. His memo had called for a platform to address the players' "core issues." But what exactly were the "core issues"? Kaepernick's unemployment? Criminal justice reform? Systemic racism? Even if league and team officials agreed on these matters, the players, it soon became evident, did not. Moreover, implicit in Goodell's proposal was the assumption that the protests would end if a platform was created. That assumption may have undersold the protests' distinct value—that they could raise awareness in unmatched ways. For players who subscribed to this view, the demonstrations were hardly barriers to "real progress," especially compared to vague promises of a platform that would be subject to league approval.

If there was one person who could sympathize with Goodell's travails, it may have been Nate Boyer, the former Green Beret who back in August 2016 had written an open letter to Kaepernick and dialogued with him, with the result being that the quarterback had knelt instead of sat during the anthem. Boyer now took up his pen again, addressing "Every Single American."[278] "[I]t seems like we just hate each other," lamented Boyer, and that extreme divisiveness, he added, "is almost as difficult to deal with as burying a fallen comrade." The problem, he continued, was that people appeared unwilling to swallow their pride, open their mind, embrace what they don't understand, and "ultimately...surrender." Instead, "It's all about winning." The contestants in this battle, thought Boyer, were not "right and wrong." Rather, they were "right and left."

Boyer had a point. The NFL had become a partisan issue.[279] Prior to Trump's September 22 speech in Alabama, Republicans and Democrats held roughly similar attitudes about the league—about sixty percent of each viewed it favorably. After Trump's remarks, Republicans soured on the NFL. By mid-October, the league was among the nation's most politically polarizing businesses, comparable to (on the one hand) Fox News and (on the other) ABC News. How had a league dominated by right-wing, white male billionaires end up being castigated by conservatives?

The answer partly concerns the way race warps political ideologies in America. Consider Kaepernick's case. Conservatives lambast Kaepernick, even though, upon closer examination, they should see likeable qualities in him. Kaepernick embodies the self-help tradition of Marcus Garvey,[280] Malcolm X,[281] and the Black Panther Party,[282] a boot-strapping philosophy that ought to appeal to conservatives. If, as the saying goes, inconsistency is a minor sin in politics, race is what often leads the guilty to commit transgressions.

Like conservatives, liberals also have reason to reassess their views on Kaepernick. For example, Kaepernick may share some characteristics with Martin Luther King, Jr., but the latter, while well-attuned to the African liberation movements of his day, never called himself "an African man," as did the former.[283] Misreading Kaepernick is one thing that liberals and conservatives have in common.

Conservatives also walked away from the NFL because the league's leaders had inadvertently built a pathway for them to do so. Team owners and league executives, by laboring to associate the NFL with militaristic patriotism, had created a brand that was susceptible to political exploitation. It was comparatively easy for a figure like Trump, who was skilled at rallying his base against those he said threatened the country's values, to frame what was happening at NFL stadiums, where a particular kind of public-spiritedness was supposed to reign, as un-American, as an affront to the nation. But the potential for the league's brand to be usurped became clear only in retrospect. Moreover, once it was co-opted, there was little that could be done about it. Even if they had wanted to, the league's powerbrokers couldn't re-write history, they couldn't go back in time and scale back on the military flyovers, soldier reunions, and other nationalistic displays.

What if the protesting players had taken a different approach? What if they hadn't involved the flag or anthem—would it have been more difficult for their opponents to change the subject from racism to patriotism? Perhaps. But the historical evidence indicates otherwise. As previously discussed, well before the Kaepernick-inspired protests, many athletes had demonstrated in ways that had nothing to do with the flag or anthem, yet their activism sparked outrage nonetheless. But what if player-protesters had expressly embraced the flag? Civil rights era activists had done so, and they were less popular than the NFL demonstrators.[284] Ultimately, it may not have mattered whether the protesters steered clear of the flag, literally wrapped themselves in it, or gestured in such a way as to dramatize the gap between the values it represents and the realities of American life, for after scanning the broad sweep of the nation's history, one would be hard-pressed to name any instance of black protest that was deemed acceptable by most white people at the time. From a historical perspective, the NFL demonstrations were distinguished not by the amount of indignation they generated, but by how much support they received.

Such long-term views about the protests' comparative popularity provided little comfort to team owners who were distressed about the here and now as they gathered in New York City on October 17 to discuss the demonstrations with Goodell, about a dozen players, and three union leaders.[285] (Why Kaepernick wasn't there was a matter of dispute.[286] That he had just filed with support from the NFLPA but independently of it a collusion grievance against the NFL may have played a role,[287] as may have the fact that some players, while sympathetic to Kaepernick's situation, did not regard his unemployment as their top priority, a distinction that would further rend the players' ranks as time passed.) Goodell worked to bridge divisions between and among the groups, insisting "We're all in this together." However, a recording of the meeting obtained by the *New York Times* showed that the participants largely talked past one another.[288] More challenges awaited the next day, when at a meeting in which the players were not present, hardliners like Jerry Jones tried to persuade their counterparts to enact a must-stand edict, while Bob McNair offered the cringe-worthy comment that "We can't have the inmates running the prison."[289] Yet despite everything, Goodell, after two difficult meetings, felt optimistic.

In the meantime, protests continued across the land, and once a person or institution weighed in on the matter, the consequences of doing so ricocheted in unpredictable ways. Take, for example, the case of the College of the Ozarks, a small Christian school located in Point Lookout, Missouri. Back in September, the school said it would not play any opponent that had player-protesters. "We're living in a culture that doesn't know right from wrong anymore," opined the college's president.[290] Now, in late October, the school, which had hosted the NAIA Division II men's basketball tournament for eighteen years, asked the NAIA, which would not compel student-athletes to stand for the anthem, to take its tournament elsewhere, thereby depriving local businesses of the economic boost that came with hosting the event.[291] The protests' political and pecuniary complexities likewise redounded against John Schnatter, the Trump-supporting CEO of Papa John's, a pizza company that was among the NFL's top business partners. In early November, Schnatter blasted the league for its handling of the demonstrations, which he blamed for the company's slumping sales.[292] Papa John's thus became the highest-profile company to pressure the league to resolve the issue. But days after Schnatter's statement, the *Daily Stormer*, a white supremacist publication, declared Papa John's the official pizza of the "alt-right." The company quickly denounced the endorsement, condemned "racism in all forms," and, the following month, sacked Schnatter as CEO.²⁹³ Thus did one man taking a knee lead to another being shown the door. The players, too, were dealing with difficulties. Reid had grown frustrated that he and Kaepernick, who had spearheaded the protests, had been supplanted by Boldin and Malcolm Jenkins as the Players Coalition's point persons in conversations with league officials.²⁹⁴ This was no minor matter, for they embraced somewhat different goals and tactics than Reid. For example, Jenkins had gone on a ride along with the Philadelphia police.²⁹⁵ He and four others (Boldin, Detroit Lions' safety Glover Quin, the aforementioned Andrew Hawkins and his white teammate, quarterback Josh McCown) also had traveled to Washington, D.C. to discuss police brutality with lawmakers (among them Republican House Speaker Paul Ryan).²⁹⁶ In an attempt to bridge the riff between the two factions, the Players Coalition reportedly agreed that any communication with the league would involve multiple players, but soon thereafter, Reid unsuccessfully attempted to arrange a meeting between Goodell, Kaepernick, and himself, an undertaking that "blindsided" other members of the group. The coalition, in short, was cracking.²⁹⁷

Amid the frayed nerves and seething resentments, the only person who seemed to delight in the situation was Trump, who continued to hammer away at the issue on Twitter. Two episodes in November seemed custom-made for the president's 280-character invective. In the first instance, when the Oakland Raiders played the New England Patriots in Mexico City, running back Marshawn Lynch stood for Mexico's national anthem but sat during the United States', prompting Trump to tweet that the next time he did so the NFL ought to suspend him for the remainder of the season.²⁹⁸ A few days later, Trump, grousing that players continued to "disrespect" the flag, anthem, and country "without penalty," retweeted an item from his social media director Dan Scavino, Jr., whose post showcased an article about New York Giants' defensive end Olivier Vernon kneeling before a game on Thanksgiving Day,[299] a story that underscored the notion that protesters were not only unpatriotic but also ungrateful. This trope had become so common that one columnist, recalling how opponents of the civil rights movement had castigated that era's activists for not "knowing their place," concluded that "ungrateful" was the new "uppity."[300] Even so, the president knew his base, claiming, with an expression reminiscent of McNair's infamous "inmates" comment, that Goodell had "lost control" of the league and that the players "are the boss!"

Trump had not always said such things. But at the time, he was, by historical standards, a hugely unpopular president and the NFL protests were among the few issues on which he polled well.[301] For him, bashing the league made political sense, even if it damaged what had been an exceedingly well-liked $13 billion American business.

Whither the Movement

As the president railed against the protests, NFL officials and player representatives edged closer to an agreement. By late November, a tentative deal had been struck. Soon thereafter, Troy Vincent, the former Eagles' safety who now served as the NFL Executive Vice President of Football Operations, sent Jenkins a final draft of the proposal.[302] On the table was an unprecedented seven-year, $89 million partnership to address causes considered important to African-American communities.

Jenkins forwarded the materials to Reid and other players, asking if they would be willing to abide by the implicit assumption that if the deal came to fruition, they would cease demonstrating. Reid just couldn't sign on. He and three other staunch protesters (Miami Dolphins' wide receiver Kenny Stills and his teammate safety Michael Thomas, along with San Diego Chargers' offensive lineman Russell Okung) soon left the Players Coalition.[303] The rupture exasperated Goodell, who feared that the negotiations would be derailed. Jenkins encouraged the commissioner to keep faith.[304] "Don't hold us all accountable for a few we can't control," he pleaded with Goodell. "Give us a chance....Together we can make a difference." Goodell concurred, and on the evening of November 29 the two sides approved the proposal.[305]

After the split in the Players Coalition, accusations and counter-accusations were levelled about the nature of the negotiations (e.g., whether Kaepernick had been purposely excluded from the conversations; whether Jenkins' communications with the league had been appropriate; whether the whole affair had been rushed to take pressure off Goodell as he entered his own fraught contract talks with the owners).[306] But even if leadership and transparency hadn't been issues, the substance of the deal had given Reid and others pause.

The agreement, they thought, had many shortcomings. Most importantly, it said nothing about Kaepernick's status (Jenkins felt for Kaepernick but concluded that the out-of-work quarterback had known that unemployment might be the penalty for protesting, and, in any case, the movement was bigger than one person.) In addition, reports indicated that the agreement called for the creation of a working group that would consist of five players, five owners, and two NFL staffers.[307] If the latter two groups worked in tandem, as one might expect, the players would be outvoted five to seven on nearly all matters. Would, for example, the league minimize its financial commitment by simply reallocating funds it had earmarked for other projects, like aiding service members and promoting youth fitness, instead of ponying up new dollars?

As Harry Edwards commented, "[T]he devil isn't in the details, it's in the delivery....Unless you substantially control the delivery, you've been took, you've been had, you've been bamboozled."[308]

There were also questions about the organizations that would receive funding. Twenty-five percent of the national donations would go to the United Negro College Fund,[309] a venerable institution, to be sure, but not exactly a grassroots outfit, nor one that has much to do with police reform. Another twenty-five percent would go to Dream Corps, an entity that works to reduce the prison population, build an "inclusive green economy strong enough to lift people out of poverty," and teach youth of diverse backgrounds to find success in the technology sector.[310] The remaining fifty percent would go to the Players Coalition, but that group, because of its legal status at the time, could not distribute the monies as it pleased, but rather would be overseen by the Hopewell Fund, a murky organization with no history of fighting racial injustice.[311] One observer compared the agreement's terms with Kaepernick's work and concluded, "It's the difference between philanthropy and activism."[312]

For these reasons, skeptics suggested that this endeavor would be as underwhelming as the NFL's comparable ventures. The league's "No More" anti-domestic violence campaign had been derided as little more than an exercise in self-congratulatory corporate branding,[313] and its Breast Cancer Awareness program allegedly wasn't much better.[314] The league had likewise trumpeted a $30 million "unrestricted" grant to the National Institute of Health to study concussions but ended up withholding over half of the money on account of it potentially going to a scientist who had criticized the NFL's handling of brain trauma.[315] Given the league's track record, remarked one doubtful commentator, it was clear that "The NFL was always going to try and co-opt this, it was only a question of exactly when, and how, and for what final amount."³¹⁶

Conservatives also disparaged the agreement. Fox News, for example, ran an op-ed that insisted the NFL's donations had nothing to do with "social causes" and "racial equality" (this argument was, ironically, similar to the critique offered by some progressives, who contended that the league's contributions neutered what had started as a bold movement against police violence).³¹⁷ It wasn't clear, however, why groups that combatted mass incarceration, enhanced black people's access to college, and trained young people of color for tech jobs weren't really, in the conservatives' minds, champions of "social causes" that advanced "racial equality." Moreover, if these groups didn't fit the bill, what other organizations would? It was also intriguing that conservative commentators didn't denounce one of the proposal's most conspicuous features—that it did not require players to stand during the anthem. If "disrespecting" the flag had been the real source of right-wing outrage over the demonstrations, one would have expected that conservatives would have lambasted this aspect of the agreement. Ultimately, conservatives' criticism boiled down to the idea that the NFL had buckled by promising to fund what they derided as "left-wing activist" organizations. If that was going to be the case, then the league ought to "stick to sports."³¹⁸

The final agreement did not end the protests. Although Jenkins, who had raised a fist during the anthem since Week 2 of the 2016 season, no longer did so, most of the twenty-five to thirty players who had demonstrated before the agreement was reached continued making such gestures thereafter.³¹⁹ Unsurprisingly, among them were Okung, who dubbed the deal a "farce,"³²⁰ and Reid, who called it a "charade."³²¹ And what did Kaepernick have to say about the matter? Characteristically, nothing. He remained focused on his own objectives.

As Kaepernick labored on, he was aided and lauded by others. Kevin Durant, Stephen Curry, Serena Williams, Snoop Dogg, Meek Mill, Usher, and other celebrities matched Kaepernick's donations with contributions of their own.[322] *Sports Illustrated* gave him its Muhammad Ali Legacy Award;[323] the American Civil Liberties Union of Southern California honored him,[324] as did the Robert F. Kennedy Foundation;[325] the *New Yorker's* cover depicted him kneeling with fellow protester Michael Bennett and Martin Luther King, Jr.;[326] and the NFLPA named him a finalist for the Byron "Whizzer" White Community MVP Award.[327] Even Kaepernick's fashion sense drew praise, particularly because he showcased black designers.[328] All the while, Kaepernick remained deflective. "It was never for or about me—it has & always will be for the people," he tweeted.[329]

Of course, Kaepernick and the other demonstrators still had many detractors. Among them was Trump, who recognized the political value of continuing to wage this culture war, and consequently took a thinly veiled swipe at the NFL protesters in his State of the Union Address on January 30, 2018.[330] From the league's perspective, the president's jab was especially ill-timed, for it came right before the NFL held its premier event, the Super Bowl. Over the course of the season, NFL viewership, while declining in absolute terms, had actually increased relative to most other programs, as nearly all broadcast and cable networks lost ground to streaming services like Netflix, Amazon Prime, and Hulu.[331] And if there was one show that could draw an audience, it was the Super Bowl, an entertainment spectacle that transcended sports and had produced nineteen of the twenty most-watched television programs in U.S. history.[332]

The Super Bowl, like the playoff games that preceded it, was perceived through the prism of the protests. When the regular season ended, five teams had at least one steadfast protester. Three of those squads, noted one commentator, had been among the twelve teams to make the playoffs in 2016 but had failed to do so in 2017, indicating that the demonstrations had caused divisions within teams that hurt their on-field performances.[333] The evidence for that argument was suspect, however. While an usually large number of squads that had made the 2016 playoffs didn't repeat the feat the following year, the attrition rate was not unprecedented, and among the teams that didn't make the cut were those that had no staunch demonstrators.[334] If anything, claimed one observer, the opposite was true: decent teams that could have made the playoffs if they had had a good quarterback opted to scuttle their season rather than sign Kaepernick, a decision that, if true, raised the question of whether franchises that received tax breaks and other public assistance had an obligation to field the best squad possible.[335] Whatever effect the presence or absence of protesters had on a team's fortunes, the two that made the Super Bowl—the Philadelphia Eagles and the New England Patriots—reflected in the popular imagination very different attitudes toward the demonstrations and the causes they symbolized.

Any generalization about an NFL franchise should be viewed warily, given that these large entities invariably include a diverse array of individuals. That said, although some players from the Patriots' 2016 championship team had skipped the traditional White House visit (among them were individuals who did so explicitly on account of their opposition to Trump),[336] the most important figures in the organization admired the president: team owner Robert Kraft was close to Trump and had donated $1 million to his inauguration committee; head coach Bill Belichick likewise regarded Trump as a friend and on the eve of the 2016 election had sent him a letter that praised him as "the ultimate competitor" and an "amazing" leader and expressed his hope for a Trump victory;[337] and star quarterback Tom Brady golfed with the president and had a "Make America Great Again" hat in his locker.[338] Trump's invective against the NFL had strained, but not severed, his ties to these Patriot leaders.

By contrast, the Eagles featured several players who, while not necessarily taking a knee, had with words and deeds been ardent activists. Among them were Malcolm Jenkins, Torrey Smith, and Rodney McLeod. This group also included Chris Long, who had been the demonstrators' earliest and arguably most stalwart white supporter, and who after the clash in his hometown of Charlottesville had donated his entire 2017 salary to organizations that promote educational equality.[339] The team's unofficial song was "Dreams and Nightmares" by Meek Mill,[340] a black artist from Philadelphia whose troubles with the law exemplified in some protesters' minds the criminal justice system's problems. Indeed, those problems seemed even more manifest after the Super Bowl, when an Eagles' victory prompted fans in Philadelphia, most of them white, to topple structures, tear down light poles, vandalize vehicles and storefronts, and engage in other disorderly acts with virtual impunity. "You can riot if you're white and your team wins," reflected a Black Lives Matter official, "but if you're black and being killed, you can't speak out."[341]

Some continued to speak out nonetheless. According to one report, there were over 1,110 instances of athlete-activism during the previous year.[342] They included protests, of course, but also episodes in which athletes made financial contributions, issued public statements, participated in collective action initiatives, joined community outreach projects, or wore special apparel. More than seventy percent of these endeavors aimed to raise awareness, particularly about racism and inequality, while the rest sought to increase underprivileged groups' access to resources, encourage civic participation, empower individuals, and protect human rights. Critics pushed back—sometimes. Athletes who raised money for victims of natural disasters, or who touted mental healthcare, usually weren't told to "stick to sports." That refrain was typically reserved for those who combatted racial prejudice or championed criminal justice reform (a cause that had taken on additional urgency with the Trump administration pursuing what the Brennan Center for Justice called a "draconian vision of law enforcement").[343] Defamed or acclaimed, some athletes came to regard advocacy as not merely "a hobby or pastime but as a career." It was central to their identity, a part of their legacy.

Among them was Colin Kaepernick. After fulfilling his pledge to donate $1 million, Kaepernick organized an encore campaign in which additional well-known individuals contributed $10,000 or more to grassroots, social justice organizations. "We can all enact change," proclaimed Kaepernick, who remains unbent.[344]

Thus black Americans continue to fight for freedom, extending a crusade that stretches back to the days of Francis Scott Key and beyond. The most recent chapter of this epic tale is comparable to the preceding ones. It features a yearning for equality and justice; athletes stepping into the historical spotlight; debates over their tactics and the unleashing of counter-tactics; and a cacophony of opinions about the activists' causes, dissent's boundaries, and patriotism's meaning. It is, as Kaepernick declared after his initial protest, "bigger than football."

Notes

1. https://www.smithsonianmag.com/smithsonian-institution/wheres-debate-francis-scott-keys-slave-holding-legacy-180959550/ [http://perma.cc/Z8ZJ-2EYG]
2. https://en.wikipedia.org/wiki/List_of_U.S._states_by_historical_population
3. http://www.inmotionaame.org/print.cfm;jsessionid=f8301458311537418609298?migration=3&bhcp=1 [https://perma.cc/P4TB-U5FZ]
4. http://users.clas.ufl.edu/davidson/Jim%20Crow%20America%20Spring%202016/Jim%20Crow%20America%20course%20readings/Week%204%20construction%20of%20jim%20crow/Rabinowitz%201988.pdf [https://perma.cc/24B6-VBM4]
5. https://www.vox.com/2015/7/13/8913297/mass-incarceration-maps-charts [http://perma.cc/6AU7-DZ9U]
6. http://www.pewresearch.org/fact-tank/2014/03/28/lower-support-for-death-penalty-tracks-with-falling-crime-rates-more-exonerations/ [http://perma.cc/DE3E-4UE2]
7. https://www.c-span.org/video/?c4612766/law-order-richard-nixon-1968-presidential-acceptance-speech [http://perma.cc/V7T3-B5AF]
8. https://www.minnpost.com/community-voices/2014/08/long-powerful-history-how-we-militarized-police/[http://perma.cc/UGF2-YRUM]
9. https://www.forbes.com/sites/adamandrzejewski/2016/05/10/war-weapons-for-americas-local-police-departments/#f2934494af4d [http://perma.cc/LMS9-C4X3];https://www.theatlantic.com/national/archive/2014/08/the-evolution-of-police-militarization-in-ferguson-and-beyond/376107/ [http://perma.cc/PRZ7-M33T]
10. https://www.pbs.org/wgbh/frontline/article/the-problem-with-broken-windows-policing/ [http://perma.cc/UGP9-TTFC]
11. https://web.archive.org/web/20170211080746/http:/oag.state.ny.us/sites/default/files/pdfs/bureaus/civil_rights/stp_frsk.pdf
12. https://www.nyclu.org/en/stop-and-Frisk-data [https://perma.cc/LGN3-JMP5]
13. http://www.pbs.org/independentlens/content/the-rise-of-swat-sources/ [https://perma.cc/FF5K-G78M]; https://www.motherjones.com/politics/2015/07/police-shootings-traffic-stops-excessive-fines/ [https://perma.cc/MP7N-PMKJ]
14. https://qz.com/356013/ferguson-is-what-happens-when-you-run-a-police-force-as-a-profit-making-business/ [http://perma.cc/LQ98-M8E7]
15. https://www.theatlantic.com/politics/archive/2014/04/a-timeline-of-the-rise-and-fall-of-tough-on-crime-drug-sentencing/360983/ [http://perma.cc/2YGL-FH6J]
16. https://www.usnews.com/news/articles/2010/08/03/data-show-racial-disparity-in-crack-sentencing [http://perma.cc/S5JL-6CVV]

17. https://www.vox.com/2015/5/27/8661045/prosecutors-mass-incarceration [http://perma.cc/56WQ-24NC]
18. https://d11gn0ip9m46ig.cloudfront.net/images/059_Bail_Report.pdf [http://perma.cc/CQ9V-4PFN]
19. https://www.bja.gov/Publications/PleaBargainingResearchSummary.pdf [http://perma.cc/4TMD-TXD4]
20. http://www.politifact.com/truth-o-meter/statements/2015/jul/31/cory-booker/was-prison-built-every-10-days-house-fast-growing-/ [http://perma.cc/2CSF-4DS8]
21. https://www.vox.com/2015/7/16/8978579/war-on-drugs-mass-incarceration [http://perma.cc/KF78-24FN]
22. https://www.motherjones.com/politics/2016/06/history-of-americas-private-prison-industry-timeline/ [http://perma.cc/4VBZ-79X8]
23. https://www.theatlantic.com/business/archive/2015/09/prison-labor-in-america/406177/ [http://perma.cc/H454-7M9H]; http://www.latimes.com/opinion/op-ed/la-oe-bozelko-prison-labor-20171020-story.html [http://perma.cc/G6AB-DA9K]; https://www.newyorker.com/business/currency/making-profits-on-the-captive-prison-market [https://perma.cc/W42Q-P4WC]
24. https://www.vox.com/cards/crime-rate-drop/prison-reduce-crime [http://perma.cc/2H3H-2H66]
25. http://newjimcrow.com/about/excerpt-from-the-introduction [http://perma.cc/2UTS-HGTJ]
26. https://www.bjs.gov/content/pub/pdf/ppus08.pdf [http://perma.cc/DT49-723H]
27. http://cepr.net/documents/publications/incarceration-2010-06.pdf [http://perma.cc/B47W-DD3Q]
28. https://sentencingproject.org/wp-content/uploads/2016/01/Trends-in-US-Corrections.pdf [http://perma.cc/7STS-7NKW]
29. http://www.prisonstudies.org/highest-to-lowest/prison-population-total?field_region_taxonomy_tid=All [http://perma.cc/DKJ4-84F8]
30. https://en.wikipedia.org/wiki/Barack_Obama_citizenship_conspiracy_theories
31. https://fivethirtyeight.com/features/inside-the-five-day-stretch-when-obama-found-his-voice-on-race/ [https://perma.cc/NK7R-TKLF]
32. http://www.people-press.org/2014/06/12/section-1-growing-ideological-consistency/#interactive [http://perma.cc/QC29-Y6PW]
33. https://www.vox.com/polyarchy/2016/8/30/12697920/race-dividing-american-politics [http://perma.cc/3C2P-FRLQ]
34. http://www.people-press.org/2017/10/05/the-partisan-divide-on-political-values-grows-even-wider/overview_1-5/ [http://perma.cc/QC29-Y6PW]
35. https://voteview.com/parties/all [http://perma.cc/DE7V-BA42]
36. https://sites.hks.harvard.edu/fs/dshoag/Documents/Political%20Protests%20--%20Evidence%20from%20the%20Tea%20Party.pdf [http://perma.cc/4KSM-R7TC]

37. https://www.indivisible.org/guide/grassroots-advocacy/ [http://perma.cc/TWM4-65HZ]
38. https://www.cheatsheet.com/money-career/amount-money-military-gives-nfl.html/ [http://perma.cc/5P27-YE97]
39. https://www.mccain.senate.gov/public/_cache/files/12de6dcb-d8d8-4a58-8795-562297f948c1/tackling-paid-patriotism-oversight-report.pdf
40. https://www.washingtonpost.com/news/made-by-history/wp/2017/10/08/good-corporate-citizenship-wont-end-racism-the-nfl-must-do-more/?utm_term=.21804adf8fbd [http://perma.cc/A8LL-9R4Q]
41. https://religionandpolitics.org/2017/10/17/the-role-of-sports-ministries-in-the-nfl-protests/ [http://perma.cc/4KMN-VZB3]
42. https://www.si.com/nfl/2017/01/18/president-barack-obama-nfl-players-activism-colin-kaepernick-donovan-mcnabb [http://perma.cc/M2C9-Y2CY]
43. https://en.wikipedia.org/wiki/List_of_Barack_Obama_presidential_campaign_endorsements,_2008#Athletes_and_sports; https://en.wikipedia.org/wiki/List_of_John_McCain_presidential_campaign_endorsements,_2008#Athletes_and_sportspeople
44. https://deadspin.com/5856237/the-stupid-moral-panic-over-mocking-tim-tebow-or-what-would-jesus-do-about-tebowing [http://perma.cc/99ZP-FZJJ]
45. https://religionandpolitics.org/2017/10/17/the-role-of-sports-ministries-in-the-nfl-protests/ [http://perma.cc/4KMN-VZB3]
46. http://www.people-press.org/2017/10/05/the-partisan-divide-on-political-values-grows-even-wider/ [http://perma.cc/D8ZG-BWX3]
47. https://soundcloud.com/chriswebbershow/sports-entertainent-emmett [https://perma.cc/87Z7-SZWS]
48. https://twitter.com/kingjames/status/183243305428058112?lang=en [http://perma.cc/VA3Z-2KM4]; https://30for30podcasts.com/episodes/hoodies-up/ [http://perma.cc/V38P-XD9U]
49. https://theundefeated.com/features/one-year-later-steve-wyche-colin-kaepernick-story/ [http://perma.cc/7SPD-47N7]
50. http://www.chicagotribune.com/news/columnists/glanton/ct-opioid-epidemic-dahleen-glanton-met-20170815-column.html [http://perma.cc/Q5MS-JKQT]
51. https://www.kff.org/other/state-indicator/opioid-overdose-deaths-by-raceethnicity/?dataView=1&currentTimeframe=0&sortModel=%7B%22colId%22:%22Location%22,%22sort%22:%22asc%22%7D [http://perma.cc/VC2Z-ZGXS]
52. https://theintercept.com/2017/01/31/the-fbi-has-quietly-investigated-white-supremacist-infiltration-of-law-enforcement/ [http://perma.cc/CC93-ZAQQ]; https://www.splcenter.org/what-we-do/fighting-hate/law-enforcement-resources [http://perma.cc/KLT7-CGLL]
53. https://infogram.com/2012-racial-breakdown-of-major-us-professional-sports-1g8djp90oxykpyw [http://perma.cc/7EQR-LUXX]

54. http://money.cnn.com/2017/09/25/news/companies/trump-nfl-owners-donations/index.html [http://perma.cc/5NYM-F8DB]
55. https://www.indystar.com/story/sports/nfl/colts/2014/09/30/nfl-fun-league-forbidden-celebrations/16500055/ [http://perma.cc/4CCZ-EHMF]
56. https://deadspin.com/why-only-the-nfl-doesnt-guarantee-contracts-1797020799 [http://perma.cc/J6CL-4USR]
57. https://www.si.com/nfl/2016/03/01/nfl-careers-shortened-two-years-data-analysis [http://perma.cc/V8ZC-TYK9]
58. https://overthecap.com/players-strike-work-nfl-players/ [http://perma.cc/QJ5V-P548]
59. http://www.nytimes.com/2012/09/15/sports/football/views-on-gay-rights-of-ravens-brendon-ayanbadejo-are-rooted-in-upbringing.html
60. https://deadspin.com/5941348/they-wont-magically-turn-you-into-a-lustful-cockmonster-chris-kluwe-explains-gay-marriage-to-the-politician-who-is-offended-by-an-nfl-player-supporting-it [http://perma.cc/AK85-5B5P]
61. http://m.startribune.com/nfl-s-matt-birk-let-s-protect-marriage-and-speech/171850721/ [http://perma.cc/4LQ6-2PWB]
62. http://www.people-press.org/2013/07/22/big-racial-divide-over-zimmerman-verdict/ [http://perma.cc/VWK5-GWTP]
63. http://www.academia.edu/9365974/Talking_about_Trayvon_in_140_Characters_Exploring_NFL_Players_Tweets_about_the_George_Zimmerman_Verdict [https://perma.cc/HEX4-VU53]
64. https://www.youtube.com/watch?v=_D_LC2mJAWY [http://perma.cc/7RGT-9D26]
65. https://deadspin.com/arian-foster-gave-the-same-answer-11-times-in-a-90-seco-1613429436 [http://perma.cc/2HFC-T659]
66. http://www.latimes.com/sports/sportsnow/la-sp-sn-marshawn-lynch-interview-20141222-htmlstory.html [http://perma.cc/SF4P-DSYM]
67. https://www.ninersnation.com/2014/12/3/7329717/colin-kaepernick-transcript-49ers-local-media [http://perma.cc/XB3T-9XL5]
68. http://houston.cbslocal.com/2014/08/14/arian-foster-continues-spat-with-reporters/ [https://perma.cc/XV5E-RFR9]
69. https://www.azcentral.com/story/sports/nfl/super-bowl/2015/01/26/seattle-seahawks-super-bowl-marshawn-lynch-media-day-nfl/22380229/ [http://perma.cc/BY7T-65A4]
70. https://www.justice.gov/sites/default/files/crt/legacy/2015/03/04/ferguson_findings_summ_3-4-15.pdf [http://perma.cc/HK9V-UHXE]
71. http://www.cleveland.com/metro/index.ssf/2014/12/hawkins_delivers_emotional_res.html [http://perma.cc/A3VW-U3RP]
72. https://ftw.usatoday.com/2014/12/kyrie-irving-i-cant-breathe-t-shirt-before-cavaliers-eric-garner-lebron-james [https://perma.cc/N383-6SU8]

73. https://www.thenation.com/article/cleveland-browns-andrew-hawkins-blacklivesmatter-and-accidental-activist/ [https://perma.cc/Q3Z5-THYY]
74. https://www.cbsnews.com/news/st-louis-rams-apologize-for-players-ferguson-hands-up-dont-shoot/ [http://perma.cc/Q4S9-JQVA]; https://www.ksdk.com/article/news/local/slpoa-condemns-rams-display/278759364 [https://perma.cc/X6GV-DBXD]
75. http://www.cleveland.com/metro/index.ssf/2014/12/cleveland_police_union_preside_1.html [http://perma.cc/A3VW-U3RP]
76. https://www.theguardian.com/us-news/2015/mar/18/police-killings-government-data-count [http://perma.cc/QN4W-3AJK]
77. https://www.bja.gov/jag/ [https://perma.cc/NGQ6-879U]
78. http://elearning-courses.net/iacp/html/webinarResources/170926/FinalReport21stCenturyPolicing.pdf [https://perma.cc/P262-4Q2F]
79. https://www.washingtonpost.com/graphics/national/police-shootings/ [http://perma.cc/E9V9-GB44]
80. https://www.theguardian.com/us-news/ng-interactive/2015/jun/01/the-counted-police-killings-us-database [http://perma.cc/DDY7-LLHE]
81. http://killedbypolice.net/ [http://perma.cc/N3ZN-BTHS]; https://www.fatalencounters.org/ [http://perma.cc/LR7H-J2RL]
82. https://www.theguardian.com/us-news/2015/jun/01/black-americans-killed-by-police-analysis [http://perma.cc/7YMH-UXA3]
83. https://theconversation.com/slow-death-is-the-trauma-of-police-violence-killing-black-women-62264 [https://perma.cc/3KZP-P7JC]
84. https://www.booker.senate.gov/?p=press_release&id=247 [http://perma.cc/DAG2-VFYW]
85. https://projects.propublica.org/represent/bills/114/s1476 [http://perma.cc/BQ58-LDGD]
86. https://www.theguardian.com/us-news/2015/oct/02/loretta-lynch-reports-killed-by-police [http://perma.cc/AR97-AVCQ]
87. http://time.com/4066558/police-shootings-data-fbi/ [http://perma.cc/XVK5-E6B7]
88. https://www.cdc.gov/flu/weekly/summary.htm [https://perma.cc/B73E-Y325]; https://www.statista.com/statistics/264396/frequency-of-going-to-the-movies-in-the-us/ [perma.cc/M7PV-53Q2]
89. http://tikiandtierney.radio.cbssports.com/2015/08/07/john-mcclain-bob-mcnair-upset-with-fosters-comments/ [http://perma.cc/VFG5-T569]
90. https://athlonsports.com/nfl/open-letter-new-pittsburgh-steelers-rb-deangelo-williams [https://perma.cc/C2W6-ZEZ5]
91. https://twitter.com/ArianFoster/status/499957451886952449 [https://perma.cc/P8A2-6ATZ]
92. https://theconversation.com/slow-death-is-the-trauma-of-police-violence-killing-black-women-62264 [http://perma.cc/PN2V-G69X]
93. https://www.usatoday.com/story/sports/ncaaf/swac/2013/10/21/grambling-players-provide-shocking-details-former-coach-swayed-them-back-out-of-protest/3144353/ [http://perma.cc/N6NN-7QUN]

94. https://www.columbiamissourian.com/news/answered-common-questions-about-jonathan-butler-s-hunger-strike/article_40c94356-84f0-11e5-a07e-536bff6722fa.html#q6 [https://perma.cc/6F7R-VEPF]
95. https://www.si.com/sports-illustrated/2016/11/21/colin-kaepernick-muhammad-ali-donald-trump [http://perma.cc/4B85-C34T]
96. https://www.sbnation.com/2017/9/24/16357206/national-anthem-protest-wnba-history-donald-trump [http://perma.cc/8676-BYD9]
97. https://twitter.com/A_Phoenix_Born/status/755958534810939392 [https://perma.cc/GQC2-GPEX]
98. https://twitter.com/kelseybone3/status/755914880058654720 [https://perma.cc/R4ZH-37N4]
99. https://bluelivesmatternyc.org/pages/frontpage [https://perma.cc/B3RN-JHBX]
100. https://www.libertariancountry.com/products/am-i-being-detained-t-shirt [https://perma.cc/9ZBM-BMFE]
101. https://www.themaven.net/bluelivesmatter [http://perma.cc/W7NH-HFJ3]
102. http://news.gallup.com/poll/192701/confidence-police-recovers-last-year-low.aspx [http://perma.cc/EAP4-KKPA]
103. https://www.nytimes.com/2017/11/20/opinion/kaepernick-protest-kneel-nfl.html
104. https://www.mrporter.com/journal/the-look/mr-colin-kaepernick/535 [http://perma.cc/4FDB-CWC5]
105. https://www.albany.edu/history/history316/webdub2.html [http://perma.cc/4FDB-CWC5]
106. http://www.maxpreps.com/athlete/colin-kaepernick/dO-Q1zPTlEeKZ5AAmVebBJg/gendersport/football-stats.htm [https://perma.cc/6F5K-L9PE]
107. https://www.gq.com/story/colin-kaepernick-cover-september-2013 [https://perma.cc/PPM8-PZH3]
108. https://www.mrporter.com/journal/the-look/mr-colin-kaepernick/535 [http://perma.cc/4FDB-CWC5]
109. https://www.nytimes.com/2017/09/07/sports/colin-kaepernick-nfl-protests.html
110. https://www.nytimes.com/2017/09/07/sports/colin-kaepernick-nfl-protests.html?smid=pl-share
111. http://www.baltimoresun.com/sports/ravens/ravens-insider/bal-san-francisco-49ers-quarterback-has-every-attribute-a-passer-needs-to-excel-20130203-story.html [http://perma.cc/LFA4-CQB4]; http://wonderlictestsample.com/nfl-wonderlic-scores/ [http://perma.cc/Z47R-RBDT]
112. https://www.si.com/2013/07/23/colin-kaepernick-49ers [http://perma.cc/JWA5-M76E]
113. http://www.espn.com/espn/story/_/id/8897116/colin-kaepernick-birthmom [http://perma.cc/JDC6-MZTM]

114. https://www.cbssports.com/nfl/news/columnist-attacks-colin-kaepernick-for-having-tattoos-compares-him-to-inmates/ [https://perma.cc/MHR8-WQKJ]
115. https://www.si.com/2013/07/23/colin-kaepernick-49ers [http://perma.cc/JWA5-M76E]
116. https://www.gq.com/story/colin-kaepernick-cover-september-2013 [http://perma.cc/HJK4-42TK]
117. https://www.mrporter.com/journal/the-look/mr-colin-kaepernick/535 [http://perma.cc/4FDB-CWC5]
118. https://www.usmagazine.com/celebrity-news/news/colin-kaepernick-details-childhood-racial-struggle-2015810/ [https://perma.cc/888E-3Z88]
119. https://ninernoise.com/2016/08/26/colin-kaepernick-lost-49ers-quarterback-competition/ [http://perma.cc/9SGR-QDGJ]
120. https://athletique.com/89431/2017/08/26/guest-column-the-true-colin-kaepernick-from-someone-who-has-been-there-and-calls-him-a-friend/ [http://perma.cc/2QT3-TCCL]
121. https://sociology.stanford.edu/publications/threshold-models-collective-behavior [http://perma.cc/MDN8-29GB]
122. http://www.nfl.com/news/story/0ap3000000691077/printable/colin-kaepernick-explains-why-he-sat-during-national-anthem [http://perma.cc/AR9R-VJMG]
123. http://www.nfl.com/news/story/0ap3000000691077/printable/colin-kaepernick-explains-why-he-sat-during-national-anthem [http://perma.cc/AR9R-VJMG]
124. http://www.snopes.com/fact-check/must-nfl-players-stand/ [http://perma.cc/CE4J-ESRT]
125. https://profootballtalk.nbcsports.com/2015/05/17/commissioners-power-under-article-46-has-been-present-since-the-first-cba/ [https://perma.cc/R9DB-UMML]
126. https://static.nfl.com/static/content/public/photo/2017/08/11/0ap3000000828506.pdf [http://perma.cc/K2MV-E7TK]
127. https://www.si.com/nfl/2018/05/08/nflpa-grievance-eric-reid-national-anthem [http://perma.cc/QUH3-LBZL]
128. https://www.si.com/nfl/2017/09/23/donald-trump-fired-roger-goodell-player-protest [http://perma.cc/53M6-DXY3]
129. https://www.gq.com/story/the-colin-kaepernick-reading-list [https://perma.cc/4Y9S-NWUK]
130. http://teachingamericanhistory.org/library/document/what-to-the-slave-is-the-fourth-of-july/ [https://perma.cc/TL6L-K3XB]
131. http://theundefeated.com/features/colin-kaepernick-know-your-rights-camp-san-franscico/ [http://perma.cc/RW7M-AYHQ]
132. https://twitter.com/mikegarafolo/status/769498231243993088 [http://perma.cc/RHZ3-HYEM]
133. https://www.youtube.com/watch?v=HRoMlcpxkhY [http://perma.cc/A2BM-D4YM]

134. https://twitter.com/jenniferleechan/status/769446898176495616 [http://perma.cc/65KK-5S8A]
135. https://theundefeated.com/features/one-year-later-steve-wyche-colin-kaepernick-story/ [http://perma.cc/Q6WD-JTNF]
136. http://www.nfl.com/news/story/0ap3000000691077/article/colin-kaepernick-explains-why-he-sat-during-national-anthem [http://perma.cc/7NLL-M67E]; https://profootballtalk.nbcsports.com/2016/08/27/kaepernick-sits-during-national-anthem/ [https://perma.cc/974T-YUZN]
137. https://theundefeated.com/features/abdul-rauf-doesnt-regret-sitting-out-national-anthem/ [http://perma.cc/5LXA-ULUY]
138. https://www.sfgate.com/49ers/article/49ers-Colin-Kaepernick-transcript-I-ll-9189548.php [http://perma.cc/Y3KJ-NKVH]; https://www.washingtonpost.com/news/early-lead/wp/2016/08/28/colin-kaepernick-criticizes-hillary-clinton-and-donald-trump-says-he-will-keep-sitting-during-national-anthem/?noredirect=on&utm_term=.e1a6d75b-40be [http://perma.cc/U3Y9-D7W4]
139. http://teachingamericanhistory.org/library/document/agitation/ [http://perma.cc/TS9F-NX57]
140. https://www.africa.upenn.edu/Articles_Gen/Letter_Birmingham.html [http://perma.cc/L5JV-Z4FV]
141. https://books.google.com/books?id=TV05BgAAQBAJ&pg=PA146&lpg=PA146&dq=the+terrible+truth+is+that+we+cannot+will+ourselves+to+an+escape+on+our+own&source=bl&ots=eqP7BEePz0&sig=UJuyx_2Jzs_SNqI6onEjmfoo3uA&hl=en&sa=X&ved=2ahUKEwjg0PH185TdAhUJ34MKHRaNBP0Q6AEwAn0ECAoQAQ#v=onepage&q=the%20terrible%20truth%20is%20that%20we%20cannot%20will%20ourselves%20to%20an%20escape%20on%20our%20own&f=false [http://perma.cc/2Q6L-5KRH]
142. https://www.theringer.com/2016/8/29/16077318/colin-kaepernick-san-francisco-49ers-national-anthem-cc0e231fdf19 [http://perma.cc/9YT6-JQER]
143. http://www.nfl.com/news/story/0ap3000000693574/article/colin-kaepernick-releases-statement-regarding-socks [http://perma.cc/WZR6-CH25]; https://www.instagram.com/p/BJ0vPsQAGZQ/.
144. https://www.armytimes.com/opinion/2016/08/30/an-open-letter-to-colin-kaepernick-from-a-green-beret-turned-long-snapper/ [http://perma.cc/62ZQ-VJJB]
145. https://www.chargers.com/news/chargers-to-host-28th-annual-salute-to-the-military-at-chargers-49ers-gam-136206 [https://perma.cc/VPW8-HV73]
146. https://www.sfgate.com/49ers/article/49ers-Eric-Reid-transcript-The-meeting-that-9199428.php [http://perma.cc/RUD4-RWUY]
147. https://www.seattletimes.com/sports/seahawks/seahawks-cornerback-jeremy-lane-sits-during-national-anthem-in-oakland/ [http://perma.cc/6D9R-UURU]

148. https://greatergood.berkeley.edu/article/item/the_psychology_of_taking_a_knee [http://perma.cc/Q7U8-26C2]
149. https://www.cbssports.com/nfl/news/heres-how-nate-boyer-got-colin-kaepernick-to-go-from-sitting-to-kneeling/ [https://perma.cc/H48V-N3W6]
150. http://www.espn.com/blog/san-francisco-49ers/post/_/id/19126/transcript-of-colin-kaepernicks-comments-after-preseason-finale [http://perma.cc/SUX3-BKVY]; https://www.breitbart.com/california/2016/09/01/colin-kaepernick-stands-god-bless-america-sitting-national-anthem/ [https://perma.cc/UK7V-UGHM]
151. http://www.espn.com/blog/san-francisco-49ers/post/_/id/19126/transcript-of-colin-kaepernicks-comments-after-preseason-finale [http://perma.cc/SUX3-BKVY]
152. https://www.sfgate.com/49ers/article/49ers-Eric-Reid-transcript-The-meeting-that-9199428.php [http://perma.cc/6QCF-TT7M]
153. https://www.cbssports.com/nfl/news/here-are-the-11-players-who-joined-colin-kaepernicks-protest-in-week-1/ [http://perma.cc/4EGK-7WMW]
154. http://www.espn.com/nfl/story/_/id/17532283/arian-foster-miami-dolphins-plans-continue-kneeling-national-anthem [http://perma.cc/7F87-J3L7]
155. http://www.espn.com/blog/new-england-patriots/post/_/id/4795724/patriots-de-chris-long-shares-perspective-on-colin-kaepernicks-protest [http://perma.cc/H3KB-E82P]
156. https://spectator.org/kaepernicks-culture-warrior-curse/ [http://perma.cc/9F5X-32V8]
157. http://www.orlandosentinel.com/sports/nfl/os-colin-kaepernick-national-anthem-david-whitley-0829-20160828-column.html [http://perma.cc/9QVA-SQ8S]
158. https://www.mercurynews.com/2016/09/11/colin-kaepernick-told-by-espns-trent-dilfer-to-be-quiet-sit-in-the-shadows/ [https://perma.cc/8CS2-SC24]
159. https://www.mercurynews.com/2016/09/11/colin-kaepernick-told-by-espns-trent-dilfer-to-be-quiet-sit-in-the-shadows/ [https://perma.cc/8CS2-SC24]; https://theundefeated.com/features/colin-kaepernick-mix-of-racism-anti-islam-rhetoric-are-increasingly-toxic/ [http://perma.cc/J2UQ-NEVV]; https://www.snopes.com/fact-check/colin-kaepernick-converts-to-islam/ [http://perma.cc/5PKY-XPK3]
160. https://www.usatoday.com/story/sports/nfl/broncos/2016/09/14/brandon-marshall-endorsement-national-anthem-protest-colin-kaepernick/90355508/ [http://perma.cc/5S5X-8CFY]
161. http://www.espn.com/nfl/story/_/id/17597992/colin-kaepernick-san-francisco-49ers-says-gotten-death-threats-protest-national-anthem [http://perma.cc/CTX9-X6DJ]

162. http://www.espn.com/nfl/story/_/id/17604958/san-francisco-49ers-qb-colin-kaepernick-most-disliked-player-nfl-according-poll-e-poll-marketing-research [http://perma.cc/TC6R-A9KJ]
163. https://www.forbes.com/sites/darrenheitner/2016/09/07/colin-kaepernick-tops-jersey-sales-in-nfl/#fd1356a7aad9 [http://perma.cc/ZZQ4-CD46]
164. http://www.espn.com/nfl/story/_/id/17485819/colin-kaepernick-san-francisco-49ers-donate-jersey-sales-proceeds [http://perma.cc/6RKW-2ABP]
165. http://www.latimes.com/sports/nfl/la-sp-colin-kaepernick-49ers-donation-20160908-snap-story.html [http://perma.cc/MND4-S4W4]
166. https://www.si.com/sportsperson/2017/12/06/colin-kaepernick-charity-giving-donations [http://perma.cc/Z2RL-EGMQ]; https://www.ninersnation.com/2018/1/31/16956016/colin-kaepernick-donations-full-list-of-organizations-one-million-dollars [http://perma.cc/3H75-563M]
167. http://www.100suits.org/ [http://perma.cc/6HN8-3VSA]
168. https://appetiteforchangemn.org/ [http://perma.cc/8E2P-FSNC]
169. https://www.lifeafterhate.org/ [http://perma.cc/P86F-3C63]
170. https://theathletic.com/89431/2017/08/26/guest-column-the-true-colin-kaepernick-from-someone-who-has-been-there-and-calls-him-a-friend/ [http://perma.cc/M3SB-BYCY]
171. http://knowyourrightscamp.com/ [https://perma.cc/E8UL-743U]
172. https://www.civilrightsteaching.org/voting-rights/exploring-history-freedom-schools/ [https://perma.cc/A3TV-EU2Q]; https://www.aaihs.org/the-black-panther-party/ [https://perma.cc/6B8Y-ZD3H]
173. http://theundefeated.com/features/colin-kaepernick-know-your-rights-camp-san-franscico/ [http://perma.cc/TM7G-4DP7]
174. https://www.thenation.com/article/colin-kaepernicks-message-to-chicago-youth-know-your-rights/ [http://perma.cc/J4KN-8ES7]
175. https://thinkprogress.org/national-anthem-sports-protest-tracker-kaepernick-284ff1d1ab3e/ [http://perma.cc/CD9P-SX7R]
176. http://www.espn.com/blog/nflnation/post/_/id/220055/eagles-malcolm-jenkins-adds-perspective-to-protest-in-ride-with-philly-police [http://perma.cc/BEV7-PYU6]
177. https://ninerswire.usatoday.com/2016/08/28/transcript-colin-kaepernick-addresses-sitting-during-national-anthem/ [https://perma.cc/7A9E-CTHC]
178. https://www.sfgate.com/49ers/article/49ers-Colin-Kaepernick-transcript-I-ll-9189548.php [http://perma.cc/M7VT-N5KB]
179. https://ftw.usatoday.com/2016/09/colin-kaepernick-donald-trump-hillary-clinton-proven-liars-quote [http://perma.cc/3CR5-LTP2]
180. https://www.politifact.com/truth-o-meter/statements/2016/aug/28/reince-priebus/did-hillary-clinton-call-african-american-youth-su/ [https://perma.cc/E2ZT-A42A]

181. https://medium.com/thewashingtonpost/inside-the-washington-posts-police-shootings-database-an-oral-history-413121889529 [https://perma.cc/7XRN-FAG8]
182. https://news.vice.com/en_us/article/xwvv3a/shot-by-cops [http://perma.cc/P4SX-3Y4V]
183. https://www.theguardian.com/us-news/ng-interactive/2015/jun/01/the-counted-police-killings-us-database [http://perma.cc/YY2F-9GQY]; https://www.washingtonpost.com/policeshootings/?noredirect=on&utm_term=.cde5d3c168a1 [http://perma.cc/BM8D-FJCF]
184. https://www.theguardian.com/us-news/2015/jun/09/the-counted-police-killings-us-vs-other-countries [http://perma.cc/7LWT-EHG7]
185. https://www.theguardian.com/us-news/2015/dec/31/the-counted-police-killings-2015-young-black-men [http://perma.cc/YY2F-9GQY]
186. https://scholar.harvard.edu/files/fryer/files/fryer_police_aer.pdf [http://perma.cc/L8UR-ZYW4]
187. https://www.theguardian.com/us-news/2015/sep/01/moving-targets-police-shootings-vehicles-the-counted [http://perma.cc/7DMQ-38EF]
188. https://www.washingtonpost.com/graphics/national/police-shootings-2017/?noredirect=on [http://perma.cc/MU9G-JGB2]
189. https://www.theguardian.com/us-news/2015/dec/31/ties-that-bind-conflicts-of-interest-police-killings [http://perma.cc/PEC8-PDBD]
190 http://time.com/4398392/obama-police-reform-report-task-force-on-21st-century-policing/ [http://perma.cc/NVA3-LRDU]
191. https://news.vice.com/en_us/article/xwvv3a/shot-by-cops [http://perma.cc/P4SX-3Y4V]
192. https://www.washingtonpost.com/graphics/national/police-shootings-2017/?noredirect=on [http://perma.cc/MU9G-JGB2]
193. https://www.theguardian.com/us-news/2015/dec/31/the-counted-police-killings-2015-young-black-men [http://perma.cc/YY2F-9GQY]
194. https://www.fbi.gov/news/speeches/the-true-heart-of-american-law-enforcement [http://perma.cc/RN2R-SCEA]
195. https://newrepublic.com/article/146940/chance-criminal-justice-reform-trump [http://perma.cc/YL59-THLS]
196. https://newrepublic.com/article/146940/chance-criminal-justice-reform-trump [http://perma.cc/YL59-THLS]
197. https://www.snopes.com/fact-check/donald-trump-racist-meme/ [http://perma.cc/SY4X-TCW6]; https://www.pbs.org/weta/washingtonweek/web-video/paul-ryan-trump-made-textbook-definition-racist-comment [http://perma.cc/W998-DJ88]
198. https://thinkprogress.org/donald-trump-on-black-lives-matter-we-have-to-give-power-back-to-the-police-6769b42e96fb/#.vlnhm9a4i [http://perma.cc/YM8A-6FM8]
199. http://dailycaller.com/2015/08/03/trump-we-have-to-give-power-back-to-the-police-video/ [http://perma.cc/6J25-8SFC]; https://www.

whitehouse.gov/briefings-statements/the-inaugural-address/ [http://perma.cc/Y5HZ-U9R8]
200. http://nymag.com/daily/intelligencer/2016/11/sessions-as-ag-means-criminal-justice-reform-is-dead.html [http://perma.cc/THU6-YNAB]
201. https://www.cnn.com/2016/08/30/opinions/where-kaepernick-lost-me-cane/index.html [http://perma.cc/49Q7-UFYN]
202. https://www.thenation.com/article/colin-kaepernick-has-a-right-to-hate-both-candidates/ [http://perma.cc/ED9X-WRJJ]
203. https://www.politico.com/magazine/story/2017/11/08/donald-trump-johnstown-pennsylvania-supporters-215800 [http://perma.cc/3GEE-8M8D]; https://morningconsult.com/form/avoiding-a-firestorm-the-political-issues-brands-should-steer-clear-of/ [http://perma.cc/ZN55-NEPJ]; https://www.mercurynews.com/2016/08/31/colin-kaepernicks-hometown-of-turlock-turns-its-back-on-native-son/ [http://perma.cc/Q2Q7-NBZ5]
204. http://www.pewresearch.org/fact-tank/2017/05/12/black-voter-turnout-fell-in-2016-even-as-a-record-number-of-americans-cast-ballots/ [http://perma.cc/3YRZ-UMYB]
205. http://www.sportingnews.com/us/nfl/news/donald-trump-colin-kaepernick-national-anthem-flag-protest/1f52ma0o08u22100zf7dpdmv0c [http://perma.cc/88TT-8CF5]
206. http://mynorthwest.com/379820/donald-trump-on-colin-kaepernick-he-should-find-another-country/ [http://perma.cc/67FS-DEZK]
207. https://www.ninersnation.com/2016/9/29/13105864/bill-oreilly-donald-trump-video-colin-kaepernick-national-anthem-protest [http://perma.cc/3KHC-TJBB]
208. https://www.reuters.com/article/us-usa-election-spending-idUSKBN1341JR [http://perma.cc/4AH5-W8W7]
209. https://thelab.bleacherreport.com/donald-trump-is-tearing-the-nfl-apart/ [http://perma.cc/6H56-LBAD]
210. https://www.270towin.com/2016_Election/ [http://perma.cc/GAN8-3DG7]
211. https://thedigitalpress.org/picking-the-president/ [http://perma.cc/FJF9-5EZP]
212. https://www.archives.gov/publications/prologue/2000/winter/garrisons-constitution-1.html [http://perma.cc/KK4F-PKN8]
213. https://wcm1.web.rice.edu/book-introduction.html [http://perma.cc/4ADS-Z5WF]
214. https://www.nbcsports.com/bayarea/49ers/kaepernick-it-would-be-hypocritical-me-vote [http://perma.cc/RVV2-CFJ8]
215. https://www.usatoday.com/story/sports/nfl/49ers/2016/11/09/colin-kaepernick-donald-trump-hillary-clinton-election/93569110/ [http://perma.cc/PMF8-QSCZ]
216. http://www.espn.com/blog/nflnation/post/_/id/227095/nfl-players-who-protested-during-the-national-anthem-in-week-17 [http://perma.cc/K5LM-FQTP]

217. http://www.espn.com/nfl/story/_/id/18818589/colin-kaepernick-opts-contract-becomes-free-agent [http://perma.cc/2MVK-96S7]
218. http://www.espn.com/espn/feature/story/_/page/enterpriseCoalition180126/colin-kaepernick-movement-endures-supporters-more-fragmented-ever [http://perma.cc/C38J-K55Y]
219. https://www.youtube.com/watch?v=1IocUTXwr-k [http://perma.cc/MN59-GNAK]
220. http://www.sportingnews.com/nfl/news/hall-of-fame-game-nfl-offseason-cowboys-elliott-jerry-jones-kaepernick/1bnpoll7fsegx1p9elzeecpxvo [http://perma.cc/BK6L-6N7L]
221. http://www.espn.com/nfl/story/_/id/18412873/nfl-tv-viewership-drops-average-8-percent-season [http://perma.cc/UTG7-25A5]
222. http://www.laweekly.com/news/nfl-faces-possible-boycott-over-colin-kaepernick-8489062 [http://perma.cc/6Z9T-DU6A]; https://www.change.org/p/nokaepernicknonfl-boycott-nfl-games-if-colin-kaepernick-doesn-t-play-this-season-nflcommish [http://perma.cc/ADW3-7WTD]
223. http://www.espn.com/espn/feature/story/_/page/enterpriseCoalition180126/colin-kaepernick-movement-endures-supporters-more-fragmented-ever [http://perma.cc/C38J-K55Y]
224. http://www.espn.com/blog/nflnation/post/_/id/244795/nfl-players-who-protested-during-the-national-anthem-of-the-2017-preseason [http://perma.cc/ELM8-D5NU]
225. https://www.si.com/nfl/2017/08/22/seth-devalve-national-anthem-protest-cleveland-browns [http://perma.cc/GGL7-S3ZP]
226. https://www.whitehouse.gov/briefings-statements/remarks-president-trump-infrastructure/ [http://perma.cc/72LV-ANTE]
227. https://www.npr.org/sections/thetwo-way/2017/12/14/570984855/first-degree-murder-charge-against-man-who-drove-into-charlottesville-demonstrat [http://perma.cc/G3FA-TKW9]; https://www.cnn.com/2017/08/13/us/charlottesville-heather-heyer-profile/index.html [http://perma.cc/895D-6F4L]
228. https://twitter.com/playercoalition [http://perma.cc/9NDN-VHHD]
229. https://abcnews.go.com/Sports/colin-kaepernicks-inclusion-players-coalition-heart-eric-reid/story?id=51477368 [http://perma.cc/ZGG7-CXDL]
230. https://theundefeated.com/features/irreconcilable-differences-why-the-nfl-players-coalition-split-apart/ [http://perma.cc/6C-QU-LPAL]
231. http://www.sportingnews.com/us/nfl/news/colin-kaepernick-supporters-hold-protest-outside-nfl-headquarters-nyc/1wyf915xwb-wo21fducokjalkvs [http://perma.cc/QCJ7-JEKK]; https://theathletic.com/89431/2017/08/26/guest-column-the-true-colin-kaepernick-from-someone-who-has-been-there-and-calls-him-a-friend/ [http://perma.cc/98ZS-GVHW]

232. http://www.espn.com/blog/nflnation/post/_/id/247658/nfl-players-who-protested-during-the-national-anthem-in-week-1 [http://perma.cc/V9VL-PFX9]; http://www.espn.com/blog/nflnation/post/_/id/248762/nfl-players-who-protested-during-the-national-anthem-in-week-2 [http://perma.cc/FT8X-9FS2]
233. http://time.com/4954684/donald-trump-nfl-speech-anthem-protests/ [http://perma.cc/6FRB-HX4R]
234. http://www.espn.com/blog/nflnation/post/_/id/249755/nfl-players-who-protested-during-the-national-anthem-in-week-3 [http://perma.cc/ZXT6-AZXG]
235. http://money.cnn.com/2017/09/24/media/nfl-unity-ad-trump/ [http://perma.cc/PR9E-BEGZ]
236. https://www.youtube.com/watch?v=JIq6dXEvGvY&sns=em [http://perma.cc/5SKF-ECUC]
237. https://twitter.com/realdonaldtrump/status/912280282224525312 [http://perma.cc/94DG-49T7]
238. https://www.nytimes.com/2017/09/25/opinion/colin-kaepernick-football-protests.html
239. https://www.snopes.com/football-fan-flag-stand-national-anthem/ [http://perma.cc/V3UE-GZWJ]
240. https://www.legion.org/flag/questions-answers/91517/it-permissible-wear-item-clothing-looks-united-states-flag [http://perma.cc/7U5H-CQVX]
241. https://www.theblaze.com/news/2010/10/20/did-sarah-palin-sign-an-american-flag [http://perma.cc/9BC8-9MQA]
242. https://forgottenhistoryblog.com/media/images/ZZ416A2017.jpg [http://perma.cc/YWD4-S27F]
243. https://splinternews.com/great-moments-in-celebrities-wearing-american-flags-1793860028 [http://perma.cc/34CV-7JAZ]
244. https://gizmodo.com/5839995/those-humungous-american-flags-at-football-stadiums-weigh-1100-pounds-and-cost-50000-to-make [http://perma.cc/L72J-MR3K]; https://www.legion.org/flag/code [http://perma.cc/M5Y4-FZEL]
245. https://twitter.com/astros/status/917504561912442880 [http://perma.cc/L3BZ-U4GE]
246. https://en.wikipedia.org/wiki/Reasonable_person
247. http://themercury.com/opinion/i-m-offended-by-butchering-of-national-anthem-but-not/article_522bcd43-4838-56be-89f6-82a5079e88e1.html [http://perma.cc/39ES-B98C]
248. http://ftw.usatoday.com/2017/10/kirk-cousins-cringed-chiefs-anthem-protest-redskins-peters-monday-night-football-nfl [http://perma.cc/455M-WHW2]
249. https://medium.com/sportspickle/baltimore-fans-yell-o-during-national-anthem-to-raise-awareness-that-they-like-the-orioles-f3ede0d98de0 [http://perma.cc/4UEW-ZQRX]

250. http://www.inforum.com/news/3818740-sioux-chants-could-mean-consequences-und [http://perma.cc/J6FP-8MFJ]
251. https://www.esquire.com/news-politics/politics/a20915719/nfl-national-anthem-protests-concessions-ex-player/ [http://perma.cc/6K7M-FBX8]
252. https://www.instagram.com/p/BZjpUNpF7iA/?utm_source=ig_embed [http://perma.cc/ET9V-NQXY]
253. https://www.nytimes.com/2017/10/01/sports/football/nfl-anthem-protest.html
254. https://www.facebook.com/Mediamatters/videos/10154972993406167/ [http://perma.cc/QTC5-G5N6]
255. http://www.bvsj.org/ [http://perma.cc/JRG4-38XA]
256. https://twitter.com/RobertKlemko/status/938545782743097345 [http://perma.cc/HCY6-JV3A]
257. https://fivethirtyeight.com/features/how-do-americans-feel-about-the-nfl-protests-it-depends-on-how-you-ask/ [http://perma.cc/CG3N-C8MX]
258. https://sports.vice.com/en_us/article/kz3kzm/five-cheerleaders-kneeled-for-the-anthem-the-scariest-thing-ive-ever-done [http://perma.cc/L5LN-Q2LX]
259. http://usatodayhss.com/2017/national-anthem-kneeling-high-school-football-protest-racial-injustice [http://perma.cc/XCH5-MQM3]
260. https://www.dailymail.co.uk/news/article-4960586/Woman-throws-drink-two-men-kneeling-anthem.html [http://perma.cc/7J3P-QRYL]
261. https://twitter.com/vp/status/917078269077413888 [http://perma.cc/6J4E-N7X3]
262. https://twitter.com/PeterAlexander/status/917094805276168192 [http://perma.cc/Q4R7-LCUJ]; https://www.si.com/nfl/2017/10/08/mike-pence-colts-tweet-national-anthem-protest-vice-president [http://perma.cc/D3DU-U3PC]
263. https://twitter.com/baratunde/status/917140377735499777?lang=en [http://perma.cc/FKJ5-5H25]
264. https://twitter.com/realDonaldTrump/status/917091286607433728 [http://perma.cc/Z3XZ-KLM4]
265. https://www.usatoday.com/story/sports/nfl/columnist/bell/2017/10/09/jerry-jones-dallas-cowboys-stand-national-anthem-very-bright-line/748375001/ [http://perma.cc/5V46-9TH6]
266. https://www.si.com/extra-mustard/2017/10/09/jerry-jones-dallas-cowboys-national-anthem-protest-kneeling [http://perma.cc/BSN8-EJVD]
267. https://sportsday.dallasnews.com/dallas-cowboys/cowboys/2017/10/09/imagine-jerry-jones-demanding-cowboys-respect-women-strongly-demands-respect-flag [http://perma.cc/S7MB-DPN8]

268. https://www.si.com/nfl/2017/09/23/donald-trump-fired-roger-goodell-player-protest [http://perma.cc/GT9G-9XMG]
269. http://www.espn.com/college-football/story/_/id/21137492/division-iii-football-player-kicked-team-kneeling-national-anthem [http://perma.cc/M9TM-Z2CT]; https://www.youtube.com/watch?v=ucAz8NqwGA4 [http://perma.cc/B7FA-3HEW]
270. https://www.cnn.com/2017/10/01/us/high-school-football-kicked-off-protest/index.html [http://perma.cc/3W6Z-QT45]
271. https://www.si.com/tech-media/2017/10/09/jemele-hill-suspend-espn [http://perma.cc/W8DA-2M2X]; https://twitter.com/jemelehill/status/917217116662763520 [http://perma.cc/P3KJ-6M97]
272. https://theundefeated.com/features/irreconcilable-differences-why-the-nfl-players-coalition-split-apart/ [http://perma.cc/6C-QU-LPAL]
273. https://www.cbssports.com/nfl/news/roger-goodell-visits-philly-to-talk-criminal-justice-reform-with-lurie-eagles/ [http://perma.cc/AK99-VQJA]
274. https://pbs.twimg.com/media/DLy4E3FWkAAzDhx.jpg [http://perma.cc/7EHH-MC9Q]
275. https://twitter.com/realDonaldTrump/status/918065431939829760 [http://perma.cc/F2W6-R3FP]
276. https://www.facebook.com/AdamSchefter/posts/1646979115354723 [http://perma.cc/A4SY-HEM6]
277. http://www.espn.com/nfl/story/_/id/20989433/gerald-mccoy-tampa-bay-buccaneers-uproar-players-forced-stand [http://perma.cc/HF2G-8BPB]
278. http://www.espn.com/nfl/story/_/id/21003968/nfl-2017-ex-green-beret-nate-boyer-writes-open-letter-president-donald-trump-colin-kaepernick-nfl-united-states-america [http://perma.cc/YW2V-X4MC]
279. https://www.nytimes.com/interactive/2017/10/11/upshot/trump-nfl-polarization.html
280. http://nationalhumanitiescenter.org/tserve/twenty/tkeyinfo/garvey.htm [http://perma.cc/U82L-Y7PF]
281. https://www.miamiherald.com/sports/spt-columns-blogs/armando-salguero/article117033883.html [http://perma.cc/F4PZ-QG94]
282. https://www.npr.org/templates/story/story.php?storyId=1128093 [http://perma.cc/2E7V-7KVJ]
283. https://www.thenation.com/article/colin-kaepernicks-message-to-chicago-youth-know-your-rights/ [http://perma.cc/5AC3-W7PP]
284. https://www.washingtonpost.com/news/the-fix/wp/2016/04/19/black-lives-matters-and-americas-long-history-of-resisting-civil-rights-protesters/?utm_term=.092ba91651bb [http://perma.cc/M6NK-3DZW]
285. http://www.espn.com/espn/otl/story/_/id/21170410/gaffes-tv-ratings-concerns-dominated-nfl-players-forged-anthem-peace-league-meetings [http://perma.cc/FEH9-UZE4]

286. http://www.slate.com/blogs/the_slatest/2017/10/29/colin_kaepernick_frozen_out_of_discussions_between_nfl_players_and_owners.html [http://perma.cc/5E72-YHCD]
287. http://www.espn.com/nfl/story/_/id/21035352/colin-kaepernick-files-grievance-nfl-owners-collusion [http://perma.cc/8ZPM-3K2Z]
288. https://theundefeated.com/features/nfl-owners-players-meet-to-talk-race-justice-and-working-together/ [http://perma.cc/U3LW-RZLZ]; https://www.nytimes.com/2018/04/25/sports/nfl-owners-kaepernick.html
289. https://www.sbnation.com/2017/10/27/16559952/bob-mcnair-houston-texans-nfl-owners-meeting-protests [http://perma.cc/KM78-3V38]
290. http://www.kansascity.com/sports/college/article176201431.html [http://perma.cc/L37L-L9LV]
291. http://www.kansascity.com/sports/college/article181351036.html [http://perma.cc/ER8D-FV2E]
292. http://money.cnn.com/2017/11/01/media/nfl-papa-johns-protests/index.html [http://perma.cc/SA7L-NQ3N]
293. https://www.washingtonpost.com/news/business/wp/2017/12/21/papa-johns-founder-replaced-as-ceo-weeks-after-blaming-the-nfl-for-sagging-pizza-sales/?utm_term=.9a78dd9d2d62 [http://perma.cc/5CFV-GK7V]
294. https://www.si.com/nfl/2017/10/29/colin-kaepernick-nfl-players-meeting-eric-reid-malcolm-jenkins [http://perma.cc/W2UN-CPGR]
295. http://www.espn.com/blog/philadelphia-eagles/post/_/id/19079/eagles-malcolm-jenkins-adds-perspective-to-protest-in-ride-with-philly-police [http://perma.cc/TB35-3T5Z]; https://www.youtube.com/watch?v=VbtLGLw12mE [http://perma.cc/SZQ3-35GL]
296. http://www.espn.com/nfl/story/_/id/18053552/nfl-players-headed-capitol-hill-talk-police-relations-race-issues-meet-paul-ryan [http://perma.cc/F79J-UFYL]; http://www.nj.com/eagles/index.ssf/2016/11/eagles_malcolm_jenkins_gets_post-meeting_shout-out.html [http://perma.cc/56RE-UWZL]
297. https://theundefeated.com/features/irreconcilable-differences-why-the-nfl-players-coalition-split-apart/ [http://perma.cc/6C-QU-LPAL]
298. https://twitter.com/realDonaldTrump/status/932570628451954688 [http://perma.cc/4GM5-37JV]
299. https://twitter.com/realDonaldTrump/status/934026050388013056 [http://perma.cc/KW94-6AF8]
300. https://www.newyorker.com/news/news-desk/from-louis-armstrong-to-the-nfl-ungrateful-as-the-new-uppity [http://perma.cc/2ACJ-B24H]
301. https://projects.fivethirtyeight.com/trump-approval-ratings/?ex_cid=rrpromo [http://perma.cc/875M-S5F7]
302. http://www.espn.com/nfl/story/_/id/21606390/nfl-offers-100-million-plan-social-justice-organizations-partnership-players [http://perma.cc/WAZ6-R8CW]

303. https://theundefeated.com/features/dolphins-kenny-stills-we-have-to-get-people-to-understand-what-racism-is/ [http://perma.cc/ZT6D-BHEN]; https://www.theplayerstribune.com/russell-okung-an-open-letter-to-all-nfl-players/ [http://perma.cc/7EHE-8KEH]
304. https://theundefeated.com/features/irreconcilable-differences-why-the-nfl-players-coalition-split-apart/ [http://perma.cc/6C-QU-LPAL]
305. http://www.espn.com/nfl/story/_/id/21614673/nfl-agrees-commit-nearly-100m-seven-years-charities-important-african-american-communities [http://perma.cc/4FGY-VMN5]
306. https://slate.com/culture/2017/11/eric-reid-was-asked-if-hed-stop-protests-if-nfl-donated-usd100-million-to-charity.html [http://perma.cc/W36A-CKF8]; http://www.espn.com/nfl/story/_/id/21606390/nfl-offers-100-million-plan-social-justice-organizations-partnership-players [http://perma.cc/WAZ6-R8CW]
307. https://deadspin.com/the-nfls-proposal-to-end-anthem-protests-gives-the-nfl-1820876878 [http://perma.cc/WYJ5-G5XS]
308. https://theundefeated.com/features/irreconcilable-differences-why-the-nfl-players-coalition-split-apart/ [http://perma.cc/6C-QU-LPAL]
309. https://www.uncf.org/ [http://perma.cc/83FE-XKBL]; https://www.insidehighered.com/news/2017/12/05/some-question-nfl-gift-uncf [http://perma.cc/SD7R-6GXJ]
310. https://www.thedreamcorps.org/ [http://perma.cc/KX7Q-9YE3]
311. https://deadspin.com/what-the-hell-is-the-hopewell-fund-1820881123 [http://perma.cc/8P27-JUXQ]
312. https://www.thenation.com/article/two-different-paths-two-different-goals-understanding-the-rift-in-the-nfls-players-coalition/ [http://perma.cc/KUQ2-G7FY]
313. https://deadspin.com/no-more-the-nfls-domestic-violence-partner-is-a-sham-1683348576 [http://perma.cc/D688-SEL4]
314. https://jezebel.com/5950971/the-nfls-campaign-against-breast-cancer-is-a-total-scam [http://perma.cc/QT22-BYV4]
315. http://www.espn.com/espn/otl/story/_/id/14417386/nfl-pulls-funding-boston-university-head-trauma-study-concerns-researcher [http://perma.cc/J9DG-TP4E]
316. https://deadspin.com/what-the-hell-is-the-hopewell-fund-1820881123 [http://perma.cc/8P27-JUXQ]
317. http://www.foxnews.com/opinion/2017/12/03/nfls-proposed-100-million-in-donations-is-foolish-political-stunt.html [http://perma.cc/DM6L-BVEZ]
318. https://www.washingtontimes.com/news/2017/dec/4/nfl-inks-deal-george-soros-linked-social-justice-g/ [http://perma.cc/F6C2-M8LA]
319. http://www.espn.com/blog/nflnation/post/_/id/264431/nfl-players-who-protested-during-national-anthem-in-week-17 [http://perma.cc/FS34-XDTP]

320. http://bleacherreport.com/articles/2747266-russell-okung-explains-players-coalition-split-says-89m-donation-plan-farce [http://perma.cc/U5X6-ZUNQ]
321. https://slate.com/culture/2017/11/eric-reid-says-nfl-wants-to-use-money-from-military-programs-to-buy-off-players.html [http://perma.cc/EWE3-VAGX]
322. https://www.sbnation.com/2018/1/31/16935356/colin-kaepernick-donate-organizations-million-dollar-pledge-10-for-10 [http://perma.cc/ZC2C-UQXH]
323. https://www.si.com/sportsperson/2017/11/30/colin-kaepernick-muhammad-ali-legacy-award [http://perma.cc/B5KV-NFFS]
324. http://www.chicagotribune.com/sports/football/ct-colin-kaepernick-honored-by-aclu-20171204-story.html [http://perma.cc/K8CN-ER6Z]
325. https://www.hollywoodreporter.com/news/robert-f-kennedy-foundation-celebrates-colin-kaepernick-harry-belafontes-activism-1067599 [http://perma.cc/AML7-BXV2]
326. https://www.newyorker.com/culture/cover-story/cover-story-2018-01-15 [http://perma.cc/HTA6-9JVB]
327. https://www.usatoday.com/story/sports/nfl/2018/01/23/kaepernick-watt-among-5-finalists-for-whizzer-white-award/109742446/ [http://perma.cc/DG7A-4NKP]
328. https://www.racked.com/2018/1/4/16846314/colin-kaepernick-nfl-clothing-media [http://perma.cc/A9ES-K7R6]
329. https://twitter.com/Kaepernick7/status/958903136223023104 [http://perma.cc/Z2W9-ZDMM]
330. https://www.usatoday.com/videos/sports/nfl/eagles/2018/02/05/nick-foles-offers-inspiring-words-advice-failure/110125750/ [http://perma.cc/DG4F-8CH2]
331. https://deadspin.com/for-the-last-time-nfl-ratings-are-not-down-theyre-up-1827378925 [http://perma.cc/6S4W-84RA]
332. https://en.wikipedia.org/wiki/List_of_most_watched_television_broadcasts_in_the_United_States
333. https://www.washingtontimes.com/news/2018/jan/15/nfls-kneeling-protesters-miss-playoffs/ [http://perma.cc/B67T-W8AY]
334. http://thecomeback.com/nfl/nfl-2018-playoffs-retain-four-teams-last-year-tied-since-1991.html [http://perma.cc/MPA8-EBMS]
335. https://www.thenation.com/article/the-nfl-chose-to-tank-its-season-rather-than-sign-colin-kaepernick/ [http://perma.cc/RBJ2-9MFR]
336. https://www.snopes.com/fact-check/patriots-white-house-attendance/ [http://perma.cc/WR6A-7TTZ]
337. http://www.espn.com/nfl/story/_/id/18006423/new-england-patriots-bill-belichick-says-letter-donald-trump-not-political [http://perma.cc/64CP-48YJ]; http://www.nbcsports.com/boston/new-england-patriots/belichick-did-indeed-write-letter-trump [http://perma.cc/F6B8-58PG]

338. https://www.elitedaily.com/p/tom-brady-donald-trumps-relationship-is-complicated-8100986 [http://perma.cc/2ANZ-W66M]
339. http://www.espn.com/nfl/story/_/id/21061905/philadelphia-eagles-defensive-end-chris-long-now-donating-entire-season-salary [http://perma.cc/S7Q4-VMGC]
340. https://www.theringer.com/nfl/2018/2/5/16973684/meek-mill-dreams-and-nightmares-philadelphia-eagles-super-bowl-lii [http://perma.cc/R3NB-R6RX]; https://twitter.com/JClarkNBCS/status/955247033815916545 [http://perma.cc/U4W9-K3XY]
341. http://www.newsweek.com/philadelphia-chaos-reveals-racial-double-standard-over-riots-critics-say-799421 [http://perma.cc/TW9R-WX-CC]
342. http://www.risetowin.org/wp-content/uploads/2018/03/Report-The-Athlete%E2%80%99s-Quest-for-Social-Justice-An-examination-of-2017-Goals-and-Impact-rev-3-9-18.pdf [http://perma.cc/N9LR-4GF2]
343. https://www.brennancenter.org/publication/criminal-justice-one-year-trump-administration [http://perma.cc/BG26-UFNH]; https://harvardlawreview.org/2017/01/the-presidents-role-in-advancing-criminal-justice-reform/ [https://perma.cc/JU8T-BVH4]
344. https://kaepernick7.com/pages/colin-kaepernicks-10for10-encore-1 [http://perma.cc/XZZ5-XU2H]

Section One

The United States and Its Anthem

"Oh Say, Can You See?": The National Anthem

Jon Foreman

This essay originally appeared on *Switchfoot* on October 13, 2017. http://switchfoot.com/the-national-anthem/ [https://perma.cc/JJ4S-66X9]

    The National Anthem of the United States of America is not a statement. It's a question. And we, my friends, are the nation in question.

    I was standing side stage with a mic in my hand getting ready to sing the national anthem at a NASCAR race. The top 8 finalists for a popular TV singing contest just got up and crushed "God bless America." And I'm supposed to just go ahead and sing the anthem. No accompaniment, just me. So I start in.

    And then halfway through the anthem, my renegade mind starts to wander. Instead of focusing on the lyrics and pitch and making it through to "the home of the brave," my brain starts to analyze the sentence structure. For the record, I'm not the guy to parse out sentence structure. Besides, even if our nation's anthem is grammatically fascinating, syntax was probably the worst thing I could be thinking about right then. Distraction from the task at hand could lead to angry NASCAR fans, and angry NASCAR fans is never the goal.

So there I was—still singing this anthem. Still thinking about grammar. It was an out of body experience. I was in three places at once; my mouth and my lungs were singing; my brain was pondering the syntax; and something beyond my brain was yelling at my brain to pay attention.

Nonetheless, that was the moment that I realized what the National Anthem of the United States of America meant to me. And it all comes down to punctuation.

Our national anthem consists of two meandering questions with a wandering statement in between. The first question is an incredibly long, run-on sentence that's especially easy to get lost in. The first part goes like this:

"Oh say can you see
by the dawn's early light,
what so proudly we hailed
at the twilight's last gleaming..."

This would be a good place to begin a new sentence but the question continues with more specifics about about the flag:

"...whose broad stripes and bright stars,
through the perilous fight
o'er the ramparts we watched
were so gallantly streaming?"

Here we get a little more context of this perilous fight and some glowing adjectives describing the flag. The second sentence talks a bit more about the battle that went on during the night:

"And the rockets red glare,
the bombs bursting in air,
gave proof through the night
that the flag was still there."

This second sentence, annunciates that even through the dark night of battle the flag was still there, (lit up by the light of exploding rockets and bombs).

It's worth noting that even though we're almost to the end of the anthem there has been almost no mention of the nation over which the flag stands. There's been a lot of specifics about the flag and the battle but nothing about liberty or justice. Or honor or patriotism. Just pride in hailing the flag in the twilight. The anthem concludes with yet another question:

"Oh say does that star-spangled banner yet wave,
o'er the land of the free and the home of the brave?"

And now, in the final two lines of the song we hear our first few details about the people who hail the flag, who are purportedly free and brave. And as I stood singing those words onstage in front of NASCAR enthusiasts, I realized something I had never thought about before. The most important, most overlooked aspect of the national anthem is this: It's not a declaration. It's a question. "Does the banner yet wave over the land of the free and the home of the brave?"

Since we're singing these words while staring at the flag, the question is not whether or not the flag is still there. The question is for us is this: are we the "land of the free and the home of the brave?" Who are we the people? What is the character of the nation underneath the flag? Do we empower and uphold the freedom and bravery of others, or does our flag wave over a different kind of land?

Lately, the posture of professional athletes during our national anthem has become a point of tension. You might see the actions of Colin Kaepernick and others as a strong non-violent protest—a beautiful way to draw the attention of the nation to parts of America that are less than beautiful. Or maybe, you are irate because you've concluded this gesture can only mean that the anthem of the country you love is being disrespected. Maybe you feel that their posture goes too far. Even though the players have carefully explained (and will continue to explain), that they aren't disrespecting the flag or the nation, perhaps their actions offend you.

For those of you who disagree with the players who are taking a knee, I ask for you to be brave and embrace the freedom that the anthem portrays. To silence all voices but your own is not strength, but weakness. It takes bravery to allow others to peacefully disagree with you. It takes courage to step outside of your comfort zone and begin to listen to another's perspective. Remember, these players are not protesting the flag or the anthem—they are using this moment to protest inequality, police brutality, and racial injustice. If these shameful elements were less present in our society, there would be no need to protest.

If you are upset about folks kneeling during the anthem, consider this: perhaps the player protesting during the anthem believes in a bigger America than you do. Maybe they believe that our freedom (particularly our freedom of speech), is larger than you believe it to be. Maybe they believe in an America whose justice fully embraces racial equality. Could it be that they are kneeling to bring attention to the parts of our land that is neither free nor brave? Hoping to see a land that lives up to our anthem, a land that is freer and braver than the America we live in?

Maybe bravery is doing the right thing in the face of danger. Even when you're scared. Maybe a land is free only when the folks in charge abstain from imposing their restrictions on the folks who disagree with them. Ask yourself an honest question, if the players were kneeling to draw attention to fallen soldiers, do you think our society would have a problem with their posture? Are we offended by the manner in which these players are protesting? Or is it the content of what they are protesting?

Yes, I'm proud of my country. I'm proud of my grandfathers, my friends, and neighbors who have fought for our freedom. Even though it's hard to sing, I truly appreciate our national anthem. And yet, blind nationalism cannot help us forward. After all, America is a nation in process. Not unlike her anthem, America is more of a question mark than a statement. Our nation is an ongoing experiment chasing after ideals like liberty, honor, and justice for all. A nation of immigrants defined by a promise, rather than a nationality or a geography or a language.

Who gets to decide what America means? They do. You do. I do. We the people choose our path. "Does that star spangled banner yet wave, o'er the land of the free, and the home of the brave?" You tell me. After all, the National Anthem of the United States of America is not a statement. It's a question. And, we are the nation in question.

Mild Protest

Clay S. Jenkinson

This essay was originally published on *The Jefferson Hour* on October 31, 2017. https://jeffersonhour.com/blog/mild [https://perma.cc/64DB-FAC2]

I know people who feel strongly that professional football players should stand during the national anthem. They feel that the anthem is a symbol of American unity, a tribute to our service men and women, and that it is that not patriotic to sit or kneel or hold up a fist during the Star-Spangled Banner. I respect people who feel this way, but I respectfully disagree with them. Here's why.

If you have been listening to the Jefferson Hour for any length of time, you know that Jefferson was a revolutionary in the full sense of the term, not just a "revolutionary" in the milder Continental Congress sense. In his carefully crafted letters, he told Abigail Adams and James Madison that he liked a little rebellion now and then.

In a letter to William Smith, written in Paris on November 13, 1787, Jefferson wrote, "God forbid we should ever be 20 years without a rebellion." He said, "What country can preserve its liberties if their rulers are not warned from time to time that their people preserve the spirit of resistance? Let them take arms. The remedy is to set them right as to facts, pardon & pacify them. What signify a few lives lost in a century or two? The tree of liberty must be refreshed from time to time with the blood of patriots & tyrants."

The NFL players in question are not shooting the referees for reaching for their penalty flags. They are not tearing down the goalposts at halftime. They are not beating up random fans in the stands. They are not blowing up the football on the 45-yard line. They are not smashing people's iPhones, or throwing flagons of beer on coaches and owners. They are not boycotting the games or walking off the field with ten seconds left in the fourth quarter to show their discontentment with America. They are not taping over the mouth of the celebrity or active military officer who sings the national anthem. They are not ripping through the giant American flag that is stretched across the field or throwing bleach or blood on it.

They are quietly kneeling, without shouting slogans or obscenities. This does not sound very incendiary or very radical. Jefferson defended the French Revolution, including the Reign of Terror, as a necessary bloodletting to restore the equilibrium and justice to life in France. I doubt that he would find the NFL protest outrageous. Nor did he ever express any sacred reverence for songs, flags, salutes, anthems, medals, or the rest of the flummery of artificial patriotism. To be patriotic is to love this country. To love this country is to want it to live up to its ideals. To want it to live up to its ideals is to be willing to criticize it when it fails to do so. If you think it never fails to do so, you have not paid the slightest attention to the wild ride of American history. If you think we never fail to live up to the promise of America you are not black, Hispanic, poor, or Native American, and you have not bothered to project your imagination beyond your own comfort zone.

When I watch the video of the athletes kneeling in silence, I see purpose, dignity, anguish, and conviction. What I don't see is people brandishing semi-automatic weapons, people wearing camouflage fatigues, people wielding openly hateful, often racist signs denouncing the president of the United States, people calling for Second Amendment solutions to America's ills. No, that was what one saw at a Tea Party rally during the Obama years, and it was always defended as a venerable American tradition drawn from the playbook of the Minutemen and the Boston Tea Party.

We need to take a deep breath. We need to have a serious and careful national conversation about the legacy of slavery and racism. We need to read and investigate. We need to take this protest seriously.

The NFL's athletes have gotten our attention. All of America is now talking about the protests. That includes people who would rather talk about anything else. In their quiet, non-violent and dignified way, the athletes have forced all of us to talk about what kinds of protests are legitimate in a sprawling continental democracy, whether corporation owners have a right to censor the free expression of their employees, whether politicians can legitimately try to coerce corporation owners to censor their employees.

But we are also talking about the *real issue*—police brutality, race profiling, whether the seemingly routine shooting of black suspects is justified, whether there is structural and institutional racism at the center of American life, or to put it by way of the slogan, whether black lives matter in American life as much as white lives matter. I wish we were talking about this issue more and the sanctity of the national anthem less, but that may still come.

Protest is a central virtue in the American experiment. Its roots are in the Boston Tea Party on December 16, 1773, in Daniel Shays' rebellion of 1786, the event that triggered the Constitutional Convention of 1787; or the dozens of slave rebellions that were a prelude to John Brown's terrorist raid on the U.S. arsenal at Harper's Ferry on October 16, 1859.

Think of the silent protest of the Underground Railroad in which an estimated 100,000 black slaves were shepherded out of the plantation south to free northern states or to Canada in response to the inhuman violation of human right that was slavery.

Think of the labor movement of the post-Civil War era, or the protests of women demanding that they be given the vote in the United States and then equal access to employment, and then control of their reproductive destiny.

Think of Rosa Parks silently refusing to move to the back of the bus—do you remember the outrage expressed then by white people who felt that this was not the time or place to raise the issue of equal access to taxpayer supported public transport? Think of the African Americans who sat in white only lunch counters, or those who marched peacefully along the roads of Alabama—subjected to water hoses and attack dogs for the crime of marching nonviolently in silence.

Think of the vast national protest against the Vietnam war, the worldwide anti-nuclear movement of the 1970s and 80s.

In each of those watersheds—some of them among the greatest moments in American history—the reactionaries have said not now, not here, not about this, not patriotic, not legitimate, not American.

Thomas Jefferson understood this better than all the rest of us combined, and he understood it back at the very beginning of our national experiment. He understood that petitions and letters to the editor do not redress the fundamental wrongs of a civilization. He understood that protest only works if you are able to get the attention of the community, and to do so you had to be willing to violate the norms of civil complacency. "I like a little rebellion now and then," said Jefferson.

The athletes who are kneeling at NFL games are not attempting to tear down American civilization. They are not moving us toward anarchy and social collapse. (The person who is flirting with that agenda now occupies the desk in the Oval Office of the White House). No, they are quietly asking the rest of us to attend to a central problem of American life—that to be born black in America means that your life is going to be more vulnerable, more marginal, more impoverished, and more dangerous, that if you are born black you are born into second class citizen status and the great institutions of the country, including the police and the judicial system, appear to line up against you more often than not.

This is a question that all people who prize equality should want to address earnestly, not reluctantly.

Section Two

The Law

Bearing Witness for Civil Liberties

Shawn Peters

Before there was Colin Kaepernick, there were Lillian and Billy Gobitas.

Bitter public controversies over an individual's right to refrain from participating in compulsory patriotic rituals are nothing new in American history. In fact, one of the greatest (if sometimes overlooked) episodes of intolerance in our history was sparked when members of a small religious group stubbornly refused to honor the flag in the traditional manner. As would be the case with the former San Francisco 49ers' quarterback, Jehovah's Witnesses like the Gobitas children paid a heavy price for holding fast to their beliefs at a time when failing to take part in patriotic rituals was seen by many as being nothing less than treasonous.

Jehovah's Witnesses believe that saluting a secular emblem like the American flag amounts to idolatry, a practice forbidden by the Christian scriptures. At the urging of their leader, members of the faith began refusing to participate in Pledge of Allegiance exercises in the 1930s. At about the same time, and for the same reason, they also started abstaining from the "Hitler salute" in Nazi Germany.

The results were, as one might expect, catastrophic. In Germany, Witnesses (who were called Bible Students there) were among the first groups targeted for extirpation by the Nazis. Conditions in the United States were better but still grim. Witnesses were expelled from public schools, fired from their jobs, denied relief benefits, and mobbed on the streets. In one fairly typical incident, a group of Witness proselytizers in West Virginia was rounded up, tied together, and forced to drink large doses of castor oil—a form of torture that had been popularized in fascist Italy under Mussolini. Specifically referencing widespread physical assaults on members of the faith, the American Civil Liberties Union stated, "Nothing parallel to this extensive mob violence has taken place in the United States since the days of the Ku Klux Klan in the 1920s. No religious organization has suffered such persecution since the days of the Mormons."

Matters came to a head in 1940 when the legal battle over the expulsion of the Gobitas children reached the U.S. Supreme Court. (The case was known as *Minersville School District v. Gobitis* because the family's name was misspelled in court records.) The timing of their case—in which they argued that their right to the free exercise of religion had been abrogated by a school measure mandating the flag salute—could not have been worse. With World War II raging in Europe, panic over spies and saboteurs gripped the United States; tales of alleged "Fifth Column" activities appeared in the news almost daily. In an opinion written by Justice Felix Frankfurter, the Supreme Court ruled against the Jehovah's Witness school children.

No Supreme Court opinion in American history has had a more direct and violent impact. Throughout the summer and fall of 1940, mobs routinely attacked Witnesses who attempted to distribute religious literature in public spaces. They were persecuted because their refusal to salute the flag made them appear unpatriotic. According to the ACLU, by September of 1940 more than one thousand members of the faith were injured in 236 separate incidents. Attacks and other forms of oppression continued for several years, prompting a prolonged investigation from the U.S. Department of Justice.

The Supreme Court's misguided ruling in the flag salute case was widely misunderstood as giving legitimacy to doubts about the loyalty of the Jehovah's Witnesses. When asked by a reporter why some Witnesses were being rounded up in his town, one police officer said, "They're traitors—the Supreme Court says so."

One useful lesson to be drawn from the persecution of the Jehovah's Witnesses is that it abated over time and for a variety of interrelated reasons. Wartime paranoia eased; the Witnesses themselves became somewhat less obstreperous in practicing and promoting their faith; and the Supreme Court changed its mind about the constitutionality of compulsory patriotic exercises. A second flag salute case reached the high court in 1943, and this time the justices ruled in favor of the Jehovah's Witnesses. "If there is any fixed star in our constitutional constellation," Justice Robert Jackson wrote for the court, "it is that no official, high or petty, can prescribe what shall be orthodox in politics, nationalism, religion, or other matters of opinion, or force citizens to confess by word or act their faith therein."

Incredibly, the Jehovah's Witnesses (who were involved in numerous Supreme Court cases during the World War II era) became unsung civil liberties heroes. Their legal efforts were seen as precursors to the "rights revolution" that flowered during the tenure of Chief Justice Earl Warren during the

1950s and 1960s. All Americans, not simply members of the faith, benefited from their persistent advocacy for judicial protections for our most basic democratic freedoms.

Of course, there is no telling how the current national anthem protests will play out, in either the short or long terms. One might gain hope by looking at the lessons of the past and hope that tolerance prevails. Perhaps Colin Kaepernick eventually will be widely regarded as a champion of free expression, a real patriot (and not one of the NFL variety). However, the very fact that this type of controversy has cropped up yet again, and in its characteristically virulent form, seems to suggest that the path toward tolerance will be a long and rocky one.

Trump's National Anthem Outrage Ignores Decades of Supreme Court Rulings

Emma Long

This essay originally appeared in *The Conversation* on September 28, 2017. https://theconversation.com/trumps-national-anthem-outrage-ignores-decades-of-supreme-court-rulings-84725 [https://perma.cc/43SR-F35Q]

When San Francisco 49ers quarterback Colin Kaepernick chose to remain seated during a pre-game national anthem in protest against racial injustice and police brutality last year, his action caused widespread controversy.[1] Now Donald Trump has reignited that controversy by suggesting at a rally that National Football League (NFL) players who take similar action should be kicked off their teams:

> Wouldn't you love to see one of these NFL owners, when somebody disrespects our flag, to say 'get that son of a b*tch off the field right now, he's fired? He's fired!'[2]

The fallout was immediate. Stephen Curry, player for the Golden State Warriors, responded that he did not want to attend an event at the White House honouring the team's success.[3] Trump fired back by publicly withdrawing the invitation.[4] In response, teams, players, and managers across the country (and at the London-based NFL games) followed Kaepernick's example and kneeled, or stood, with arms locked in protest as the anthem was played before their games.⁵

And so the debate rages on. But if anyone defending the players' right to kneel (or #TakeAKnee) needs some backup for their arguments,⁶ there's an obvious place for them to look: the judgements of the U.S. Supreme Court, which has heard a number of major cases involving the Pledge of Allegiance and the treatment of the American flag, all touching on the obligations of patriotism and the right to refuse to participate in national rituals. And more than that, the court is generally supported by the people it serves—even when they disagree with its decisions.⁷

So as the Trump-NFL national anthem controversy continues, let's look at some of what the court has said on this subject over the decades.

Compulsory unity

In January 1942, shortly after the attack on Pearl Harbor and America's entry into World War II, West Virginia's State Board of Education adopted a resolution requiring the state's children to salute the flag as part of their daily school activities. Much as did Trump in his recent tweets about players' refusal to stand for the national anthem at sporting events,⁸ the board argued that the salute would "honour the nation represented by the flag" and that refusal to participate would be "regarded as an act of insubordination".

The board's actions were inspired by a ruling two years earlier. In Minersville School District v. Gobitis (1940),⁹ it was found that a compulsory flag salute and recitation of the Pledge of Allegiance did not violate the constitutional rights of Jehovah's Witness children, who objected to the actions on the grounds that it violated their faith's requirements not to worship graven images. The fallout from that decision included laws and resolutions similar to West Virginia's, increased reports of physical assaults on Witness children, and threats to send non-conforming children to reformatories.[10]

But the backlash wasn't long in coming, and in 1943, the court reversed its decision in West Virginia State Board of Education v. Barnette, holding that such compulsory activities did violate the U.S. Constitution.[11]

The court recognized that the flag symbolised adherence to the government and that national unity was an important value: "National unity as an end which officials may foster by persuasion and example is not in question." It also noted that the case involved an emotional issue and was difficult "not because the principles of its decision are obscure, but because the flag involved is our own." But the court also argued that "to sustain the compulsory flag salute we are required to say that a Bill of Rights which guards the individual's right to speak his own mind, left it open to public authorities to compel him to utter what is not in his mind."

Recognising that the Board of Education had acted in good faith, the court nevertheless issued a stark, eloquent warning:

> Struggles to coerce uniformity of sentiment in support of some end thought essential to their time and country have been waged by many good as well as by evil men ... Those who begin coercive elimination of dissent soon find themselves exterminating dissenters. Compulsory unification of opinion achieves only the unanimity of the graveyard.

The justices also had a message for those who saw the children's refusal as a threat to American patriotism and unity: "To believe that patriotism will not flourish if patriotic ceremonies are voluntary and spontaneous instead of a compulsory routine is to make an unflattering estimate of the appeal of our institutions to free minds."

Individuals might disagree with the actions taken, the court argued, but that does not mean such actions threaten the nation's future, strength, or unity. In fact, the freedom to disagree is at its strongest when such disagreement touches on the most controversial issues.

Protecting contempt

Those most upset about players who choose not to stand for the national anthem might also do well to revisit a 1990 case, Texas v. Johnson, in which the court struck down a Texas law banning the burning of the American flag.[12]

In concurrence with the decision, Justice Anthony Kennedy expressed his difficulty with the case:

> The hard fact is that sometimes we must make decisions we do not like. We make them because they are right, right in the sense that the law and the Constitution, as we see them, compel the result. And so great is our commitment to the process that, except in the rare case, we do not pause to express distaste for the result, perhaps for fear of undermining a valued principle that dictates the decision. This is one of those rare cases.[13]

"I agree," Kennedy continued, "that the flag holds a lonely place of honor in an age when absolutes are distrusted and simple truths are burdened by unneeded apologetics." But, he argued, "it is poignant but fundamental that the flag protects those who hold it in contempt."

Kennedy's words have a particular message for those who see the players' actions as an affront: sometimes those same American values demand you accept actions of which you don't approve.[14] You don't have to like the decision to kneel during the national anthem, but you do have to accept that people have the right to do so without fear of retaliation. The court has time and again recognized that the American people think differently about issues, and that they can express those differences so long as others are not prevented from exercising their own right to reply. Those caught up in the current debate should take heed.

Notes

1. https://www.theguardian.com/sport/2016/aug/27/colin-kaepernick-national-anthem-protest [https://perma.cc/2EYN-CZBS]
2. https://www.youtube.com/watch?v=8JMnfmxA_Q0 [https://perma.cc/F77K-AD89]
3. https://theconversation.com/the-surprising-connection-between-take-a-knee-protests-and-citizens-united-84645 [https://perma.cc/XJG2-46Q2]
4. https://www.nytimes.com/2017/09/23/sports/stephen-curry-trump-nba-.html
5. http://www.bbc.co.uk/sport/american-football/41381896 [https://perma.cc/9L8J-Z3SW]
6. https://twitter.com/hashtag/takeaknee?lang=en) [https://perma.cc/GQQ7-RHHE]
7. http://democracyinstitute.la.psu.edu/documents/PollReportJusticeReappointmentfinal.pdf [https://perma.cc/JXX3-N6BV]; https://theconversation.com/in-trumps-america-is-the-supreme-court-still-seen-as-legitimate-84242 [https://perma.cc/NUZ5-YWE5]
8. https://twitter.com/realDonaldTrump/status/912280282224525312 [https://perma.cc/GPZ3-9E29]; https://twitter.com/realDonaldTrump/status/912037003923005440 [https://perma.cc/P5D6-M995]; https://twitter.com/realDonaldTrump/status/912443924979077120 [https://perma.cc/Y63T-5FRQ]
9. https://www.oyez.org/cases/1940-1955/310us586 [https://perma.cc/4DRK-67ZR]
10. https://www.pbs.org/wnet/supremecourt/personality/landmark_minersville.html [https://perma.cc/44NR-FC8E]
11. https://supreme.justia.com/cases/federal/us/319/624/case.html [https://perma.cc/Q5WS-9P39]; https://constitutioncenter.org/blog/west-virginia-v.-barnette-the-freedom-to-not-pledge-allegiance [https://perma.cc/YG33-YKQL]
12. https://constitutioncenter.org/blog/inside-the-supreme-courts-flag-burning-decision [https://perma.cc/8ASR-2PJR]

13. https://supreme.justia.com/cases/federal/us/491/397/case.html [https://perma.cc/A49T-6RWA]
14. https://twitter.com/search?q=%23boycottnfl&src=typd&lang=en [https://perma.cc/X48Q-BACC]

Anthem Protests in High School Athletics

Mark Rerick

The national anthem protests taking place in professional sports were inevitably going to trickle down to collegiate and high school athletics. Unlike professional athletes who are paid employees, collegiate and high school athletes are held to a separate standard of care. Furthermore, because high school athletics do not generate the large amount of institutional revenue like collegiate athletes, there is further scrutiny of the actions of high school athletes. Whereas professional and collegiate athletes' actions are judged against their ability to raise revenue, high school athletes' actions occur within a well-established legal precedent.

Participation in high school athletics is not a constitutionally protected right. Rather, it is a privilege afforded to high school students who meet a certain set of criteria. With the explosion of social media alongside the unfortunately high stakes nature of youth sports today, it has become even more important to remind families and athletes that participation in athletics is a privilege. Unlike students in the classroom who are constitutionally protected (unless there is a substantial disruption to the educational process), athletes can be held to a stricter standard.

You will find no mention of education in the U.S. Constitution; however, the Tenth and Fourteenth Amendments combine to determine, in part, that a person's right to life, liberty, and the pursuit of happiness (which includes the right to be educated) are based in state law. North Dakota establishes the right to a free, public education in Article VIII of its constitution. Nowhere in either the United States or the North Dakota Constitutions will you find reference to any athletics programming, meaning an individual is not guaranteed the right to participate in extra-curricular activities beyond the equal protection parameters set by the Fourteenth Amendment and several federal laws such as Title VI (race equity) and Title IX (gender equity).

Generally, there are four constitutional amendments—First, Fourth, Fifth, and Fourteenth—that are challenged in relation to extra-curricular activities, and case law for all of them has reinforced athletics as a privilege. Although the Fourth Amendment has little to do with establishing guidelines for such actions as national anthem protests, the other three are integral in providing schools with guidance for regulating students' actions. As will be noted below, school districts do still have a standard of care to allow for those aspects of due process and equal protection that are guaranteed to students.

Combining the First and Fifth Amendments, several cases have challenged courts attempting to show that athletic program regulations violate an individual's property rights and/or have not allowed sufficient due process to the athlete:

> The 1987 case *Brands v. Sheldon Community School* established that when a school district applies consistent consequences that are neither arbitrary nor capricious, those conse-

quences do not deprive a student of property rights regardless of his or her athletic ability.

Using the Brands case as a guideline, *Thompson v. Fayette County Public Schools* denied a student's appeal to reverse a suspension for academic ineligibility.

Letendre v. Missouri HSAA ruled against a student attempting to swim for a club team during the high school season by noting that due process in executing the suspension and equal protection for students on athletic teams do not apply because the student was not deprived of life, liberty, or property.

James v. Tallassee High School found that schools and coaches can publish their own set of standards and guidelines without violating constitutional rights because participation in teams is a voluntary activity. Like the Brands case, this case also found that a student's ability to earn a college scholarship has no bearing on the court's decision.

Mancuso v. Massachusetts IAA established that athletic teams are separate from a school's required physical education curriculum and are therefore allowed to set additional rules and regulations.

Tenets of the Fourteenth Amendment requiring due process and equal protection for citizens' life, liberty, and the pursuit of happiness run through many of the above cases. School districts and participants need to remember that (1) the loss of voluntary participation does not constitute a loss of Fourteenth Amendment rights, but (2) schools need to treat all participants equally within their extra-curricular rules. Furthermore, as is good practice for all school regulations, schools are best-served by publishing a handbook and requiring written verification from athletes and parents that it has been received.

Although many of these cases are more recent, courts have been attempting to make sense of schools' role in student liberties for a long time. The decision summary in the 1975 *Goss v. Lopez* case foreshadowed the necessity of courts limiting their decision-making powers for every small infraction in schools. As we see more and more cases related to high school athletics being brought to court, we are realizing how visionary that summary was. Establishing high school athletics as a privilege, not a right, has allowed multiple courts to dismiss cases quickly rather than miring themselves in the inner workings of high school administration. As such, we can reasonably expect court cases based on high school athlete protests to similarly be dismissed.

Can a school punish an athlete for an action of protest while representing the school? The simple answer is, yes, such punishment is protected by legal precedent. The longer answer is that schools would be best-served by publishing a student-athlete Code of Conduct and then holding all students equally accountable to that Code. Further, schools need to remember that the purpose of high school athletics is to use competition in sports as a catalyst for teaching usable life lessons. While schools appear to be within their legal rights to punitively react to a national anthem protest, the better route may be to use such an incident as a teachable moment regarding civic duty and peaceful protest.

Celebrity Voices are Powerful, But Does the First Amendment Let Them Say Anything They Want?

Shontavia Johnson

This essay originally appeared in *The Conversation* on December 11, 2017. http://theconversation.com/celebrity-voices-are-powerful-but-does-the-first-amendment-let-them-say-anything-they-want-69467 [https://perma.cc/KCW4-5LN8]

When NFL player Colin Kaepernick refuses to stand for the national anthem,[1] or the cast of the Broadway musical "Hamilton" confronts the vice president-elect, or the Dixie Chicks speak out against war,[2] talk quickly turns to freedom of speech. Most Americans assume they have a constitutional guarantee to express themselves as they wish, on whatever topics they wish. But how protected by the First Amendment are public figures when they engage in political protest?

Recently, celebrities have become increasingly vocal regarding the collective Movement for Black Lives, for instance.

Coming out publicly, whether for or against some disputed position, can have real consequences for the movement and the celebrity. However helpful a high-profile endorsement may be at shifting the public conversation, taking these public positions—particularly unpopular ones—may not be as protected as we assume. As a professor who studies the intersection of law and culture, I believe Americans may need to revisit their understanding of U.S. history and the First Amendment.

Harnessing the power of celebrity

Far from being just product endorsers, celebrities can and do use their voices to influence policy and politics.[3] For example, some researchers believe Oprah Winfrey's early endorsement of Barack Obama helped him obtain the votes he needed to become the 2008 Democratic nominee for president.[4]

This phenomenon, however, is not new. Since the birth of the nation, celebrities have used their voices—and had their voices used—to advance important causes. In 1780, George Washington enlisted the help of Marquis de Lafayette, a French aristocrat dubbed by some "America's first celebrity," to ask French officials for more support for the Continental Army.[5] Lafayette was so popular that when he traveled to America some years later, the press reported on each day and detail of his yearlong visit.[6]

Social movements also have harnessed the power of celebrity influence throughout American history. In the early 1900s, after the National Woman Suffrage Association was founded to pursue the right of women to vote, the group used celebrities to raise awareness of the cause.[7] Popular actresses like Mary Shaw, Lillian Russell and Fola La Follette, for example, brought attention to the movement, combining their work with political activism to push the women's suffrage message.[8]

Celeb actions can move the needle

The civil rights movement of the 1960s benefited from celebrities' actions. For instance, after Sammy Davis Jr., a black comedian, refused to perform in segregated venues, many clubs in Las Vegas and Miami became integrated. Others—including Ossie Davis and Ruby Dee, Dick Gregory, Harry Belafonte, Jackie Robinson and Muhammad Ali—were instrumental in the success of the movement and passage of the Civil Rights Act of 1964.[9] These actors planned and attended rallies, performed in and organized fundraising efforts and worked to open opportunities for other black people in the entertainment industry.

By the 1980s, you could watch Charlton Heston and Paul Newman debate national defense policy and a potential nuclear weapons freeze on television.[10] Meryl Streep spoke before Congress against the use of pesticides in foods.[11] Ed Asner and Charlton Heston publicly feuded about their differing opinions of the Reagan administration's support of right-wing Nicaraguan militant groups.[12]

Whatever you think of how well thought out their opinions are (or aren't), celebrities have the ability to draw attention to social issues in a way others do not. Their large platforms through film, music, sports and other media provide significant amplification for the initiatives they support.

There is, in particular, a measurable connection between celebrity opinions and young people.[13] Most marketing research shows that celebrity endorsements can improve the likelihood that young consumers will choose the endorsed product.[14]

Antagonism toward celebrity activism

Celebrities have been important partners, strategists, fundraisers and spokespeople for social movements and politicians since the earliest days of modern America. Recently, however, celebrities speaking out about policy and politics have received some harsh responses.

Kaepernick, in particular, has received scathing criticism.[15] Fans of his team have burned his jersey in effigy.[16] Mike Evans, another NFL player, drew so much criticism for sitting in protest of Donald Trump's election to the presidency that he was forced to apologize and say he would never do it again.[17] #BoycottHamilton trended on Twitter after the cast of the Broadway show Hamilton addressed Mike Pence.[18]

> Tonight, VP-Elect Mike Pence attended #HamiltonBway. After the show, @BrandonVDixon delivered the following statement on behalf of the show.[19]

President-elect Donald Trump jumped into the fray, tweeting that he does not support the public expression of sentiments like those of the "Hamilton" cast.

> Our wonderful future V.P. Mike Pence was harassed last night at the theater by the cast of Hamilton, cameras blazing. This should not happen![20]

> The Theater must always be a safe and special place. The cast of Hamilton was very rude last night to a very good man, Mike Pence. Apologize![21]

Unprotected speech

All of this raises significant questions about speech, protests and the law. Often celebrities, commentators and pundits talk about being able to say whatever they want thanks to their right to freedom of speech. But this idea is based on common misconceptions about what the U.S. Constitution actually says.

What is allowed under the law starts with the text of the First Amendment, which provides that:

> Congress shall make no law respecting an establishment of religion, or prohibiting the free exercise thereof; or abridging the freedom of speech, or of the press; or the right of the people peaceably to assemble, and to petition the Government for a redress of grievances.[22]

The language essentially allows for freedom of expression without government interference. The right to free speech includes protests and distasteful speech that one might find offensive or racist.

But, the First Amendment as written applies only to actions by Congress, and by extension the federal government. Over time, it's also come to apply to state and local governments.[23] It's basically a restriction on how the government can limit citizens' speech.[24]

The First Amendment does not, however, apply to nongovernment entities. So private companies—professional sports organizations or theater companies, for instance—can actually restrict speech without violating the First Amendment, because in most cases, it doesn't apply to them (unless the restriction is illegal for other reasons).[25] This is why the NFL could ban DeAngelo Williams from wearing pink during a game in honor of his mother, who had died from breast cancer, and fine him thousands of dollars when he later defied the rules and did it anyway.[26]

How does all of this affect celebrities? In a nutshell, if a celebrity is an employee of, or has some kind of contract with, a nongovernment entity, his speech actually can be restricted in many ways. Remember, it's not against the law for a nongovernment employer to limit what employees can say in many cases. While there are other more limited protections based on state and federal law that protect employee speech, they are incomplete and probably wouldn't apply to most celebrity speech.[27] Any questions about what a public figure can or cannot express, therefore, will start with the language of any contracts she has signed – not the First Amendment.

For better or worse, celebrities can make significant impacts on policy, politics and culture, and have been doing so for centuries. But speaking out can put them at risk. Celebrities can be fined by their employers, like DeAngelo Williams, have their careers derailed, like the Dixie Chicks,[28] or receive death threats, like Colin Kaepernick.[29] Even so, their involvement can provide an influential platform in promoting and creating societal change.

Notes

1. https://theconversation.com/the-oppressive-seeds-of-the-colin-kaepernick-backlash-66358 [https://perma.cc/9MMP-2GZE]
2. http://www.dailykos.com/story/2013/3/11/1193171/-Ten-Years-Ago-This-Week-the-Dixie-Chicks-Found-Free-Speech-Comes-at-a-High-Price [https://perma.cc/KP2B-ZE9B]
3. http://dx.doi.org/10.1007/s10551-009-0090-4
4. http://www.stat.columbia.edu/~gelman/stuff_for_blog/celebrityendorsements_garthwaitemoore.pdf [https://perma.cc/G6BN-453M]
5. https://newrepublic.com/article/123170/marquis-de-lafayette-americas-first-celebrity) [https://perma.cc/A4G9-GD98]
6. http://www.jstor.org/stable/4233634
7. http://www.historynet.com/womens-suffrage-movement [https://perma.cc/6LZ7-N8QV]
8. https://books.google.com/books?id=QO79UClRsDMC&pg=PA7&lpg=PA7&dq=national+woman+suffrage+movement+actress&source=bl&ots=EKlau1ccmV&sig=bERJBYmVA4vtMwKoZZhoQ5RorZU&hl=en&sa=X&ved=0ahUKEwi-3rvW6OXQAhULjlQKHZOjAZoQ6AEINTAE#v=onepage&q=national%20woman%20suffrage%20movement%20actress&f=false [https://perma.cc/SPE5-5NRE]
9. https://news.vcu.edu/article/Hollywood_celebrities_unsung_role_in_the_civil_rights_movement [https://perma.cc/6ZLH-88GG]
10. https://books.google.com/books?id=7Q3QE-n8q4UC&pg=PA154&lpg=PA154&dq=Charlton+Heston+and+Paul+Newman+nuclear&source=bl&ots=-eRL7vFhFg&sig=rb4q3wEvuYDCpF9ztOnT3mSkfgs&hl=en&sa=X&ved=0ahUKEwjTx9SN9OXQAhVKw1QKHaa9BDkQ6AEIRjAL#v=onepage&q=Charlton%20Heston%20and%20Paul%20Newman%20nuclear&f=false [https://perma.cc/T4F6-JGCB]
11. http://www.pbs.org/tradesecrets/docs/alarscarenegin.html [https://perma.cc/3KHD-CC7Y]
12. https://books.google.com/books?id=-OHQCwAAQBAJ&pg=PA299&lpg=PA299&dq=Nicaraguan+contras+ed+asner+heston&source=bl&ots=dwjrs01QRO&sig=yj8m00S3JrWqTKiL7_4PyqZ4-hY&hl=en&sa=X&ved=0ahUKEwjAmYfD9eXQAhUhrFQKHFbcD94Q6AEIzAB#v=onepage&q=Nicaraguan%20contras%20ed%20asner%20heston&f=false [https://perma.cc/3NGA-Q5H8]

13. https://doi.org/10.1017/S0021849904040206
14. http://dx.doi.org/10.1086/209029
15. http://www.esquire.com/news-politics/news/a48246/tomi-lahren-kaepernick-facebook/ [https://perma.cc/E7JS-4VYU]
16. http://www.dailymail.co.uk/news/article-3762239/You-never-play-NFL-Canada-49ers-fans-burn-Kaepernick-jerseys-national-anthem-114million-sport-star-refused-stand-protest-black-oppression.html
17. https://www.washingtonpost.com/news/early-lead/wp/2016/11/15/nfl-player-who-knelt-in-protest-of-donald-trumps-election-pledges-to-stand-for-anthem-again/?utm_term=.7c6cdf41259a [https://perma.cc/32FK-VNQR]
18. http://www.nytimes.com/2016/11/19/us/mike-pence-hamilton.html
19. https://twitter.com/hashtag/HamiltonBway?src=hash; https://twitter.com/HamiltonMusical/status/799828567941120000 [https://perma.cc/5MSN-87AV]
20. https://twitter.com/realDonaldTrump/status/799972624713420804 [https://perma.cc/9T2X-7HL2]
21. https://twitter.com/realDonaldTrump/status/799974635274194947 [https://perma.cc/4JL3-PTTC]
22. https://www.law.cornell.edu/wex/first_amendment [https://perma.cc/2PR4-W6WP]
23. http://faculty.smu.edu/jkobylka/supremecourt/Nationalization_BoRs.pdf [https://perma.cc/FBV9-5B53]
24. https://fas.org/sgp/crs/misc/95-815.pdf [https://perma.cc/HK5C-SZB9]
25. http://scholarlycommons.law.hofstra.edu/cgi/viewcontent.cgi?article=1135&context=hlr
26. http://www.michiganreview.com/the-nfl-vs-freedom-of-expression/ [https://perma.cc/E2VQ-WK8E]
27. http://www.americanbar.org/publications/insights_on_law_andsociety/15/winter-2015/chill-around-the-water-cooler.html [https://perma.cc/N4JT-NQUM]
28. http://www.savingcountrymusic.com/destroying-the-dixie-chicks-ten-years-after/ [https://perma.cc/P7Z9-3DNY]
29. http://edition.cnn.com/2016/09/21/sport/colin-kaepernick-death-threats/ [https://perma.cc/8F4A-RHZG]

The Surprising Connection Between 'Take a Knee' Protests and Citizen United

Elizabeth C. Tippett

This essay originally appeared in *The Conversation* September 26, 2017. https://theconversation.com/the-surprising-connection-between-take-a-knee-protests-and-citizens-united-84645 [https://perma.cc/HL9V-LP6H]

Citizens United, the Supreme Court ruling that some fear is destroying American democracy, may also be showing us how to heal it.[1]

The most recent example of this is the reaction to President Donald Trump's comments suggesting that sports owners should fire players who kneel during the national anthem.[2] As the president does so often, he placed business leaders in the difficult position of deciding whether to speak out at the risk of alienating customers and courting further controversy.

In this case, many league officials and owners chose to do just that, labeling Trump's words "divisive"[3] and defending their players' right to "express themselves freely on matters important to them."[4] Some owners "took a knee" alongside their players.[5]

While corporate speech is often assumed to favor only conservative causes, my research on attorney advertising reveals the extent to which free speech rights for companies also advances causes important to liberals.[6]

I would argue that *Citizens United*—a Supreme Court opinion that has produced bitterly partisan reactions—ironically offers a pluralistic vision of corporate speech as well as a full-throated defense of the kind of political speech we are now witnessing from business leaders.[7]

Speaking out in the age of Trump

Whether to speak out when Trump takes a position that is at odds with the rights of their employees or their own or company's values has become a fundamental dilemma for many business leaders in the Trump era.

Many have on Charlottesville,[8] climate change,[9] transgender service in the military,[10] and Deferred Action for Childhood Arrivals.[11] Others have stayed silent,[12] seeming to support the notion that inserting themselves into political controversies would be to step out of bounds.

In this view, business should be separate from politics, and corporations should leave political discourse to private citizens. But for better or worse, our system protects business leaders speaking up. And the Supreme Court's ruling in *Citizens United* describes why it's so important.

Citizens United, the left's bete noir

In 2010, Citizens United v. Federal Election Commission overturned a law that limited corporate finance of certain political ads on First Amendment grounds.[13] The reaction from liberals and those who favor limits on campaign finance was fierce.[14]

President Barack Obama famously criticized the opinion during a State of the Union address, with the justices who issued the ruling sitting a few feet away:

"I don't think American elections should be bankrolled by America's most powerful interests, or worse, by foreign entities. They should be decided by the American people."[15]

According to a *Time* magazine survey of law professors, the opinion ranks among the worst since 1960.[16] And yet, like any political lightning rod, *Citizens United* is both less and more than it seems.

Constitutional scholar Justin Levitt characterized the opinion as an incremental change from previous law,[17] which offered corporations no shortage of options for political influence. Another study found that companies spent more on politics after *Citizens United* but it ultimately hurt shareholders —it was essentially a form of corporate waste.[18] Spending additional corporate dollars on campaigns awash in advertising may not produce much of a return on investment.[19]

Beyond its legal impact, *Citizens United* offered a vision of democracy that embraces the unique and important role that business leaders play in political discourse. In other words, exactly what we've seen when business leaders stand up to Trump.

Business leaders bridging divides

Citizens United stands in part for the idea that the First Amendment provides strong protection for political speech, even if it originates from a company. Corporations may not be people,[20] but, to paraphrase the movie *Soylent Green*, they are made of people.[21]

In this view, corporations are groups of people on par with labor unions or nonprofits, and their joint viewpoints are deserving of protection.

At a time of deep partisan division, business leaders may be the rare voice deemed credible across the political spectrum. Small businesses are among the few remaining institutions that inspire a high level of confidence from both Republicans and Democrats.[22] Tech companies also still enjoy high levels of trust.[23] Importantly, among those who are losing confidence in the "system," business is seen as the most trusted institution.[24]

To this, one might respond, why ruin a good thing? Perhaps business leaders should lie low and preserve their reputation. But it is a mistake to assume that any statements in opposition to Trump are themselves divisive.

In this regard, even diluted corporate rhetoric offers the comparative benefit of articulating a few things that Americans have in common. After Charlottesville, the CEO of Campbell Soup—a symbol of mainstream values if there ever was one—issued a statement that "racism and murder are unequivocally reprehensible."[25] It may not be revolutionary, but at least it's a point upon which virtually every American can agree.

Citizens United also argued that corporations have a unique viewpoint in the marketplace of ideas.[26] In this conception of speech, corporate voices are worth protecting because voters find them valuable or important. As the Supreme Court explained:

> "On certain topics corporations may possess valuable expertise, leaving them the best equipped to point out errors or fallacies in speech of all sorts, including the speech of candidates and elected officials."[27]

In this vein, corporations represent a credible source of information and context on policy matters.

The Trump administration's decision to terminate DACA is often invoked as a moral issue. However, in a lawsuit against the administration, tech leaders explained that it was also a business issue, describing how its termination will affect their ability to recruit and retain top talent.[28] Likewise, when NFL owners and coaches defend their players, it's an opportunity to provide context for how the kneeling controversy relates to racial justice.

For business leaders, it's personal

To be sure, *Citizens United* has had some of the negative impact liberals feared. In particular, one study estimated that corporate spending following *Citizens United* measurably improved Republican prospects in state legislatures.[29]

When corporations have the option to engage in unlimited spending, it gives them a louder voice than others in the electoral process.[30]

Nevertheless, the kind of statements we've heard from NFL and NBA team owners offers a counterpoint to the kind of corporate speech most feared by commentators following *Citizens United*—that of faceless corporations pouring money into elections in service of their "greedy ends." Instead, these statements have an intensely personal character. They show leaders sharing their own personal experiences and how those experiences are reflected in the organizations they run.

When NFL team owner Shahid Khan linked arms with his players during the national anthem before a game, it sent a symbolic message to his players—and to everyone watching – about his vision of an inclusive America that honors diversity "in many forms—race, faith, our views and our goals."[31]

It may not be the kind of corporate speech that we imagined. But it's exactly what we need.

Notes

1. http://time.com/4922542/democrats-citizen-united/ [https://perma.cc/3TGH-92NF]
2. https://www.nytimes.com/2017/09/24/sports/nfl-trump-anthem-protests.html
3. https://twitter.com/NFLprguy/status/911580084141772801/photo/1 [https://perma.cc/8QFG-8A3L]
4. https://twitter.com/WarriorsPR/status/911671456928382976/photo/1 [https://perma.cc/CG42-FCTZ]
5. https://www.washingtonpost.com/news/early-lead/wp/2017/09/25/cowboys-players-take-a-knee-with-owner-jerry-jones-before-standing-for-anthem/?utm_term=.d00ae10138dc [https://perma.cc/R8CK-8U4J]
6. https://papers.ssrn.com/sol3/papers.cfm?abstract_id=2445771 [https://perma.cc/3Y3E-KCUY]
7. https://scholar.google.com/scholar_case?case=6233137937069871624 [https://perma.cc/Y3AT-X6HW]; https://theconversation.com/how-corporate-ceos-found-their-political-voice-83127 [https://perma.cc/C3SE-ZFQ7]
8. http://fortune.com/2017/08/14/ken-frazier-trump-charlottesville-response/ [https://perma.cc/P77J-2NSK]
9. http://www.telegraph.co.uk/news/2017/06/01/elon-musk-quits-donald-trumps-advisory-councils-paris-accord/ [https://perma.cc/QTG9-Y2TJ]
10. https://twitter.com/sundarpichai/status/890247543686397952 [https://perma.cc/5VRV-PPUU]
11. https://www.washingtonpost.com/news/the-switch/wp/2017/09/06/amazon-and-microsoft-are-supporting-a-15-state-lawsuit-to-protect-daca/?utm_term=.988cbc9f1414 [https://perma.cc/62T5-Z55W]
12. https://www.newyorker.com/news/john-cassidy/corporate-americas-awkward-embrace-of-trump-will-continue [https://perma.cc/P3ME-384Z]
13. https://scholar.google.com/scholar_case?case=6233137937069871624 [https://perma.cc/H63P-D3UR]
14. http://www.nybooks.com/articles/2010/02/25/the-devastating-decision/ [https://perma.cc/5EUD-F96J]
15. https://www.youtube.com/watch?v=deGg41IiWwU [https://perma.cc/5YP6-S22X]; http://abcnews.go.com/Politics/State_of_the_Union/state-of-the-union-2010-president-obama-speech-transcript/story?id=9678572 [https://perma.cc/UHS2-C85L]
16. http://time.com/4056051/worst-supreme-court-decisions/ [https://perma.cc/FT99-H5XM]
17. https://www.jstor.org/stable/41308528
18. https://doi.org/10.1111/j.1740-1461.2012.01265.x
19. https://www.google.com/url?sa=t&rct=j&q=&esrc=s&source=web&cd=1&cad=rja&uact=8&ved=0ahUKEwjNg9CAssPWAhVBXWM-KHVp8D_8QFggmMAA&url=http%3A%2F%2Fpeople.umass.

edu%2Fschaffne%2Flaraja_schaffner_spendingbans.pdf&usg=AFQ-jCNGCK5ryfKuvJ9A-bvaLmbV7efoUyA [https://perma.cc/2KRA-X7ES]
20. https://www.youtube.com/watch?v=E2h8ujX6T0A [https://perma.cc/7WR7-9VUF]
21. https://vimeo.com/193955387 [https://perma.cc/P8C8-ZMQT]
22. http://news.gallup.com/poll/212840/americans-confidence-institutions-edges.aspx
23. https://www.nbcnews.com/meet-the-press/poll-little-confidence-major-american-institutions-n697931 [https://perma.cc/2JYY-G8TY]
24. https://www.edelman.com/global-results/ [https://perma.cc/8C9X-WBUX]
25. https://www.campbellsoupcompany.com/newsroom/press-releases/campbell-ceo-resigns-from-presidents-manufacturing-jobs-initiative/ [https://perma.cc/KZQ6-9UD4]
26. http://scholarlycommons.law.case.edu/cgi/viewcontent.cgi?article=3484&context=caselrev
27. https://scholar.google.com/scholar_case?case=6233137937069871624 [https://perma.cc/6A89-F7KP]
28. https://www.washingtonpost.com/news/the-switch/wp/2017/09/06/amazon-and-microsoft-are-supporting-a-15-state-lawsuit-to-protect-daca/?utm_term=.fb7cf1118ac6 [https://perma.cc/QEJ3-23SJ]
29. https://doi.org/10.1086/685691
30. http://heinonline.org/hol-cgi-bin/get_pdf.cgi?handle=hein.journals/gslr27&section=43 [https://perma.cc/29QQ-UZ6L]
31. https://www.washingtonpost.com/news/sports/wp/2017/09/24/shahid-khan-the-jaguars-owner-who-stood-with-his-team-has-long-espoused-the-american-dream/?utm_term=.40c47b159691 [https://perma.cc/2ARW-P6LJ]

Section Three

Athlete-Activists

#PlayingWhileWhite: The Colin Kaepernick Saga and the (A)political White Athlete

David J. Leonard

This essay was originally published in *The Society Pages* on August 14, 2017. https://thesocietypages.org/engagingsports/2017/08/14/playingwhilewhite-the-colin-kaepernick-saga-and-the-apolitical-white-athlete/ [https://perma.cc/T587-S73D]

With NFL training camps well underway, teams looking to sign a quarterback have passed over Colin Kaepernick time and time again. It appears he may be serving his ultimate punishment following a year of protest and activism. Amid those who defend NFL decision-makers as simply making choices for "football reasons," there has also been a chorus of critics who see (black) players as responsible for his remaining on the sidelines.

"If the black players would unite, and say, 'We will not play Game 1 this year,'" Skip Bayless noted as part of a discussion about Kaepernick on Fox Sport's *Undisputed*, "I promise you, it would have an impact and would get something done."[1]

Bayless isn't alone in putting the responsibility and risks in the laps of the league's black players.

"As a result, the only way that NFL owners would be threatened by a protest was if it came from the players," argues A.R. Shaw. "If all of the Black NFL players threatened to sit out a game, the NFL owners would immediately find a way to sign

Kaepernick. About 70 percent of all players in the NFL are Black. The NFL product would suffer tremendously without its Black players."[2]

In response to such commentaries, we should question why it is the responsibility of black players to refuse to play. Why do Bayless and others see the burden of protest as one held by black players rather than those who cash in on racially codified privilege on and off the field? Imagine if Tom Brady spoke out. What about Drew Brees, J.J. Watt, or countless other white NFL players? Imagine if they refused to play in protest of the treatment of Colin Kaepernick. What if they, like Malcolm Jenkins and Marshawn Lynch,[3] continued Kaepernick's protest against persistent anti-black racism? Yet, white players are neither expected nor chastised for failing to protest racial injustice, for failing to account for the decisions of their employers.

#PlayingWhileWhite means having the ability to remain silent amid zero expectations of doing what is morally/politically righteous. As noted by Howard Bryant, "The White players in the NFL should be ashamed of themselves. If you're a union…You have to send some type of message that this isn't acceptable."[4] Yet Bryant has been one of the few voices demanding action from ALL players.

Seemingly ignoring the countless black players who have spoken truth to power over the discrimination and persecution of Kaepernick, much of the discourse focusing on "player silence" continues to center the failures of black players to speak up. Some have even gone as far as to call out specific players for not kneeling with Kaepernick last season or standing up against the owners.[5] Most of those named are African-American, ostensibly giving white superstars a pass.

As I argue in *Playing While White*, one of the privileges of whiteness, on and off the field, is being seen as a leader.[6] Yet, when it comes to leading the fight against racial injustice, against the discrimination of one's football peers, these white leaders are nowhere to be found. And while their black peers are chastised for selfishly not standing up for Kaepernick, for not speaking, whites inside and outside of football are not held accountable.

#PlayingWhileWhite is also having the privilege to speak out without fear of punishment; in fact, #PlayingWhileWhite is having the ability to speak out about racial injustice without widespread accusations of "playing the race card," "selfishness," "ignorance," "childishness," or "ungratefulness." To be white and woke is to be insulated from the demonization and criminalization that is commonly applied to black athletic protest. While black athletes, whether in the WNBA,[7] among the collegiate ranks,[8] or in countless other spaces,[9] are routinely told to shut up and play, white athletes are told over and over again, "we love when you use your voice, your intelligence, and your place to be role models and facilitators of social good #ThankYou #TruthToPower." To be white and woke is to garner celebration for one's courage, leadership, and selflessness.

When New England Patriots' defensive lineman Chris Long voiced his support for Kaepernick, he was rightly praised as an accomplice doing necessary political work. Long went beyond the clichéd "I support his right to kneel," never mind the issues of racial injustice and anti-black violence, reflecting on his own whiteness.[10] "I play in a league that's 70 percent black, and my peers—guys I come to work with, guys I respect, who are very socially aware, intellectual guys," Long noted. "If they identify something that they think is worth putting their reputations on the line, creating controversy, I'm going to listen to those guys." Such comments didn't prompt outrage or endless debates within the sports media; rather they prompted praise, shock and awe, and celebrations. He's not alone.

San Antonio Spurs' coach Gregg Popovich, who has expressed support for Kaepernick and disdain for the "45th President of the United States," and who has discussed white privilege and systemic racism,[11] has not been called a distraction. His opinions have not been dismissed as baseless; he has not been routinely told to shut up because he is alienating fans and sponsors. Instead, he has been widely celebrated as "woke,"[12] as intelligent and knowledgeable, and for using his power and privilege to advance change. Like Steve Kerr and Stan Van Gundy,[13] Pop is held up as an example of how sports figures can use their platforms to foster critical conversations about racism. While their platforms emanate from their place in the coaching ranks, from their power as fixtures within the sporting landscape, their whiteness is central. To coach while white empowers them to speak out in ways that their black peers rarely dream; the wages of whiteness amplify their voices, promoting praise and celebration of their courage, wokeness, and sacrifice.

The widespread celebration of Josh Rosen (and Johnny Manziel),[14] compared to Cardale Jones or Nigel Hayes,[15] all of whom have in different ways shone a light on the hypocrisy, moral bankruptcy, and complicity of the NCAA, its partner schools, and collegiate coaches in the exploitation of college athletes, elucidates the ways whiteness matters.

#PlayingWhileWhite is also engaging in political projects without fanfare, media scrutiny, or accusations of distraction and disrespect. Look no further than America's golden boy, the ultimate modern-day great white hope, whose leadership is praised as much as his intelligence and work ethic, Tom Brady. Over and over again, he exhibits the power and privileges of whiteness not simply in the narratives that render his screaming on the sideline as evidence of his passion, that refashioned accusations of cheating as proof of his competitiveness and victimization, that imagine him as the ultimate leader because of his determination, intellect, and commitment to team, but in his ability to be vocal and silent on political issues at his choosing.

#PlayingWhileWhite is standing for the national anthem, while black peers kneel or raise a fist, and never having to answer why he stands in silence. It is never having to explain how his whiteness shapes his understanding of the national anthem, the Kaepernick protest, or the broader issues of racism in America. It is the ability to put a "Make America Great Again" hat in his locker in the midst of the election and then rebuff inquires and criticisms. Like countless college coaches who embraced then-candidate Donald Trump,[16] questions about appropriateness, about feelings of fans, sponsors, and teammates, and about these political choices were few and far between for Brady. As I write in *Playing While White*, "Race helps us to understand how Colin Kaepernick and countless black athletes are demonized and threatened for bringing their disrespectful politics into sports at the same time that countless white athletes and coaches are empowered to support Donald Trump with few questions about respect, the values of his campaign, or the message they sent in their support. Whiteness is privilege on and off the field. Whiteness matters." It matters for those who remain silent; it matters for those speak out; and it matters for those whose rhetoric and actions serve to normalize white supremacy. If the recent events in Charlottesville, Virginia taught us anything, it should be that white America,[17] from the football fields to stands, from the halls of government to the classrooms of higher education, need to speak out, kneel and stand up, collectively in opposition to the politics of white nationalism and endemic realities of racial violence.

Notes

1. http://ijr.com/the-declaration/2017/08/943463-skip-bayless-says-black-nfl-players-refuse-play-kaepernick-signed/ [https://perma.cc/NK73-KNHL]
2. https://rollingout.com/2017/08/10/colin-kaepernick-protests-wont-mean-thing-unless-black-players-boycott-games/ [http://perma.cc/C9RM-2PVE]
3. http://www.espn.com/nfl/story/_/id/20307080/malcolm-jenkins-philadelphia-eagles-continue-national-anthem-demonstration-2017[https://perma.cc/7LMM-35ZB]; http://www.espn.com/nfl/story/_/id/20327882/oakland-raiders-marshawn-lynch-remains-seated-national-anthem [https://perma.cc/78NF-U8ZJ]
4. http://www.ebony.com/news-views/finally-someone-calls-football-players-not-standing-behind-kaepernick#axzz4pSrkJBII [https://perma.cc/P447-NGWL]
5. http://www.nydailynews.com/sports/football/allies-colin-kaepernick-hiding-behind-helmets-article-1.3391548 [https://perma.cc/THZ3-D3EW]
6. http://www.washington.edu/uwpress/search/books/LEOPLA.html [https://perma.cc/K33X-VZFB]
7. https://www.thenation.com/article/wnba-teams-show-what-blacklivesmatter-solidarity-looks-like/ [https://perma.cc/9WPR-FT2B]
8. https://thinkprogress.org/national-anthem-sports-protest-tracker-kaepernick-284ff1d1ab3e/ [https://perma.cc/53GD-4D4Y]
9. https://www.thenation.com/article/6-times-athletes-spoke-out-in-support-of-blacklivesmatter-this-week/ [https://perma.cc/HGM6-UT3E]
10. http://bleacherreport.com/articles/2663608-chris-long-comments-on-colin-kaepernick-and-national-anthem-protests [https://perma.cc/88CN-T9PV]
11. https://www.sbnation.com/nba/2017/2/3/14496934/gregg-popovich-black-history-month-white-privilege-race-trump [https://perma.cc/6DK5-UZTP]
12. https://theundefeated.com/features/san-antonio-spurs-gregg-popovich-is-the-nbas-most-woke-coach/ [https://perma.cc/E5ZW-LK68]
13. https://www.washingtonpost.com/news/early-lead/wp/2016/09/22/steve-kerr-defends-colin-kaepernick-expects-similar-protests-in-the-nba/?utm_term=.3c4754c0f9a6 [https://perma.cc/HK85-2WVW]; http://www.sportingnews.com/nba/news/racist-donald-trump-stan-van-gundy-tirade-quotes-video/1imgxlldr0jvp175h5rvowjo45 [https://perma.cc/ZS4A-RQAP]
14. https://www.si.com/college-football/2017/08/08/ucla-quarterback-josh-rosen-student-athlete [https://perma.cc/F9S7-MDMP]; http://www.foxsports.com/collegefootball/story/johnny-manziel-case-was-tipping-point-in-ncaa-hypocrisy-080813 [https://perma.cc/CK8V-KAJ4]

15. http://www.espn.com/college-football/story/_/id/8466428/ohio-state-buckeyes-cardale-jones-tweets-classes-pointless [https://perma.cc/8E38-P734]; http://www.sportingnews.com/ncaa-basketball/news/wisconsin-nigel-hayes-college-gameday-sign-broke-badger-venmo/9c3wcm9q84f71ns5k6ejoqy7m
16. https://www.sbnation.com/nba/2017/2/3/14496934/gregg-popovich-black-history-month-white-privilege-race-trump [https://perma.cc/BQZ9-3SAY]
17. https://www.theguardian.com/us-news/2017/aug/12/virginia-unite-the-right-rally-protest-violence [https://perma.cc/9ZHF-M4XE]

Black Women Athletes, Protest, and Politics: An Interview with Amira Rose Davis

Ashley D. Farmer

This essay originally appeared in *Black Perspectives* on October 14, 2016. https://www.aaihs.org/black-women-athletes-protest-and-politics-an-interview-with-amira-rose-davis/ [https://perma.cc/P35A-Z3RQ]

The country is now recognizing black athletes as protest leaders and the sports field as a viable space for resistance and politics. High school,[1] college,[2] and professional athletes are currently engaging in various forms of demonstrations,[3] many inspired by Colin Kaepernick's protest of the National Anthem. Often overlooked, however, is the key role black female athletes have played and continue to play in making sports arenas places of political and ideological protest. This month, I spoke with Amira Rose Davis, a Postdoctoral Fellow at the Africana Research Center at Penn State University, who examines the ideological and institutional development of recreational, competitive, and professional sporting opportunities for black women in the United States. Her recent article, "No League of their Own: Baseball, Black Women and the Politics of Representation," appears in the latest issue of the *Radical History Review* (Ed. Note: May 2016).[4]

Ashley Farmer (AF): Athletes today are becoming more vocal about racism and police brutality. Most credit Colin Kaepernick with starting this latest wave of protest. Where do you place the origins of it?

Amira Rose Davis (ARD): I think the emergence of the *collective* athletic protests we are seeing now can really be mapped on to the rise of Black Lives Matter (BLM) and grassroots organizing that has kept the issues of racism and state violence visible and present in public discourse,[5] from the Miami Heat's hoodie photo following the death of Trayvon Martin to the St. Louis Rams' players putting their hands up after the death of Mike Brown and the smattering of professional and collegiate athletes who donned "I Can't Breathe" shirts after Eric Garner.[6]

Of course, individual athletes have taken stands on these issues for decades. I think it is important to situate this moment on a continuum of black athletic activism. There is a tendency to think of the 1960s as the golden age of athletic activism and then act like nothing has happened and no athlete has been vocal or politically engaged since then. But even in the 1990s when Michael Jordan was selling shoes to Republicans, you have Mahmoud Abdul-Rauf refusing to stand for the national anthem and salute the flag.[7] Or Etan Thomas's anti-war activism in the early 2000s,[8] and Toni Smith-Thompson, a mixed-race woman who played basketball at Manhattanville College who staged a silent protest during the National Anthem in 2003.[9]

AF: Who were the foremothers of current day black athlete protests?

ARD: I like to think of the history of black women's protest in two ways. First, their symbolic protest—that is, the meanings that people project onto their athletic success. I think it is mainly in this way that we remember black women athletes as trailblazers and barrier breakers, like Althea Gibson and Wilma Rudolph,[10] whose achievements were—and continue to be—celebrated as moments of black excellence or racial advancement. I find their legacy in the way we celebrate the successes of the Williams sisters, Gabby Douglas,[11] and Allyson Felix.[12]

However, there is a second strand of black women's athletic protest that is often less visible. It is found in Wilma Rudolph insisting her town's celebratory parade be integrated or Olympian Earlene Brown being vocal about civil rights and women's rights in the 1960s.[13] It is the legacy of Erosenna Robinson's 1959 anthem protest and tax resistance, and Wyomia Tyus's push for racial equality and equal pay and professional opportunities for women athletes.[14]

I think this legacy can be seen in contemporary black women athletes who use their platforms to speak on an intersection of issues. Venus Williams fighting for equal pay at Wimbledon, for example. Or Brittany Griner's LGBTQ advocacy. Or Serena's return to Indian Wells 13 years after experiencing racist heckling and accusations of match fixing, where she publicly partnered with Bryan Stevenson and the Equal Justice Initiative to raise funds and vocalize concerns about systemic racism and the death penalty.

AF: What are the similarities and differences between black male and female athletes' protest options and decisions? What do you think accounts for these differences?

ARD: Black male athletes, by and large, have much larger platforms to speak from, but they also tend to stand to lose more in terms of endorsements. Because of the underfunding and lack of visibility of women's sports, black women athletes oftentimes wouldn't have as many endorsement offers and large contracts available to them. That being said, this summer [*Ed. Note*: 2016] the WNBA attempted to fine the teams and individual players who engaged in protests. It took a public uproar to prevent the league from seizing money from already underpaid players.

Because sports is still largely understood as a masculine enterprise, women athletes, save the high-profile few, often receive less attention and therefore have a smaller platform on which to generate discussions. Indeed, much current coverage of athletic protest simply mentions the protests of women athletes as a footnote or bullet point to the larger discussion of black males protesting when in fact black women have been some of the most vocal and persistent activists. Just look at the WNBA teams who not only staged collective protest and wore BLM shirts,[15] but also initiated a media boycott, refusing to answer questions unless they related to police brutality and racism.

AF: How would you describe the intersection of black women athletes' protest and political ideologies like black nationalism and black feminism?

ARD: It's interesting because when I study black women athletes of the 1950s and 1960s I find myself asking what the possibilities and function of black nationalism is within national projects, which is to say that often the most prominent athletic space available to black women was in international competitions, particularly during the Olympic games. This in many ways remains true today. But also in the Cold War these same athletes were tapped to be part of the US State Department's cultural diplomacy tours. So the biggest opportunities for competition, for travel, for visibility, were usually done with a huge USA jersey on or as a cultural ambassador for the nation. This reality very much framed their protests. Black women athletes used their roles as both unofficial and official ambassadors of the country to argue for their piece of the American dream and demand their rights as fully protected citizens.

    I do think you see tenets of black feminism embedded in black women's athletic protest, particularly in the protests that insist on the intersectional aspect of their identities. In her autobiography Wilma Rudolph is critical of the burgeoning (at that time) Women's Liberation Movement. Rudolph notes the ways in which women's liberation is speaking for and about issues facing white middle-class women that alienate her and many of the black women athletes she knows. Yet the fight for professionalization and later equal pay is something that black male athletes aren't fighting for or dealing with at the same level. Indeed, as the Williams sisters have fought for equal pay as women tennis players they also have constantly dealt with the fact that their white, often inferior competitors can get more endorsements and are considered more marketable.

    I also think black women athletes have had to be ever conscious about how they perform black femininity. Certainly in the mid-20th century there was an insistence from the men who were coaches and sportswriters and really gatekeepers of black sporting industry that black women athletes carefully avoid playing into any racial stereotypes about the animalistic de-feminized a-sexual black woman. I think black women continue to wrestle with what it means to be a woman in a space that is often read as masculine—women from Flo Jo to Serena Williams who have forcefully asserted their athleticism, sexuality, and traditional femininity as all bound up together and complementary rather than contradicting.

AF: What do you see as the future of black women athletes and protest?

ARD: I think we will continue to see black women athletes speak out and protest both individually and collectively. The real issue is if we as a public listen to them and engage with them instead of only highlighting their actions as supplemental to those of black males, particularly because black women athletes continue to vocalize critiques of systemic racism *and* sexism, and increasingly homophobia as well. I think it is great that the collective actions of black women athletes are getting attention right now and I hope that the interest and solidarity will remain moving forward, especially if protest is also aimed at dismantling patriarchy as well as white supremacy.

Notes

1. https://www.nytimes.com/2016/10/04/us/national-anthem-protests-high-schools.html?id=17686039
2. https://web.archive.org/web/20161005080803/http://www.espn.com/video/clip?id=17686039
3. https://thinkprogress.org/nfl-anthem-protests-911-ea51717ca59a#.mvfpz5dtr [https://perma.cc/2V3Y-K7X4]
4. https://doi.org/10.1215/01636545-3451748
5. https://www.aaihs.org/black-lives-matter-a-legacy-of-black-power-protest/ [https://perma.cc/LY2S-V44B]
6. http://www.espn.com/nba/truehoop/miamiheat/story/_/id/7728618/miami-heat-don-hoodies-response-death-teen-trayvon-martin[https://perma.cc/XDQ3-KQVM]; http://ftw.usatoday.com/2014/11/rams-hands-uppregame [https://perma.cc/GX7X-4S4T]; http://abcnews.go.com/Sports/pro-athletes-don-breathe-shirts-support-eric-garner/story?id=27437509 [https://perma.cc/S2YF-2S98]
7. https://web.archive.org/web/200012071512/http:/www.nba.com/playerfile/bio/mahmoud_abdul-rauf.html

8. http://etanthomas.com/ [https://perma.cc/X5YJ-TBEL]
9. http://www.nytimes.com/2003/02/26/sports/college-basketball-players-protest-over-the-flag-divides-fans.html
10. https://www.tennisfame.com/hall-of-famers/inductees/althea-gibson/ [https://perma.cc/5G2W-PYZA]; https://www.olympic.org/wilma-rudolph [https://perma.cc/6ZQZ-BLYX]
11. http://gabrielledouglas.com/ [https://perma.cc/V4Z6-RUDV]
12. http://www.allysonfelix.com/ [https://perma.cc/5TA3-GJKY]
13. https://www.olympic.org/earlene-brown [https://perma.cc/KE7E-94DK]
14. https://www.olympic.org/wyomia-tyus [https://perma.cc/VXT7-9PKH]
15. https://www.washingtonpost.com/news/early-lead/wp/2016/07/22/wnba-players-refuse-to-talk-basketball-in-protest-of-fines-for-black-warmup-shirts/ [https://perma.cc/VXT7-9PKH]

Voices Beneath the Helmets: Athletes as Political Outsiders

Joseph Kalka

As Michael Bennett stood in the Seattle Seahawks' locker room, speaking with reporters on the ongoing injustice against people of color, he strongly cast another voice into the discourse on both the state of African Americans in the United States and that of athletes addressing such matters. Bennett was stopped by Las Vegas police officers in August of 2017, and he claimed to have been racially profiled. Bennett stated the officers used excessive force and pointed a gun at him. A subsequent investigation found no wrongdoing by the officers, and the sheriff stands by his officers' actions, but Bennett had a clear message for his community and anyone willing to listen: something had to change regarding the treatment of African Americans in the United States.[1] While views on Bennett, Kaepernick, and their cohort have varied from depictions as brave champions of change to destructive millionaires, one response continually sticks out: "Athletes should stick to sports."

Since the summer of 2015, American life had been inundated with politics, so this type of response was understandable. What made this historical moment unique is that recent frustration brought with it the rise of the political outsider.[2] Individuals from varying political backgrounds gravitated toward candidates beyond the mainstream in an attempt to make politics better serve their needs. While Donald Trump's election likely had as much to do with crowded primary fields, political timing, and unpopular candidates as it did his rogue status,[3] it demonstrated the power of political outsiders to affect the current landscape. Trump, Bernie Sanders, and others associated with the concept channeled the frustration of their bases to strive for political change. Justin Gest argued that this political frustration and outsider status is the reason many working-class white people still support Donald Trump. They believe he gives them a voice.[4] It seems as though this is the common thread amongst political outsiders: they provide unheard groups with a voice.

The rise of outsiders is a context with which one can view the 2016–2017 National Football League player protests. Beginning with Colin Kaepernick, the demonstrations started as a movement to bring attention and discussion to issues the protesters believed were falling on deaf ears: the mistreatment of African Americans by police and racial injustice in general. While later efforts shifted the attention against the suppression of free speech or displays of team unity, the most intentional moments stand out. How then did these athletes fit into the discourse on political outsiders, and how can one view them historically alongside other figures? They were non-mainstream political agents, giving a voice to otherwise unheard groups, using unconventional means to do so. These athletes are certainly political outsiders, but reactions to their protests reflect some of the very reasons that the kneeling began.

The multitude of protests brought with them severe backlash from several communities. Rationale for opposition branched into discussions of three main topics: patriotism and honoring veterans, politics in sports, and the underlying message. Backlash was perhaps most noticeable regarding the first category. Pundits, critics, citizens, and veterans showed their disapproval of acts they saw as disrespectful to the flag, the military, and the country in general. American Legion commander Denise R. Rowan showed her disapproval of the politicization of the anthem on behalf of veterans, urging unity on the subject instead.[5] Market researcher Diane Hessen argued that basic patriotism fueled much of the disapproval regarding kneeling and other anthem protests along with tradition; standing for the anthem is a hallmark of sports, and it represents a moment of unity prior to heated conflict. Hessen identified sports as an escapist moment for fans tired of the onslaught of politics.[6] This is important to note: while some members of the public readily accepted political outsiders into the mainstream, that did not mean they wanted mainstream politics in all facets of their lives. As sports were one of the last sanctuaries from the torrent of division that was 2016 and 2017, fans often opposed a further inundation of partisanship.

What is possibly the most important category to explore when analyzing athletes' place in the category of political outsiders is reactions to the original claims of the protests. Many of the protests strayed from the core purpose to focus on unity, free speech, labor autonomy, and opposition to President Trump, but those acts did less to set up athletes as political outsiders acting in politics than to make some other kind of statement, so they are less relevant. The lessons from reactions to the original protests, or those which shared the original intent, likely shed light on more deeply held opinions that other responses to the protests may have covered up. Some individuals in the U.S. simply did not believe the injustices Kaepernick originally referenced. In statements directly following his original demonstrations in August of 2016, Kaepernick explicitly outlined the problem of police misconduct and brutality against African Americans, citing "bodies in the street" and more broadly critiquing the mistreatments of African Americans in the United States.[7] These are two focuses on which to anchor an understanding of the discourse.

Recent data from Pew Research Center sheds light on different issues germane to Kaepernick's claims. Thirty-six percent of white people believed that racial discrimination was a major reason black people struggled to get ahead, a figure, again, nearly doubled when posed to African Americans (seventy percent). The same poll found that white people were almost twice as likely (forty-one versus twenty-two percent) to believe that too much attention is placed on race. That figure jumped to fifty-nine percent for white Republicans (twenty-one percent for their Democratic counterparts). This essay is not interested in a discussion of data that would support or negate these claims, but rather examines the effect perception has on public opinion.[8] Additional data suggests that such figures were exacerbated when pollsters asked working-class white individuals, many of whom felt that they have received unfair treatment in society.[9]

While these were groups that mainly backed outsider candidates, their reactions to the protests show what is fairly obvious, yet still illuminating. It was not the outsider status of athletes that led to a degree of public backlash, it was what they were claiming and how they went about it. Support for the military and sports as escapism certainly played a role in the disapproval, but the underlying argument for many was that those protesting do not have anything to be protesting about. The wave of supporters for Trump did not espouse the idea of political outsiders simply because they gave those who were unheard a voice; they did so because he gave them a voice.

When Michael Bennett and his colleagues kneeled during the anthem and worked with fellow players to come to an agreement with the National Football League regarding the protests, they too fought to give individuals a voice. This schism between these two groups reflects the very nature of changes to public policy: if all parties agreed change was necessary, it probably would have occurred prior to that conclusion. Recognizing this allows individuals to look back on these moments to view the manner in which specific athletes acted as political agents.

The protests yielded their most promising result in late November 2017. NFL owners proposed a partnership in which the league reportedly would contribute $89 million to assist African-American communities and causes, and in return, players presumably would stand for the national anthem. Although some players saw the move as an attempt to buy loyalty, the leadership of the newly formed Players Coalition, the group representing athletes' efforts for social change, believed that the money, which would be split between the United Negro College Fund, the Dream Corps, and the Player Coalition itself, was the first step in acting out real change.[10] As the outsider among outsiders, Colin Kaepernick chose not to officially serve with this group, but sought to support the broader causes moving forward.

Much like those businessmen, doctors, and celebrities who impacted politics from 2015–2017, athletes identified those who needed an outlet. With their status as political agents comes necessary differences. These men simply took a knee and spoke out against injustice. It is reasonable to argue that these acts did not require the level of planning and coordination, although planning was certainly involved, that campaigns and officeholding do and were therefore less tactful or groundbreaking. They spoke largely on one subject, rather than on a host of problems facing America. Some, like Kaepernick, even refrained from voting, a move he described as representative of the multiple avenues of social change.[11] These athletes are clearly a different type of political outsider, but nonetheless, they fit into the discussion of how new voices in public debates affect issues that matter.

Whatever comes of these efforts, they will stand out historically as a moment when sports transcended the field and entered broader public discussions. The claims of Kaepernick, Bennett, and a host of other athletes fit into the evolving landscape of political outsiders. Their words and actions emboldened some and deeply offended others. In the process, America engaged in a lively conversation on race, sport, patriotism, and free speech. These political outsiders got people talking, and it is their hope that they will help people change.

Notes

1. Steve Almasy and Tony Marce, "Michael Bennett Stop: Las Vegas Police Deny Race Played Role," Cable News Network, September 30, 2017.
2. Shermichael Singleton, "The Rise of Political Outsiders," *The Hill*, September 15, 2015.
3. Noah Berlatsky, "2016 isn't the 'Year of the Political Outsider,'" *The Week*, March 1, 2016.
4. Justin Gest, *The New Minority: White Working Class Politics in an Age of Immigration and Equality* (New York: Oxford University Press, 2017).
5. "The American Legion Calls for Unity," The American Legion, September 25, 2017.
6. Samantha Raphelson, "Many Americans Side with President Trump on NFL Anthem Protests," National Public Radio, October 4, 2017.
7. Steve Wyche, "Colin Kaepernick Explains Why He Sat During National Anthem," NFL.com, August 27, 2016.
8. Pew Research Center, "On Views of Race and Inequality, Blacks and Whites are Worlds Apart," *Social and Demographic Trends*, June 27, 2016. While this data was compiled before the 2016 election and the NFL pro-

tests themselves, it is the most complete set with which one can gain a comparative understanding on demographics' view on race relations.
9. Ryan Struyk, "Blacks and Whites See Racism in the United States Very, Very Differently," Cable News Network, August 18, 2017.
10. "Can 100 Million End the NFL's Problem with Colin Kaepernick and Anthem Protests?" Reuters, November 30, 2017.
11. Nick Wagoner, "Colin Kaepernick on Not Voting: There's More than One Way to Create Change," ESPN, November 15, 2016.

The Oppressive Seeds of the Colin Kaepernick Backlash

J. Corey Williams

This essay originally appeared in *The Conversation* October 7, 2016. https://theconversation.com/the-oppressive-seeds-of-the-colin-kaepernick-backlash-66358 [https://perma.cc/J5RH-DZVQ]

Ever since San Francisco 49ers quarterback Colin Kaepernick said, "I am not going to stand up to show pride in a flag for a country that oppresses black people and people of color,"[1] he's been in the media spotlight. Before every game, the TV cameras fixate on him as he kneels in protest. And with each passing week, more and more players around the league have joined him in an act of solidarity.[2]

In addition to troves of internet trolls and media commentators, the fierce opposition has included a handful of NFL owners and a California police union that threatened to stop working at the home games.[3] Even Donald Trump said his bit, suggesting that Kaepernick leave the country.[4]

Some might think that Kaepernick's words and actions, together with the subsequent backlash, represent a watershed moment. They don't. Spanning back to America's founding, there's an entire history of blacks stepping outside of the social order – or protesting it – only to be told they can't.

As a psychiatrist, I've long been interested in how racial identity affects mental health, and the chronic stress that racial minorities experience when they're exposed to racist messages, particularly in the media. In the controversy swirling around Kaepernick, I see racially encoded messages about power, place and punishment of black people. Obviously, there's a difference between antebellum lynching and social media outrage. But though the overt responses may have changed, the underlying hatred, disgust and impulses to punish prominent, "poorly behaved" black figures still remains.

Taming the black male?

During Reconstruction, blacks who stepped outside the social order risked their lives.

To enforce the racial hierarchy and police the boundaries of what blacks could say and do, whites often resorted to lynching. Although no one is exactly sure, it's estimated that over 3,400 blacks were lynched or publicly murdered from 1882 to 1968.[5] One of most famous examples was Emmett Till, who was murdered in Mississippi in 1955 for allegedly flirting with a white woman.

Economist Dwight Murphey has written that lynching was different from other forms of violence.[6] Unlike, say, a domestic dispute or an act of revenge, it functioned to maintain the social order. It was, Murphey wrote, "motivated by a desire to vindicate the moral sense of community, and has as its target a specific person or persons." In other words, it was used to enforce a racial hierarchy, foster a sense of community among whites, and ensure that black men knew their place.

Although the methods of lynching varied, it was common practice for white mobs, seeking to reaffirm the racial order, to hang or castrate the victim. (A number of psychoanalytic theories have sought to account for the phenomenon of castrations, but many scholars agree that castration served as the ultimate act of "taming" the black male, assuaging the fears and anxieties about uncontrolled black masculinity).[7]

As the number of lynchings decreased in the early 20th century, the mechanisms of enforcing the boundaries of black identity were reshaped. White majorities enforced social and civic confinement for most of the African-American community through redlining,[8] voting restrictions and Jim Crow laws.

Jack Johnson put in his place

For the few black athletes who had become famous by the early 20th century, the boundaries of acceptable black behavior continued to be publicly policed through racist media portrayals, searing criticism and public outrage.

Boxer Jack Johnson, after defeating Tommy Burns in 1908 to become the first black heavyweight champion, was publicly shamed. One boxing magazine called him "the vilest, most despicable creature that lives."[9]

With his dominant beatings of his white opponents, brash personality and lavish lifestyle, Johnson was one of the first black celebrity athletes to defy the social mandate that a black man must be subject to the white man's power. He was also often seen in public with white women, which was an appalling display for the time. After his defeat of Jim Jeffries (nicknamed the "Great White Hope") in 1910, race riots broke out across the country.[10] Some white men even committed suicide,[11] resulting in the film of the fight being banned in many cities and states.

Johnson was eventually sentenced to one year in jail under the Mann Act,[12] which had made it illegal to transport a woman "for the purposes of prostitution or debauchery, or for any other immoral purpose." In truth, he had saved a young girl from a life of prostitution. Using trumped up charges, police had leveraged the woman into testifying against Johnson, and an an all-white jury convicted him on basis of train tickets he bought for her.

But in truth, this case was about punishing Johnson for disobeying the racial order inside and outside the boxing ring; even the Justice Department lawyers decried his relationship with a white woman.[13]

After Johnson skipped bail and fled the country, civil rights activist W.E.B. Du Bois prophetically wrote:

> Why then this thrill of national disgust? Because Johnson is black. Of course, some pretend to object to Mr. Johnson's character. But we have yet to hear, in the case of white America, that marital troubles have disqualified prize-fighters or ball players or even statesmen. It comes down, then, after all to this unforgivable blackness.[14]

The *Los Angeles Times* essentially demonstrated Du Bois' point when it wrote to the black community, following Johnson's win over Jeffries, "Remember you have done nothing at all... Your place in the world is just what it was."

Throughout the 20th century, the media continued to relegate black athletes to a place of inferiority. Examples include sportscaster Brent Musburger calling the 1968 Olympic protesters Tommie Smith and John Carlos "a pair of dark skinned storm troopers" and *Time* magazine featuring a cover that darkened O.J. Simpson's face to make him appear more menacing during his murder trial.[15] Then there were the countless media portrayals of Muhammad Ali as unpatriotic for refusing to be drafted.[16]

Michael Jordan, submissive superstar

On the opposite pole are the black athletes who are widely embraced by the American public and media. Not surprisingly, they are deemed "acceptable" because they are docile and uncontroversial (at least, off the court or field).

Perhaps the best illustration of this phenomenon is Michael Jordan, the NBA star who is arguably responsible for the basketball league's global popularity. He's the perfectly packaged ambassador for the sport. The media portrayed him as apolitical, tame and well-mannered—an acceptable black athlete who was "black but not really black."[17] Image-conscious corporate advisers had effectively divorced him from inner city, hip-hop culture, placing him opposite from other more "street" players like Philadelphia 76ers star Allen Iverson, who was once described as the "living embodiment of hip hop in a basketball uniform," a player who "refused to bend over backwards to accommodate the tastes of the mainstream."[18]

In 2011, long after Jordan's playing career ended, a Nielsen and E-Poll Market Research study that measured appeal, public likability and awareness found that his personality attributes were off the charts: 93 percent of those surveyed said they liked him.[19]

Yes, Jordan's otherworldly talent explained a huge portion of his popularity. But it was arguably also due to his ability to be uncontroversial and seemingly disconnected from his race.

In 1990, when asked why he wouldn't endorse Harvey Gantt, a black Democratic candidate for Senate in North Carolina, Jordan simply said, "Republicans buy shoes, too."[20] (In 2001, the *Washington Post* described Gantt's opponent, Jesse Helms, as "the last prominent unabashed white racist politician in this country.")[21] When given the opportunity to use his power and influence, he reduced himself to a shoe salesman.

Prior to his murder trial, O.J. Simpson was another superstar that exhibited appropriate, acceptable forms of black behavior. He was lauded as "the first [black athlete] to demonstrate that white folks would buy stuff based on a black endorsement,"[22] while the CEO of Hertz rent-a-car, which featured Simpson in a famous TV ad, said he thought of the star running back as "colorless."²³

Then there was Tiger Woods, who, before his marital infidelities, was worshiped as "The Chosen One" in *Sports Illustrated* and "A Universal Child" due to his multiracial identity.²⁴

Like Jordan, they had stuck to the same script: be humble, grateful and—most importantly—nonthreatening to the racial order.

Where are we today?

Just months before the Kaepernick saga started to unfold, Carolina Panthers quarterback Cam Newton found himself, like Kaepernick, weathering criticism for not behaving appropriately. First he was celebrating too much in the end zone.²⁵ Then, after he lost the Super Bowl, he didn't act like a good enough sport.²⁶

Critics of black athletes often claim they have "character" concerns—that they're bothered by arrogance or poor sportsmanship.²⁷ But I wonder if the same social and psychological processes that fueled the phenomenon of lynching are the undercurrent of so much public disgust with Newton and Kaepernick.

As Newton told the *Charolotte Observer* earlier this year, "I'm an African-American quarterback that may scare a lot of people because they haven't seen nothing that they can compare me to."²⁸

It's almost like there's a reflexive visceral reaction toward successful black males who step outside their socially prescribed boundaries. There is evidence that supports the pervasiveness of racial attitudes in the American psyche. In the 1990s researchers at Washington University and Harvard College developed a test to measure implicit, or unconscious, bias for a number of characteristics, including race.²⁹ When a large nationally representative sample of people took the test for racial bias, investigators found the majority of people had preference for whites over minorities. Today no one can lynch a professional athlete, so the pressure to conform must be exerted more subtly. In this way, old expressions of racism are simply being recrafted and reshaped in modern, more socially acceptable forms.

Notes

1. http://www.nfl.com/news/story/0ap3000000691077/article/colin-kaepernick-explains-why-he-sat-during-national-anthem [https://perma.cc/V7AN-9ARK]
2. http://www.sbnation.com/2016/9/11/12869726/colin-kaepernick-national-anthem-protest-seahawks-brandon-marshall-nfl [https://perma.cc/G8J9-97G4]
3. http://www.cbssports.com/nfl/news/an-anonymous-nfl-exec-reportedly-calls-colin-kaepernick-a-traitor/ [https://perma.cc/9CJW-SF7Y]; http://time.com/4478542/colin-kaepernick-police-union-boycott-games/ [https://perma.cc/DC6E-9T59]
4. http://www.cbssports.com/nfl/news/donald-trump-fires-back-at-colin-kaepernick-after-qb-calls-him-a-racist/ [https://perma.cc/3WN9-KHRA]
5. http://law2.umkc.edu/faculty/projects/ftrials/shipp/lynchingsstate.html [https://perma.cc/U4AJ-2YJS]
6. http://www.dwightmurphey-collectedwritings.info/mono/mono1.htm [https://perma.cc/J5WM-CV9Q]
7. http://www.jstor.org/stable/pdf/3704016
8. https://www.washingtonpost.com/news/wonk/wp/2015/05/28/evidence-that-banks-still-deny-black-borrowers-just-as-they-did-50-years-ago/ [https://perma.cc/3NQZ-UTB9]
9. https://sports.vice.com/en_uk/article/the-war-on-jack-johnson-boxing39s-first-black-heavyweight-champion-versus-the-world-uk-translation) [https://perma.cc/8AW6-PMKN]
10. http://www.jstor.org/stable/43609313
11. http://fightland.vice.com/blog/the-war-on-jack-johnson-boxings-first-black-heavyweight-champion-versus-the-world [https://perma.cc/KP96-BV8K]
12. https://en.wikipedia.org/wiki/Mann_Act [https://perma.cc/9AV9-QVXM]
13. http://www.cnn.com/2009/US/04/22/jack.johnson.pardon/index.html?eref=time_us [https://perma.cc/T2SC-BFVR]
14. https://books.google.com/books?id=1AXZsjjRujAC&pg=PA81&lpg=PA81&dq=Why+then+this+thrill+of+national+disgust?+Because+-

Johnson+is+black.&source=bl&ots=vUSkiO1aqv&sig=XtsaQO3dO-eV8SM6rLnqpV4wTAUs&hl=en&sa=X&ved=0ahUKEwiEqM_kosHPAhUJ9WMKHQivB-AQ6AEIJzAD#v=onepage&q=Why%20then%20this%20thrill%20of%20national%20disgust%3F%20Because%20Johnson%20is%20black.&f=false [https://perma.cc/Y98H-7RGW]
15. https://www.thenation.com/article/after-forty-four-years-its-time-brent-musburger-apologized-john-carlos-and-tommie-smith/ [https://perma.cc/2CEG-ANGE]; http://www.nytimes.com/1994/06/25/us/time-responds-to-criticism-over-simpson-cover.html
16. http://www.jstor.org/stable/43610014
17. https://www.youtube.com/watch?v=EihcRDRAy9o) [https://perma.cc/B3RJ-KCRZ]
18. https://doi.org/10.1080/17430437.2010.491267
19. http://www.forbes.com/sites/kurtbadenhausen/2011/09/22/the-business-of-michael-jordan-is-booming/#5be003143955 [https://perma.cc/9E7Q-ES49]
20. https://books.google.com/books/about/Second_Coming.html?id=B-A5mPwAACAAJ [https://perma.cc/6KLD-WXJJ]
21. http://www.washingtonpost.com/wp-dyn/content/article/2008/07/06/AR2008070602321.html [https://perma.cc/4Q4H-YC2W]
22. http://www.adweek.com/news/television/new-espn-series-shows-how-oj-simpson-changed-advertising-and-it-changed-him-171919 [https://perma.cc/W7SV-9U88]
23. https://www.youtube.com/watch?v=7W1hnR3kLwo [https://perma.cc/YJV2-ENZ6]
24. http://www.si.com/vault/1996/12/23/220709/the-chosen-tiger-woods-was-raised-to-believe-that-his-destiny-is-not-only-to-be-the-greatest-golfer-ever-but-also-to-change-the-world-will-the-pressures-of-celebrity-grind-him-down-first [https://perma.cc/A7ZG-YDXY]
25. http://www.si.com/nfl/2016/01/29/cam-newton-controversy-dab-dance-celebrations [https://perma.cc/K8WE-MAF7]
26. http://www.cbssports.com/nfl/news/watch-cam-newton-abruptly-leaves-super-bowl-50-postgame-interview/ [https://perma.cc/FC68-5W9Y]
27. https://theconversation.com/when-it-comes-to-baseballs-ethnic-tensions-the-problems-run-deeper-than-bat-flips-49089 [https://perma.cc/RF6H-LLJQ]
28. http://www.charlotteobserver.com/sports/nfl/carolina-panthers/nfl-blog/article56857428.html#storylink=cpy [https://perma.cc/Q3NR-W6HZ]
29https://implicit.harvard.edu/implicit/demo/background/posttestinfo.html [https://perma.cc/9TYB-JJZF]

A Former NFL Player Explains Why We Need More Colin Kaepernicks [An Interview with Chris Kluwe]

Matt Connolly

This essay originally appeared in *The Aspen Institute* on September 18, 2017. https://www.aspeninstitute.org/blog-posts/professional-sports-needs-colin-kaepernicks/ [https://perma.cc/6WVV-345K] © Apsen Institute. All rights reserved.

Former NFL player Chris Kluwe took the stage at the Aspen Institute Sports & Society Program's 2017 Project Play Summit to discuss the rise of esports and how best to get kids interested in more traditional organized sports.[1] Afterward he spared some time to answer our quest
ions about athlete activism, NFL culture, and the saga of Colin Kaepernick, who has yet to be signed by an NFL team after protesting during the national anthem and speaking out against police violence and racism last season.[2] Kluwe was outspoken in his support for same-sex marriage during his football career, and he thinks that activism may have led to the loss of his punting job four years ago.[3] He had a lot to say about being an activist in the NFL, the difficulties facing Kaepernick, and what he wishes fans understood about why players stand up for what they believe in.

Can you talk a little bit about what it's like speaking up politically as a professional athlete?

Speaking up politically as a professional athlete is something I wish more professional athletes did. I understand why they don't. One look at what Colin Kaepernick is going through and what I ended up having to go through four years ago, is there's a risk because the professional sports world wants to be a very corporate world. It wants to be, "Don't offend anyone. Go out, sell jerseys, sell shoes. Make sure the fans come back for this game and the next game."

And I think that's unfortunate because the framework that sports is built on is our societal framework, and if our societal framework breaks down because people are denied their rights and are not allowed to experience life the same way as everyone else then there won't be that framework for sports. And it doesn't matter how many stadiums you have or how many jerseys you've sold — none of it means anything anymore because people are focused on getting food and shelter and trying to survive. So, I would say to any corporate sports person who might possibly be watching this, take a moment and think about the society that allows you to exist and maybe do things that perpetuate that society instead of tearing it down.

It seems like those challenges are somewhat more present in the NFL than, let's say, the NBA. What is it about the NFL that you think makes it harder to speak out?

The NFL is probably harder to speak out in for a couple of reasons. One is the players union is the weakest players union out of the four major sports. And that's because there are so many players. It's very hard to get 1,800 players to organize and work in unison, especially if those players have a limited career span. On average, they're going to play three, three and a half years. If you have to give up a year of your playing career, 33 percent of your potential earnings, to go on strike, that's a pretty hefty sacrifice. Now hopefully guys will do that in order to make changes, but I can understand why they don't.

The second problem with the NFL is that the majority of the owners are rich, old white guys and they have very specific points of view that might have been points of view in the 50s and 60s, but are not necessarily great points of view in our modern society. So, until people with those viewpoints either cycle out or are replaced with someone with more progressive points of views, then it's going to be hard to effectuate any sort of change.

It seems like there are more players who are willing to protest and speak up right now. Do you think that's been the trend?

I think a lot more players have been willing to speak out and protest because they understand that they have a lot to lose. And they're starting to understand that there's safety in numbers. If there's just a lone voice speaking out, it's very easy to quash that voice, but if there are multiple voices speaking out, then there's strength in numbers and it becomes very obvious at that point that what the league is doing is trying to silence players from speaking out on social issues.

In my case it was, "Oh here's just a punter who's speaking out on same-sex rights. Well, we can cut him and a lot of people will accept the fact that it was due to his play performance dropping or it saved us some money." But when you have someone like Colin Kaepernick get cut for speaking out on police brutality, not getting picked up by any other teams, you see all these other quarterbacks get picked up by those teams that are clearly worse than he is and now other players are speaking up on that, all of a sudden it makes it a lot harder for those same excuses to be made because people see through the charade, they see through the lies. They're like, "No. This isn't why he's not playing anymore. He's not playing because he spoke up on this issue that needs to be addressed and you don't want us to talk about it." And so hopefully that drives a lot of people to continue talking about it and make some change.

How important is it for the league for Colin Kaepernick to be speaking out the way he is?

I think it's very important for Colin Kaepernick to be speaking up the way he is because he's a role model. He is someone that hundreds of thousands of kids and adults look up to and will model their behavior after. He has the stage, he has the platform. And by using it to try to make society a better and fairer place, then that helps other people realize, "Hey I can do the same thing. I can work towards positive change in my community. I can work towards positive change in my society. I'm not the only one who feels this way." And the more of us that do that, the healthier our society becomes, the more likely it is to withstand the test of time.

What do you wish that people, especially everyday fans, understood about what you went through four years ago and what Kaepernick is going through now?

What I wish that everyday fans understood about what I went through and what Kaepernick is going through now is that when someone tells you that something is happening, odds are they're probably not lying about it, specifically as it relates to an NFL job where there's really no incentive for us to make things up and tell you that there's a problem that doesn't exist. If we're telling you that there's a problem, that problem does exist and it needs to be addressed.

I wish more fans understood that sports were secondary to human life and human society, and that, in the grand scheme of things, sports really don't matter. What matters is how you are as a human being, how you treat the human beings around you. That's what's important. So, any athlete who speaks up on that I think is doing a very helpful service to society at large and to everyone around them.

Notes

1. https://www.aspeninstitute.org/programs/sports-society/ [https://perma.cc/6WBM-8HKP]
2. https://www.sbnation.com/2016/9/11/12869726/colin-kaepernick-national-anthem-protest-seahawks-brandon-marshall-nfl [https://perma.cc/CJ7L-NSYN]
3. http://deadspin.com/i-was-an-nfl-player-until-i-was-fired-by-two-cowards-an-1493208214 [https://perma.cc/V9ZX-Q35B]

What Does It Mean to be Important?

Jack Russell Weinstein

The NFL doesn't just want to be popular; it wants to be important. It doesn't just want to make money; it wants to be influential. And it doesn't just want to be entertainment; it wants to embody America. For all of these reasons, it has both a moral obligation and an existential need to celebrate protests on the field.

Consider the myth of the student quarterback: the popular high school kid who dates the head cheerleader, the heroic leader who personifies school spirit and carries the student body's reputation on his shoulders. He is the golden boy in the prime of his life. His time on the field is, in Bruce Springsteen's words, his glory days. In order for this to be believable, football has to either eclipse or provide all of his other needs. It must inspire his parents to love him and his friends to admire him. It must give him honor in battle, teach him to be a man, educate him, and, above all, get him laid.

But history tells us that the quarterback isn't so pure. He is a date rapist and bully. He is arrogant and enabled. Parents, schools, and whole towns hide his misdeeds. People whisper the truth while his victims cower, but he is given everything because his victory is their validation. Team sports were supposed to teach him responsibility and give him a sense of community, but all that football actually did was hold him above all the others. Even when he gives lip service to the power of the offensive linemen or praises the defensive backs, even when he thanks Jesus for his victory, it is a show.

The quarterback is a selfish gladiator who is entitled to all the spoils, no matter whom it hurts. The townspeople, in turn, disavow the rape victims because they have invested too much in the rapist and only condemn themselves by pointing their fingers. Economists tell us that "sunk costs"—the amount of money a person spends on a failing endeavor—do not justify spending more money, but few believe it. The loyalty and the lies are the sunk costs that the community paid for the conviction that football is goodness.

For all this to succeed, the quarterback must not protest. He must not complain or feel incomplete, or the illusion is shattered. He must accept football in his heart, sacrificing his body and his spirit. Heaven can and will wait for him. His soul is the property of the game. He must trust in the coach and the league. He must be subservient to their decisions. He must bend both knees to their wills, and herein lays the problem. Colin Kaepernick only bends one.

My account of the quarterback and his relationship with others is an oversimplification, of course. No football player is only one thing and condemning all those who play because of the misdeeds of some is profoundly unfair. However, I am discussing the football *mythos* here, not any given individual. Statistics don't tell us anything about specific cases; they reveal patterns. These are the stories that brighten our Friday night lights. These are the invincible dreams that teach our boys all the right moves. Our midwestern boys. Our rural and, occasionally, our suburban boys. Football myth is purified by the heartland and soiled by the inner-city. Knute Rockne, the white all-American; Rudy, the Irish-catholic team-conscience; Mox, *Varsity Blues's* unappreciated backup; and even Bobby Boucher, *The Waterboy's* special-needs tackling-machine, are all stories of potential realized. The urban teams, in contrast, the black teams—The Rock's *Gridiron Gang*, Denzel Washington's Titans, Cuba Gooding Jr.'s Rod Tidwell—are all tales of redemption disguised as stories of acceptance. (Tidwell has to redeem not just himself, but Jerry McGuire and Bob Sugar—no small task.) Again, Colin Kaepernick runs against the grain. He is uninterested in his own redemption; he is concerned with America's. He is stepping over the lines. He is uppity.

Uppity is the right word, by the way. As Taylor Branch has convincingly argued in *The Cartel*, college sports—football especially—is particularly exploitative of African-American men. By naming their employees student-athletes, the NCAA takes away players' abilities to make money off of their own images, get adequate post-college health care, and even self-advocate. As Branch puts it, "College athletes are not slaves.... Yet to survey the scene—corporations and universities enriching themselves on the backs of uncompensated young men, whose status as 'student-athletes' deprives them of the right to due process guaranteed by the Constitution—is to catch the unmistakable whiff of the plantation."

High school diminishes the player's humanity, and college commodifies them, but the NFL asks for worse. With the crushing blows against their poorly protected heads, the NFL demands its players damage their intellect and their very experiences of the world. The injuries sustained from the game produce headaches, torpor, inability to focus, and limit the attention span. They make it hard to move and to lift things. They take away players' agency and, in some cases, cause depression so powerful that some former players' only escape is suicide. The NFL knew of these consequences as early as 1994[1], possibly earlier. Yet they denied it, and did little to protect their players.

Their youth gone, their education wasted, their physicality impaired, their profits stolen, and their individualism disregarded, NFL players have only their relationships to call their own. They have their families, they have their citizenship, and they have their group self-identification. But these too are exploited, for example, when the families are shown celebrating victories, or when athletes shout out to their loved ones (and God) after they win, or when the NFL and the U.S. military stage well-publicized reunions of cheerleaders and deployed service members on the field.[2] The U.S. military paid more than five million dollars for four years of "moments" honoring the troops. Players are tools for propaganda as well as profit.[3]

All of these are challenged by Colin Kaepernick when he kneels on the field in protest, and this is the real reason why his actions should be celebrated. There are other reasons to do so as well: football's role in democracy, players' positions as role models, football's being of such influence that its fields have become, in essence, a public sphere. But these are all secondary to the fact that the NFL should celebrate Kaepernick's actions because it is the moment when he reclaims his humanity. It is the act that allows him to give larger meaning to a pastime that is, in the end, just a game. It is the recognition that his personal history is always embedded in a world that he, too, has a responsibility to contribute to.

The NFL wants to be important, but all it has managed to be is prominent. It has confused moral authority with wealth and ubiquity. We remember the classical Greek Olympics as a bridge between athletic excellence and human betterment. It was an endeavor of peace and optimism. In contrast, we remember the Roman colosseum as a place of cruelty, corruption, and distraction. If the NFL can only be the latter, if it is just bread and circus, then it is indistinguishable from Wal-Mart and Verizon. All it will ever be is a commercially successful corporation created for private gain, an exploitative and racist feudal lord that is itself exploited for jingoistic purposes. But if it can be more—if it can celebrate protest on its field by honoring the humanity of its players, the citizenship of its viewers, and its role in educating a global audience—then it can have meaning. It can have moral worth. It can, when all is said and done, be justified.

Notes

1. "Timeline: The NFL's Concussion Crisis," *Frontline (PBS)*, accessed August 21, 2018, https://www.pbs.org/wgbh/pages/frontline/sports/league-of-denial/timeline-the-nfls-concussion-crisis/ [https://perma.cc/5AXJ-AKDX]
2. "Surprise Military Reunions At NFL Games Reach Peak Bullshit," *Deadspin*, accessed August 21, 2018, https://deadspin.com/surprise-military-reunions-at-nfl-games-reach-peak-bull-1727940877 [https://perma.cc/4HU6-JU78]
3. "Jets' salutes honor N.J. National Guard but cost taxpayers," *NJ.com*, accessed August 21, 2018, https://www.nj.com/politics/index.ssf/2015/05/taxpayers_pony_up_for_jets_salutes_to_nj_national.html [https://perma.cc/V34X-8DPT]

Section Four

Tactics

Allen's Knee

Richard Newman

Famed black minister Richard Allen once took a knee to protest racial injustice. When he got up, Allen launched perhaps the most important institution in African-American life: the African Methodist Episcopal Church. That church helped spread antislavery ideas in antebellum America; it recruited black soldiers during the Civil War; it remained a key institutional base in the long Civil Rights movement. Frederick Douglass gave his last speech in an AME church. Rosa Parks was an AME disciple. An AME church in Mississippi hosted protest meetings after Emmitt Till's savage murder. AME adherents in South Africa fought Apartheid. The AME Church is legendary and still growing in the twenty-first century.

And it all began when Allen took a knee to protest racial injustice.

Allen had not planned on kneeling in protest. A former slave who gained his freedom by literally paying for himself—he saved enough money to pay his master for freedom—Allen was a teenage convert to the Methodist Church. When he kneeled, Allen honored an Almighty power that had long since intervened in history to vanquish tyranny and wickedness. Like many other African Americans, he loved the Old Testament story of Exodus, in which a just God punished unrepentant Egyptian slaveholders. As a boy, Allen heard revivalist preachers near his Delaware home talk about the righteousness of an all-powerful God, as well as spiritual equality in Heaven. Such words inspired Allen to attend Methodist camp meetings and then Bible study sessions. He often crossed the color line, clasping hands with white believers of the Gospel and sharing intimate space with men and women of all races and backgrounds interested in the Word. When he became a preacher, Allen roamed the mid-Atlantic countryside in search of new adherents to his gospel of freedom and equality. He worked and prayed with white as well as black itinerants. He thought the American republic was dedicated to liberty and justice for all. He believed in an early version of the American Dream.

That vision crumbled when white leaders at his new church in Philadelphia decided that black members were becoming a problematic presence. Allen had arrived at St. George's Church in the mid-1780s hoping to expand black membership and communal opportunities with white congregants in the City of Brotherly Love. Preaching several times a day, Allen brought new vigor and membership to the church. He thought this was God's way: a church of interracial fellowship that practiced what he preached.

At worship one morning, Allen and other black members discovered that St. George's had other plans. After relegating African Americans to the back of the church, they would build a new gallery upstairs designed exclusively for black members.

Segregation had come to St. George's church—to Allen's church.

Allen wanted to prove that this violated church policy, Methodist conscience, the Lord's way, and the American Dream.

So, he and others took a knee.

Allen and his colleague Absalom Jones kneeled in prayer and refused to rise when white people tried to physically pull them up. Nothing should interrupt the sacred act of prayer, Allen thought.

But this prayer also had a design: he would challenge white congregants to stand tall against racism. If the congregation got up and told white leaders to stop, then Allen would know that his church was righteous and true. If it did not, he would walk out from a racist institution.

As one scholar has put it, Allen wanted to demonstrate that he was the best representative of Christianity and a true disciple of American democracy. When St. George's church failed to support him—to support these ideals—Allen left and launched his own church.

And so, the AME Church was born on Allen's bended knee.

In football, one knee equals two feet. In Richard Allen's world, one knee launched a revolution. He would be smiling today.

Colin Kaepernick and the Power of Black Silent Protest

Ameer Hasan Loggins

This essay originally appeared in *Black Perspectives* on September 4, 2017. https://www.aaihs.org/colin-kaepernick-and-the-power-of-black-silent-protest/ [https://perma.cc/U5YS-3663]

On July 28, 1917, thousands of Black children, women, and men stoically marched in silence down Fifth Avenue in New York City in what was called the "Negro Silent Protest Parade."[1]

The silent protest was in response to the ubiquitous horrors of Jim Crow terrorism, placing a spotlight on the horrifying reign of terror that took place in East St. Louis,[2] where within a three-day period, an estimated 100 black people had been killed by white mobs and more than 6,000 black people were burned out of their homes.

Reporter Carlos F. Hurd published an eyewitness report in the *St. Louis Post-Dispatch* regarding the domestic terror attacks where he recounted, "The East St. Louis affair, as I saw it, was a man hunt, conducted on a sporting basis, though with anything but the fair play which is the principle of sport," Hurd wrote. "There was a horribly cool deliberateness and a spirit of fun about it. 'Get a n*****' was the slogan, and it was varied by the recurrent cry, 'Get another.'"

Though vocally silent, the protesters spoke in volumes with their presence, and the signs that they carried, one of which read that, "America has lynched without trial 2,867 Negroes in 31 years and not a single murderer has suffered."[3] On an average, 39 black people were lynched per year during the Old Jim Crow era. In 1892, the worst year, 161 Black people in America were lynched and a 2015 report from the Alabama-based nonprofit Equal Justice Initiative found that white mobs murdered a total of 3,959 black persons in 12 southern states between 1877 and 1950, which is 700 more than previously reported.[4] During the New Jim Crow Era, *Quartz* states more Black men were shot dead by police in 2015 than were lynched in the worst year of the Old Jim Crow era.[5]

Just as the lynching of Black people was heavy on the hearts of Black America in 1917 during the Negro Silent Protest Parade,[6] so to are the deaths of Black children, women, and men at the hands the police in America a century later. And just as the Negro Silent Protest Parade marched because they deemed, "it a crime to be silent in the face of such barbaric acts," as lynching, Colin Kaepernick silently protested, because:

> I am not going to stand up to show pride in a flag for a country that oppresses black people and people of color. To me, this is bigger than football and it would be selfish on my part to look the other way. There are bodies in the street and people getting paid leave and getting away with murder.[7]

Kaepernick—like the participants in the Negro Silent Protest Parade—represents a complex collision of being tactically silent as a direct action method of protest, while serving as a voice for those muted by untimely deaths.

Let me explain.

When we think of the term silence it produces various intellections. On a purely definitional level we see silence as the absence of sound or noise, but when applied to the human condition, the presence of silence takes on different meanings. At one end of the spectrum of silence, it is associated with the silenced (group or individual) experiencing intimidation, fear, embarrassment, a lack of knowledge, and/or powerlessness.[8] Being silenced is almost always conceptualized as negative. Examples of this type of silencing include the silencing of trauma in general and violent trauma in particular. Trauma survivors describe a "conspiracy of silence" where they feel a need to testify to their experiences, to make them real and to make themselves whole again, but society will not let them speak, leading to a fragmented or shattered self.

In the case of those that are victims of fatal encounters with the police, they are permanently silenced.

In contrast to being silenced (by force), being silent (by choice) can have unifying benefits. We see this at the cultural level, for example, during moments of silence, used to commemorate great losses, serving as a form of soundless remembrance. Moments of silence have been used to unite people in communal mourning and reflection, and in many cases, when grieving those that have lost their lives due to systemic social injustices; moments of silence serve as the calm before the storm that leads to communal mobilization.

Moments of shared silence can also provide space for the impetus of a new communal unification, a unification born out of mourning, revolving around reflection, leading to resistance, and thus giving rise to mobilizing via protest.

In the cases of the Negro Silent Protest Parade, and Kaepernick, these silences by choice serve as convergences of mourning, reflection, and protest, all taking place in a single action, providing a voice for the silenced without saying a single word. But unlike the Negro Silent Protest Parade—which took place on one day—Kaepernick's silent protest took place every week for the entirety of an NFL season. Kaepernick's tactical silence is a calculated action being used as a means of exercising agency. His utilization of wordless communication should be viewed as an exercise in patience and perseverance, as well as a source of strength and calm.

Kaepernick's silence in 2017, screams in the same tone as his ancestors in 1917 parading through New York to protest the lynching of Black children, women and men in America. His silence speaks the same language as John Carlos and Tommie Smith as they stood atop the medal podium at the 1968 Summer Games in Mexico City with their Black fists firmly fixed in the air.[9] His silence, like those silently protesting before him, is in honor of all of those who were silenced for simply being born Black in America.

Notes

1. http://www.blackpast.org/aah/naacp-silent-protest-parade-new-york-city-1917 [https://perma.cc/LL2D-VTKH]
2. https://www.smithsonianmag.com/smithsonian-institution/east-st-louis-race-riot-left-dozens-dead-devastating-community-on-the-rise-180963885/
3. https://nationalhumanitiescenter.org/pds/maai2/forward/text4/silentprotest.pdf [https://perma.cc/648C-JHQ4]
4. http://www.dailymail.co.uk/news/article-2947828/Jim-Crow-lynchings-common-thought-new-report-adding-700-murdered-African-Americans-total-nearly-4-000.html [https://perma.cc/B6G2-RFTF]
5. https://qz.com/726245/more-black-people-were-killed-by-us-police-in-2015-than-were-lynched-in-the-worst-year-of-jim-crow/ [https://perma.cc/GC39-A8L8]
6. https://www.aaihs.org/ida-b-wells-police-violence-and-the-legacy-of-lynching/ [https://perma.cc/X6QP-WUC6]
7. https://www.aaihs.org/black-protest-white-backlash-and-the-history-of-scientific-racism/ [https://perma.cc/25NF-VL8H]
8. http://www.proactiveteaching.org/pdfs/92.pdf [https://perma.cc/T7V3-XEKP]
9. http://www.blackpast.org/aah/john-carlos-1945 [https://perma.cc/ED4P-XC2Y]; http://www.blackpast.org/aaw/smith-tommie-1944 [https://perma.cc/37N9-TSM3]

African American Patriotism during the World War I Era*

David F. Krugler

As political science professor Michael Tesler recently observed, "American patriotism has always been racialized." In 1995, for example, an NBC poll cited by Tesler found that just two percent of respondents envisioned the ideal patriot as an African American; fifty percent pictured a white man or woman. (The poll asked: "When you hear about someone being 'patriotic,' do you think of a white man, a white woman, a black man, or a black woman?") Tesler also reviewed contemporary social science research demonstrating the tendency to associate American national identity with whiteness.[1] Does this mean that African Americans who fight against racial inequality are likely to be seen as unpatriotic and un-American, even if they demonstrate their patriotism through military service and support for a war?

Historically the answer is yes, as a brief look at the World War I era reveals. In April 1917, President Woodrow Wilson asked the nation to enter the war on the Allied side to make the world "safe for democracy." Military service and the pur-

* This essay is in part adapted from my book: David Krugler, *1919, The Year of Racial Violence: How African Americans Fought Back* (Cambridge: Cambridge University Press, 2014).

chase of liberty bonds were two major ways in which Americans contributed to the war effort. For African Americans, the war posed a unique challenge: should they fight for a nation that disfranchised, segregated, exploited, and lynched them? Despite the denial of democracy at home, a majority of African Americans supported the war. "He, the American Negro—is a loyal, patriotic, undiluted American!" proclaimed the *Denver Star*.[2] Almost 370,000 black men served in the military. Black citizens flocked to industrial cities to work in factories producing war-essential goods and bought the bonds that funded the war. By August 1918, for example, African American women "had subscribed $5,000,000 for Liberty Loan bonds."[3]

The U.S. government did not, however, regard African Americans' war service as equal to that of white people. Consider the treatment of black recruits and draftees, most of whom served in segregated units in the Army. Opposed to the training of black people as officers and combat soldiers, the War Department created all-black labor battalions led by white officers. Some stateside battalions resembled chain gangs more than military units: the officers hired out their men to civilian contractors and kept their wages.[4] Discrimination greatly devalued black patriotism and demeaned African Americans while still requiring the same level of contribution and sacrifice expected of white people. Conscription was color-blind, but race mattered very much in the Army.

The sight of black men in uniform threatened white supremacy, especially in areas where local white authorities used their power to oppress African Americans. In August 1917 in Houston, a white police officer struck a black private from the Twenty-fourth Infantry, Third Battalion, after the soldier challenged his rough arrest of a black woman. Tensions were already high between the men of the Twenty-fourth and the Houston police, who had beaten several other soldiers for defying Jim Crow rules on streetcars. Rather than view the soldiers as patriots, the police saw them as a menace to the established, racist social order. In this instance, black soldiers fought back, leaving their base because they believed a white mob was forming. Armed clashes with white people in Houston led to swift and harsh reprisals by the Army—courts sentenced thirteen soldiers to death. The black press acknowledged that the soldiers had committed crimes; at the same time, it observed that the Houston police's mistreatment of the soldiers, and the failure of the men's white commanding officers to respond, had pushed the soldiers to a breaking point.[5] In another, smaller incident, a white Charleston policeman struck a black soldier whom he was arresting. When an observer rebuked the officer for "hitting a United States uniform," he angrily retorted, "Fuck the uniform! These sons of bitches should not be in them."[6] These episodes—and there were many more like them during the war—starkly showed how the association of whiteness with patriotism was an integral part of the oppression of African Americans. The Charleston officer's vehement, hateful statement put into words the widespread fear of white people that African Americans could use military service and patriotism as a pathway to equality of rights and opportunities. The willingness of black soldiers to use force heightened this fear.

African Americans responded by working to end as much wartime Jim Crow as possible and by preparing for a full-fledged effort to secure their rights and equality after the war ended. Howard University led a campaign that successfully lobbied the War Department to train African Americans as officers; the National Association of Colored Graduate Nurses pressured both the War Department and the Red Cross to end the ban on accepting black nurses.[7] A wartime slogan advised African Americans, "*first* your Country, *then* your Rights."[8] If this sounded militant—would black veterans fight for their rights after the war?—then Emmett J. Scott, Booker T. Washington's former secretary, struck a conciliatory tone in a February 1919 speech. Black soldiers, Scott declared, were coming home "to perform their full duties as citizens and to live in peace with their fellow men, asking in return only the full protection of the law of their land—the guarantee of life, liberty, and the pursuit of happiness."[9]

But acceptance of African Americans as patriots and equal citizens was not forthcoming. The wartime abuses of black soldiers in Houston and Charleston presaged a national white backlash against African Americans for transgressing white supremacy or asserting their rights. In 1919, white lynch mobs murdered more than seventy-five black people, including eleven veterans.[10] Such violence fulfilled the ominous promise of Congressman James Byrnes (Democrat, South Carolina): "There are in this country 90,000,000 white people determined not to extend political and social equality to the 10,000,000 Negroes" no matter how much African Americans had contributed to the war.[11]

Black patriotism and military service did not bring an end to or even abate white supremacy. Throughout 1919 and into 1920, racial violence—to be precise, organized white-on-black attacks—broke out in Chicago, Omaha, Washington, D.C., and Phillips County, Arkansas, among other locations. White mobs used violence to enforce the boundaries of all-white neighborhoods, punish perceived slights against white people, carry out rough justice (that is, mob killings of black people accused of crimes against white people before court proceedings could take place), or protect the economic exploitation of black sharecroppers.

The ferocious reassertion of white supremacy did not go unchallenged. As NAACP co-founder W.E.B. Du Bois wrote in May 1919: "We return from fighting. We return fighting. Make way for Democracy! We saved it in France, and by the Great Jehovah, we will save it in the United States of America, or know the reason why."[12] Where mobs attacked, black people resisted, often led by veterans. When police failed to protect black residents from roving white gangs during Chicago's weeklong outbreak of anti-black collective violence, local black veterans took up arms to stop the gangs. Although a Chicago jury later commended these men for "their valuable service in patrolling, quieting the excited colored population, and relieving the grave fears of the women and children that white mobs were about to break through," local newspapers falsely described the men as marauders who had randomly fired on white people.[13]

Black armed self-defense in Chicago and elsewhere greatly alarmed the Bureau of Investigation (BI), forerunner of the FBI. Ignoring the root cause of white-on-black violence, the BI decided that African Americans were carrying out a national uprising even though they could find no reliable evidence to support this conclusion. Still, the BI continued to assert that "propaganda of a radical nature" was a cause of racial violence.[14]

In one sense, the BI was correct: during and after World War I, African Americans' quest for equality of rights and opportunity, an expectation validated by their wartime service, was "radical" in a nation that practiced racial discrimination and white supremacy. Patriotism was highly racialized, as recognized by Hubert Eaves, a black teenager living in Des Moines, Iowa. Eaves was arrested for refusing to salute the American flag at school because, as he said in court, "America is a White man's country" and so he had no nation.[15]

This occurred in 1916. One hundred years later, Colin Kaepernick continued, so to speak, Hubert Eaves's protest by silently kneeling during the playing of the National Anthem before a NFL game. The condemnation of the black quarterback for being unpatriotic has overshadowed his and other players' motive for the protest, to draw attention to police brutality against African Americans, and suggests that, despite the gains of the civil rights movement, there is still a strong tendency in the United States to associate patriotism with whiteness, as happened during World War I.

Notes

1. Michael Tesler, "To Many Americans, Being Patriotic Means Being White," *Washington Post*, October 13, 2017, accessed November 15, 2017, https://www.washingtonpost.com/news/monkey-cage/wp/2017/10/13/is-white-resentment-about-the-nfl-protests-about-race-or-patriotism-or-both/ [https://perma.cc/885Q-Y6A4]
2. "Rocking the Boat," *Denver Star*, July 1, 1916, available at Library of Congress, Chronicling America: Historic American Newspapers, accessed November 15, 2017, http://chroniclingamerica.loc.gov/lccn/sn84025887/1916-07-01/ed-1/seq-1/ [https://perma.cc/R5A2-DMBD]
3. Cleveland G. Allen, "Negro Proves Worth in War Service," *New York Tribune*, August 25, 1918, available at Library of Congress, Chronicling America: Historic American Newspapers, accessed November 15, 2017, http://chroniclingamerica.loc.gov/lccn/sn83030214/1918-08-25/ed-1/seq-25/ [https://perma.cc/B44S-UN7Z]. For more details of African Americans' home front contributions, see Nina Mjagkij, *Loyalty in Time of Trial: The African American Experience during World War I* (Lanham, MD.: Rowman and Littlefield, 2011), 121–40. Two additional, full-length studies of African Americans during World War I are Adriane Lentz-Smith, *Freedom Struggles: African Americans and World War I* (Cambridge, MA: Harvard University Press, 2009) and Chad L. Williams, *Torchbearers of Democracy: African American Soldiers in the World War I Era* (Chapel Hill: University of North Carolina Press, 2010).
4. Arthur E. Barbeau and Florette Henri, *The Unknown Soldiers: Black American Troops in World War I* (Philadelphia: Temple University Press, 1974), 89–101, 191–201.
5. Krugler, *1919*, 21. For an in-depth examination of the Houston mutiny as a fight over racialized citizenship and manhood, see Lentz-Smith, *Freedom Struggles*, 43–79.
6. Krugler, *1919*, 36–7.
7. Emmett J. Scott, *Scott's Official History of the American Negro in the World War* (Chicago: Homewood Press, 1919), 82–90; Andrea Patterson, "Black

Nurses in the Great War: Fighting for and with the American Military in the Struggle for Civil Rights," *Canadian Journal of History* 47, no. 3 (Winter 2012): 545–66.

8. W.E.B. DuBois, "Our Special Grievances," *Crisis* 16, no. 5 (September 1918), 217, cited in Mjagkij, *Loyalty in Time*, xxii.

9. "The Negro and the South after the War," *Kansas City Sun*, February 1, 1919, available at Library of Congress, Chronicling America: Historic American Newspapers, accessed November 15, 2017, http://chroniclingamerica.loc.gov/lccn/sn90061556/1919-02-01/ed-1/seq-1/ [https://perma.cc/5UEL-9K4F]

10. "The Lynching Industry, 1919," *Crisis* 19, no. 4 (February 1920), 183–6.

11. The Editors, "A Reply to Congressman James F. Byrnes of South Carolina," *Messenger* 2, no. 10 (October 1919), 13.

12. W.E.B. Du Bois, "Returning Soldiers," *Crisis* 18, no. 1 (May 1919), reprinted in Robert T. Kerlin, *The Voice of the Negro 1919* (New York: E. P. Dutton, 1920; reprint, New York: Arno Press, 1968), 35–7.

13. Peter Hoffman, Coroner, *Report of the Coroner's Jury on the Race Riots*, November 3, 1919, box 38, folder 1980, Graham Taylor Papers, Newberry Library, Chicago, 5; "Troops Moving on Chicago as Negroes Shoot into Crowds," *Chicago Daily News*, July 29, 1919 (home edition), 1; "One Death in 14 Hours Puts Total at 26," *Chicago Tribune*, July 31, 1919 (final edition), 1–2.

14. As the BI observed (though not publicly) in 1920, "to date the Department [of Justice] has not found any concerted movement on the part of the negroes to cause a general uprising throughout the country." See Krugler, *1919*, 198 n. 7.

15. "Negro Boy Again Refuses to Salute American Flag," *Broad-Ax*, March 25, 1916, available at Library of Congress, Chronicling America: Historic American Newspapers, accessed November 15, 2017, http://chroniclingamerica.loc.gov/lccn/sn84024055/1916-03-25/ed-1/seq-1/ [https://perma.cc/XS48-CYT6]

We Interrupt This Program

Sharon Carson

"It should go without saying that I love my country and I'm proud to be an American. But, to quote James Baldwin, 'exactly for this reason, I insist on the right to criticize her perpetually.'"

Eric Reid, Strong Safety, San Francisco 49ers,
New York Times, Op-Ed, September 25, 2017.[1]

"The politics of disruption—where activists have interrupted the daily functioning of American life—have brought into full view the contradictions that drive the current social crisis in this country."

Eddie Glaude Jr., *Democracy in Black*.[2]

"Can't you understand that this is the perspective from which we are now speaking? It isn't as if we got up today and said, you know, 'what can we do to irritate America?'"

Lorraine Hansberry, "The Black Revolution and the White Backlash," Town Hall Forum, New York City, June 15, 1964.

It's no surprise that the NFL player protests have sparked debate among African-American activists about protest tactics more generally. When San Francisco 49er Eric Reid met early on with Colin Kaepernick to deliberate about the best way to use their place on a very visible stage to protest racial injustice and police brutality against black citizens, they were clearly aware that their protest was part of a longer tradition of debate about political strategy.

Reid said in his September 2017 Op-Ed: "After hours of careful consideration, and even a visit from Nate Boyer, a retired Green Beret and former NFL player, we came to the conclusion that we should kneel, rather than sit, the next day during the anthem as a peaceful protest. We chose to kneel because it's a respectful gesture. I remember thinking our posture was like a flag flown at half-mast to mark a tragedy."[3]

This somber intention has been respected, ignored, and denigrated in the ensuing controversy. As Reid put it in the same Op-Ed: "It baffles me that our protest is still being misconstrued as disrespectful to the country, flag and military personnel. We chose it because it's exactly the opposite. It has always been my understanding that the brave men and women who fought and died for our country did so to ensure that we could live in a fair and free society, which includes the right to speak out in protest."

Television audiences have since watched players, coaches, and owners take a range of physical stances during the opening ceremonies before NFL (and other) games, and those varied choices illustrate the diversity of opinion about tactics and their symbolic meanings among those participating in the protests. Such debates have been part of every historical moment in the African-American struggle for civic equality and racial justice, from the colonial era to the present. In 1964, another protest illuminated such internal debate, and did so on a similarly public entertainment stage.

It's a complex story in its own terms, but in 1964, civil rights activists abruptly interrupted the commercialized leisure of their fellow Americans on the opening day of the World's Fair in New York City. What became known as the "stall-in" actually morphed into two separate protests, but the original stall-in aimed to shut down transportation across the city by having hundreds of cars strategically run out of gas and block traffic, while hundreds of activists would block bridges and pull emergency brakes to stop the subways.

The 1964 World's Fair protests share with the current NFL player protests an intent to highlight racial inequity by startling audiences who have gathered to view a Grand American Entertainment. The aim in both historical moments has been to disrupt American leisure in order to shake peoples' complacency and turn their attention toward serious and persisting racial injustice.

In his 2016 book *Democracy in Black*, philosopher Eddie Glaude Jr. calls this injustice "the value gap":

> The crisis currently engulfing black America and the country's indifference to the devastation it has wrought illustrate what I call *the value gap*. We talk about the achievement gap in education or the wealth gap between white Americans and other groups, but the value gap reflects something more basic: that no matter our stated principles or how much progress we think we've made, white people are valued more than others in this country, and that fact continues to shape the life chances of millions of Americans. The value gap is in our national DNA.[4]

A key focus for Glaude is the refusal of too many white Americans to look at, let alone address, the realities of the value gap. The protests in 1964 and today deploy a time-honored tactic in American democratic dissent: they aim to force a look, to redirect the gaze, disrupt the status quo, to interrupt regular programming and interrupt habits of perception and action which perpetuate the value gap. In both historical moments, activists aim to very intentionally disrupt the "peace" when said peace is built on unjust social practices.

It's obvious from some virulent white backlash in both eras that for some Americans, any protest by black citizens is condemned and dismissed, peaceful or not. But both the NFL player protests and the 1964 World's Fair protests also got the attention, even action, of supporters in each audience. Just as critically, both protests also sparked important debates among African-American activists, especially ones about strategy. These debates will persist within a range of American social justice movements.

When activists of the Brooklyn chapter of the Congress of Racial Equality (CORE) proposed their massive stall-in to tie up city traffic and disrupt attendance for the opening day of the 1964 World's Fair, not all African-American civil rights activists supported the tactic. The stall-in was meant to draw public support for the Civil Rights Act, to dramatize racial discrimination in hiring (including at the Fair) and housing, and to protest police brutality in New York City. But critics *within* the black civil rights movement argued that the tactic targeted and "disrupted" the wrong people—i.e. working citizens—not those in power, and that a better strategy would be to disrupt the World's Fair opening ceremony itself, a glitzy symbol of American enterprise and the fruits of segregated commerce.

In fact, CORE national leader James Farmer and longtime "angelic troublemaker" Bayard Rustin organized their own counter-protest within the fairgrounds for the same day, a protest that actually drew significantly more participants as the stall-in faltered. This alternative protest at the opening ceremonies resulted in the arrests of Rustin and many others for "disturbing the peace." Longer and politically distinct accounts of the stall-in controversy can be found in coverage by the *New York Times* and *Slate*.[5]

That following summer, playwright and activist Lorraine Hansberry spoke at a June 1964 New York City forum entitled "The Black Revolution and the White Backlash," sponsored by The Association of Artists for Freedom. She opened her commentary by sharing her initial skepticism about the stall-in: "I said, 'Oh My God, now everybody's gone crazy, you know, tying up traffic. What's the matter with them? You know. Who needs it?' And then I noticed the reaction, starting in Washington and coming on up to New York..."

The June forum was an attempt to hash out tensions between African American activists and white liberals. Most of Hansberry's commentary focused on those tensions, but she concluded her remarks by returning to the tactics of the stall-in and civil disobedience more generally, and she did so in terms that echoed the strategy of NFL players who take a knee:

> This is why we want the dialogue, to explain [the viewpoint of African Americans] to you, you see. It isn't a question of patriotism and loyalty. My brother fought for this country, my grandfather before that and so on and that's all a lot of nonsense when we criticize. The point is that we have a different viewpoint because, you know, we've been kicked in the face so often and the vantage point of Negroes is entirely different and these are some of the things we are trying to say.[6]

Both of these historical moments, the 1964 World's Fair stall-in and the NFL protests today, invite further careful analysis of the particulars, especially the detailed thought, deliberation, and planning behind both actions. But more critically, both protests ask American citizens to pay attention to conditions in their country and to extend basic respect to those who are speaking up about serious racial and social problems in our nation. The viewing public is being asked to change the channel and listen up. As James Baldwin put it so succinctly in 1962: "Not everything that is faced can be changed, but nothing can be changed until it is faced."[7]

Notes

1. Eric Reid, "Why Colin Kaepernick and I Decided to Take a Knee," *New York Times*, September 25, 2017, https://www.nytimes.com/2017/09/25/opinion/colin-kaepernick-football-protests.html
2. Eddie Glaude Jr., *Democracy in Black: How Race Still Enslaves the American Soul* (New York: Broadway Books, 2016), 243.
3. Eric Reid, "Why Colin Kaepernick and I Decided to Take a Knee," *New York Times*, September 25, 2017, https://www.nytimes.com/2017/09/25/opinion/colin-kaepernick-football-protests.html
4. Glaude Jr., *Democracy in Black*, 31.
5. See Tamar Jacoby, excerpt from Chapter One of *Someone Elses's House: America's Unfinished Struggle for Integration*, New York Times, June 21, 1998, http://www.nytimes.com/books/first/j/jacoby-house.html and Joseph Tirella, "A Gun to the Heart of the City," *Slate*, April 22, 2014, http://www.slate.com/articles/news_and_politics/history/2014/04/core_s_1964_stall_in_the_planned_civil_rights_protest_that_kept_thousands.html. [https://perma.cc/8PGS-PDRQ]
6. Here is the full transcript of Hansberry's commentary at the forum: http://americanradioworks.publicradio.org/features/blackspeech/lhansberry.html [https://perma.cc/G5AC-KAJB]
7. James Baldwin, "As Much Truth as One Can Bear," *New York Times*, January 14, 1962, https://www.nytimes.com/1962/01/14/archives/as-much-truth-as-one-can-bear-to-speak-out-about-the-world-as-it-is.html; two additional pieces of interest: A November 25, 2017 post on Lorraine Hansberry and others entitled "Civil Rights Playwrights as Black Intellectuals" from the *Black Perspectives* blog of the African American Intellectual History Society: http://www.aaihs.org/civil-rights-playwrights-as-black-intellectuals/ [https://perma.cc/M78X-JS8A] and a retrospective *Democracy Now!* interview (audio and transcript) with Velma Hill and Norman Hill, two participants in the 1964 World's Fair actions: https://www.democracynow.org/2014/4/25/protesting_the_1964_world_s_fair [https://perma.cc/DK8W-4H6T]

E Kaepernick Unum: How Our Changing Media Habits Have Left Sports Our Place for Diverse Debate

Sarah Cavanah

Colin Kaepernick reminds us that there is one entity out there, striving to hold a fragmenting America together. And that entity is...ESPN.

In truth, it's sports broadcasting writ large, which is why we all care so much about Colin Kaepernick. He's important because most of us agree that he exists.

Most media scholars are fairly certain that our media consumption has some impact on how we view the world, even if the question of "how much" is still contested. Those that follow George Gerbner's theory of cultivation believe our media use, especially if we consume a lot of media, means that we can start to impose the reality of media onto how we view the real world. This is often illustrated with violence. People who watch a lot of television—with all its crime chases, detectives, and lawyers—tend to think there's more crime than there really is, even if they know of little crime firsthand.

Many believe this readjusting of reality extends to other aspects, as well. Mainstreaming was Gerbner's idea that media consumption starts to push viewers toward a general consensus about our life and our reality. The issues on TV are the issues we encounter. The problems are our problems. The views are our views. The problem is Gerbner wrote in 1976, and we live in 2017.

Gone are the days of 1974 when Americans watched deplorable Archie Bunker argue with his meathead liberal son-in-law about a variety of racially based gripes on *All in the Family*. Almost as many would tune in to watch those same gripes flipped another way on *Sanford and Son*. You could count on at least a quarter of a group being able to follow discussions of the collision of class and race on *The Jeffersons*. To reach that size of audience, these shows brought in black and white, conservative and liberal, young and old. Everyone had the same TV reality to muse over.

We have plenty of chances to use TV to talk social issues. I'd love to use Captain Raymond Holt from *Brooklyn Nine-Nine* as a way of talking about the stress of resisting self-stereotyping, but chances are only one out of fifty people in a random group will recognize his name. *Westworld* is a perfect chance to talk about how free we can be in a media-drenched world, but only 1.5 percent of TV viewers ages 18–49 regularly tune in. I could probably use the hit *Empire*, but, like most people, I don't watch it.

These aren't obscure shows. In fact, they are among the one hundred most successful shows of 2017. Even if we give up on the more interesting examples and go for sheer mass appeal, we're still likely to fail. The number one show for ages 18–49 was *The Walking Dead*, which does have a multiracial cast roaming its post-apocalyptic South, but also only regularly brings in eight percent of U.S. viewers.

If you want to hold a collective conversation about media or what's presented in it—good luck. Young women are watching celebrity reality shows on basic cable. Young men are playing Call of Duty. Young liberals tune in to *Last Week Tonight*. Young conservatives follow Tomi Lahren on social media. For every unique combination of identities, there's a unique collection of media to match. We still have mainstreaming in media, but now there are multiple mainstreams, matching the viewing patterns of smaller and smaller segments of society. Those mainstreams move to the center of their audiences, not the center of society, and the realities they present may not share much in common with each other. Policing problems in regard to minorities is part of the reality created for me in my TV viewing, which includes CBS's nightly newscast, *Last Week Tonight*, and complex societal dramas like *The Wire*. If your mainstream is comprised of *Wheel of Fortune*, *NCIS*, and cable news, your mainstream may be constructing a reality that emphasizes crime and order.

Our best bet for something in common would be to go for the content making up 2016's number two, three, four, and eight shows: professional football. We don't really watch sports more now than we used to, but the way we watch media in general has left sports one of the last things we watch in common. Sports are broadcast live, and the enjoyment of them is largely dependent on not knowing what's going to happen. You can't be part of the conversation the next day if you're time-shifting the game to next week. We also binge-watch most content alone, but watch sports with others. All this means that sports, particularly football, dominates the top of the ratings, when it wasn't even on the list in 1974. Sports can also cut across these growing multiple mainstreams, giving a place where different created realities can come into contact.

In February 2016, the TV comedy *Black-ish* directly dealt with a conversation on African Americans and policing. It was well-scripted, well-received, and thought-provoking. But only a fraction of the U.S. audience saw it, and the ones who did were already more likely to agree the issue was important. When Kaepernick took a knee, he did it for a bigger audience, and, more importantly, one full of different perspectives and backgrounds. These viewers took different positions on Kaepernick, and they spread those views to others like them on social media. There may not have been as much debate across positions, but there is awareness that there is a debate. It's likely not something anyone other than a professional athlete—and probably a professional football player—would be able to achieve.

Section Five

Counter-Tactics

"They Will Use This Against You": The Context and Legacy of the 2001 France vs. Algeria Protests

Andrew N. Wegmann

It started with the second song. As the players lined up on October 6, 2001, as is customary in any international friendly, nothing seemed out of the ordinary. First came the Algerian national anthem, "Kassaman" ("We Pledge"), a song of revolution, pride, and virtuous dedication to a homeland granted independence in 1962 by others but claimed internally for centuries. Green and white flags waved. Thousands sang, "*Fa-shaddü! Fa-shaddü!*" ("Bear witness! Bear witness!") as the music came to an end and cheers, whistles, and applause filled the air. Then came the home anthem, it too a revolutionary song, but from 170 years earlier than its predecessor. As the drums rolled in preparation, blue, white, and red flags waved, the team, clad in blue shirts and white shorts, a *coq sportif* newly crowned with a single cherished star on each left breast, stood together, arms linked. This was the hymn of the revolution that created this team, this stadium, this match, and, in a strange and tragic way, the day's opponent.

"Allons enfants de la Patrie
Le jour de gloire est arrivé!"

The first notes of the French revolutionary march, "La Marseillaise," met an unexpected chorus. Instead of the resounding chant, "*Allons enfants de la Patrie*" ("Onward children of the fatherland"), deep tones formed in the crowd, broken by whistles and jeers, quickly overcoming the hum of players and fans singing along. This was not supposed to happen. The faces of the players betrayed a universal confusion as they turned their heads to each other and then back to the crowd. National anthems were and remain sacred in international football. They represent the individuality of states, their players, and the fans and citizens who give it all meaning. Usually met with powerful, complimentary silence, the ritual of mutual respect that night went wrong. Something had changed, but no one on the field knew exactly what. This type of protest simply did not fit the scene.

"Qu'un sang impur
Abreuve nos sillons!"

"La Marseillaise" finished, the chorus of boos shifted to supportive joy, the captains met, shook hands, exchanged gifts, and the game began. But something was off. The match, indeed, had a purpose far beyond an exhibition between two vastly unequal sides—the French had won the most recent World Cup in 1998 and were the number one ranked team in the world. Algeria sat at eightieth, having failed even to qualify for each of the previous three World Cups. No one expected Algeria to score, much less win. And in the end, France emerged the victor by a 4-1 score line. But that was not the point. The match was organized as a statement of solidarity and binding wounds. Until 1962, when "Kassaman" became the Algerian national anthem, the country sat beneath the yoke of the French colonial empire. For seven full years, the Algerians fought for their independence against a French force brutal in its desire to retain the prized North African colony.

The war, fought between 1954 and 1962, served as fuel for a wider anti-colonial discourse that ultimately brought about the collapse of European colonialism on the African continent. It gave rise to some of the most profound and influential thinkers of the twentieth century—Frantz Fanon, Thomas Sankara, Aimé Césaire, and others. Perhaps most importantly, though, it created a relationship between France and Algeria that neither, it seemed, wanted to have. Because the fighting took place entirely in Algeria, refugees of the violence sought shelter in the colonial metropole of France, a nation that never entirely accepted them as its own but could not justly turn them away.

The match between the two nations in October 2001, then, stood as a reconciliation of sorts, an attempt at finding a common language and a common cause between nations once linked only by force. "A football game, chosen voluntarily, requires a kind of pacification in the relationship," anthropologist Christian Bromberger told the French newspaper *L'Humanité*. "You don't play a football game against a country you are at war with."[1] A month prior, two airliners hijacked by terrorists declaring *jihad* against the United States slammed into the World Trade Center in New York, killing more than 2,600 people in the worst terrorist attack in modern U.S. history. The world, it seemed, recognized the tragedy as an opportunity to make change and come to grips with differences allowed to fester too long with others. The France-Algeria match was supposed to do just that—reconcile the violent, oppressive past and share the excitement and friendship that only football could bring.

The peace lasted seventy-six minutes. France, led by their talisman Zinedine Zidane, the French-born son of two Algerian refugees, and the black Guadeloupe-born defender Lilian Thuram, had hoisted the World Cup trophy in that same stadium just three years earlier. Indeed, the 3-0 victory over Brazil in the World Cup final in Paris was a watershed moment for France as a whole. A team made up of immigrants and children of immigrants, nearly half of African descent, conquered the world of football for a nation that just a single generation before would have never recognized them as their own. This, it seemed, was the "New France" journalists celebrated in the streets that night. "There was no more red light, no bus lane, no forbidden direction," Annick Cojean famously wrote in *Le Monde*. "No more social classes, provincials, *banlieusards*. Nothing but the extraordinary, like a world turned upside down.... It was madness Paris, laughter Paris, delirious Paris. Paris the brothel. Paris the joyful. Paris the loving...colored and multi-colored, fraternal."[2]

France was still riding this high when the first of "pitch invaders" arrived on the field. Exactly thirty-one minutes into the second half, with Algeria on the attack and defender Moulay Haddou streaking up the left flank, a young man, clad in red and waving a white flag, sprinted across the field, a bevy of docents stumbling desperately behind him. From the right, another made his start. Then another, this time from the opposite touchline. Then another, and another, and another, each one simply running, some waving flags, all refusing to leave. Within two minutes the field was a chaotic mess, an anthill disturbed from above, each colorful dot a young man or woman of Algerian descent running aimlessly so long as the match did not continue.

Both teams, fearful and confused, quickly abandoned the match and left the field. But Lilian Thuram, the tall, dark French defender and public advocate for immigrants' rights, remained, his face twisted with rage, his finger lifted in accusation just inches from the chest of a young Algerian "invader" now startled with fear. He screamed furiously at the teenager, maintaining eye contact as docents and minders pulled him away and down the tunnel to the locker room.[3] The match was not supposed to end this way. There should never have been any boos or jeers. There should never have been any invaders. This was football. This was sacred. This was the New France, the "colored and multi-colored" France. This was "Paris the joyful, Paris the loving." What had become of this holy place, this nation of one, this reconciliation of past ills? As the commentators screamed of respect and shame, the embarrassment they believed the "invaders" ought to feel, and as the Algerian sports minister calmly declared, "This has nothing to do Algeria," the Algerian players smiled and took pictures with Zidane in the tunnel, their national hero clad in the French kit.

The protest that day had a strange feel to it, as though the point was not entirely clear. Lilian Thuram's fury as he left the field became a symbol of several sides—anger at the "invaders," frustration with the effects of the protest itself, an expression of the pent-up isolation that led to the protests in the first place. The next day, it was Thuram who graced the front pages of *Le Monde*, *L'Equipe*, and other national newspapers. Regardless of individual position, the entire nation seemed to balk at a universal reaction. Indeed, many French viewers feared that politics would get in the way, with the French Right increasingly arguing for a more closed off France and the Left seeking to open borders to former colonies and repent, at least in theory, for the damage done in the past.

Thuram, oddly, stood at the center, though he had nothing to do with the protest. A black native of Martinique, Thuram was something of a spokesman for the World Cup-winning team of 1998, taking every opportunity he could to point out and celebrate the diverse roots of the squad. He rightly took offense when Jean-Marie Le Pen, the founder and leader of the Right-wing Front National, attributed the World Cup victory to "*Les Noirs*" (the blacks) rather than to France.[4] And he feared that this same sentiment would seep into the events he had just witnessed in Paris. Indeed, Thuram's response to the protests, when it came to light, was a bit unexpected, at least to those who interviewed him after the fact.

While white French commentators lamented the "betrayal" committed by the "Algerian thugs" who invaded the pitch at the Stade de France, Thuram saw "idiots...ruining everything."[5] But he did not see betrayal. He saw immaturity, yes, but no ill motives. In fact, Thuram knew exactly why the young Algerians interrupted the match and jeered "La Marseillaise" that night. He too had felt the way they felt—shut off from a nation that did not allow them to be who and what they were expected to be, former "colonials" not part of France but irrevocably, and to some innately, tethered to it. When he won the World Cup for his nation, he became *un noir*, rhetorically and physically distanced from the Gallic nation whose jersey he wore, whose language he spoke, and whose anthem he sang.

The young, French-born Algerians whose arms he grabbed, whose stunned faces glared back at him on the field in October 2001, were in some ways more his compatriots than the white Frenchmen sitting peacefully and apolitically in the stands, or even those who shared the field with him that night. Thuram knew well the feeling of the colonized. He knew that "La Marseillaise" said nothing about him or his people, however they were and are defined. He was black. His blood came from Africa, not France. The words of his nation's anthem and the rhetoric of its politicians explicitly rejected this type of *sang impur* (impure blood) and celebrated its letting. Even as Thuram screamed in anger at the stunned protestors, their skin a different color than his own, he did not scream words of hatred or denial. He did not reject their sentiment or the point they were trying to make. He only rejected the way they acted and the fuel it would give to those most likely to act in response.

As he grabbed the "little idiot's" arm and placed his finger inches from his face, Thuram condemned nothing. He knew they both had the wrong audience, but he could not contain his fury with everything that had led to that moment. "Do you realize what you are doing?" he yelled, smacking the protestor's cheek with his palm. "Do you realize that television is filming you, that you are throwing yourself into shit, and pushing all your friends there too?" Thuram's eyes never left the boy's face.[6] He knew what the kid meant. He knew what he wanted to say. He knew that he wanted to be on TV, seen by those who treated him still as a colonized subject in the nation of his birth. But Thuram thought that maybe this idealistic teenager, wild with the adrenaline of doing something he knew was socially improper but needed to be done, did not realize the actual result this protest would cause. Thuram knew. He had lived it for twenty-nine years, a black man in a white man's country. And as docents and minders pried him away from his own youth before him, he made his final point to the young man: "They will use this against you!" he yelled, turning to the tunnel where his teammates waited, taking pictures and joking with their former opponents.[7] The match was over.

Notes

1. Christian Bromberger, interview by François Escarpit, "Le foot a toujours eu des fonctions ambiguës et contradictoires," *L'Humanité*, October 6, 2001, quoted in Laurent Dubois, *Soccer Empire: The World Cup and the Future of France* (Berkeley: University of California Press, 2010), 201.
2. Annick Cojean, "A la Bastille, un 14 juillet «en plus drôle»," *Le Monde*, July 14, 1998.
3. Live footage of the pitch invasion can be seen at https://www.youtube.com/watch?v=5xrYu5kUM7M [https://perma.cc/H9DY-5FPM]. For an interview with Lilian Thuram along with clips from the pitch invasion and

his reactions to it, see *Les Bleus—une autre histoire de France, 1996-2016*, directed by Pascal Blanchard, Sonia Dauger, and David Dietz (Poitiers, France: Antenne 2 France, 2016), DVD and Netflix. https://www.netflix.com/title/80164075.
4. Dubois, *Soccer Empire*, 2–5.
5. "Fans Force Abandonment of Watershed France v Algeria Match," *The Guardian*, October 8, 2001; Bruce Crumley, "Booing the *Marseillaise*: A French Soccer Scandal," *Time*, October 15, 2008.
6. Crumley, "Booing the *Marseillaise*," *Time*, October 15, 2008; James Gheerbrant, "France: Fear, Faith and Football," *BBC News*, June 8, 2016; Dubois, *Soccer Empire*, 206.
7. François Durpaire, *France blanche, colère noire* (Paris: Odile Jacob, 2006), 174–176; Lilian Thuram, *8 Juillet 1998* (Paris: Editions Anne Carrière, 2004), 161; "Fans Force Abandonment of Watershed France v Algeria Match," *The Guardian*, October 8, 2001.

Unite the Right, Colin Kaepernick, and Social Media

Azmar K. Williams

This essay originally appeared in *Black Perspectives* on September 8, 2017. https://www.aaihs.org/unite-the-right-colin-kaepernick-and-social-media/ [https://perma.cc/B36X-YUZC]

On April 22, 1820, Thomas Jefferson captured the crux of America's race problem in a letter to Maine politician John Holmes: "As it is, we have the wolf by the ears, and we can neither hold him, nor safely let him go. Justice is in one scale, and self-preservation in the other."[1] Jefferson penned those words at a time when the frontier was still open, the market revolution was in its early stages, and the continent-wide, landed white yeoman independence he longed for still seemed possible, if not inevitable. In Charlottesville on August 11, 2017, nearly 200 years later and just 10 miles away from Monticello, throngs of white nationalists gathered at "Mr. Jefferson's University" to tighten their grip on the wolf's ear.[2]

Chanting "We Will Not Be Replaced" and invoking the "Blut und Boden" ("Blood and Soil") ideology popularized by nineteenth-century German nationalists, the intent of the marchers was clear: to tip the scale, yet again, in favor of the preservation of a system of white racial domination they claimed to be under siege. Living in Jefferson's dystopian nightmare, these men, in their largely unchecked displays of lawlessness, seemed to have taken to heart words from President Donald J. Trump's Warsaw speech.³ They were not going to allow "paperwork and regulations" to deny them their right to "chase their dreams and pursue their destinies." Their march on Charlottesville symbolized their intention to make manifest those dreams and destinies.

Social media has played a central role in efforts to identify the rally's participants and to notify their employers in the hopes of securing their termination. This drive to get rally attendees fired raises issues about the relationship between social media, social movements, and the market and helps to uncover the limitations of the market and its satellites (e.g., social media) as instruments in the Black freedom struggle. To be sure, the use of social media does not constitute or wholly characterize a social movement. It does, however, shape how the public perceives those movements. As such, its role in the Charlottesville rally and its aftermath are worthy of scrutiny.

Journalist Angela Helm recently wrote that there were "calls on social media to identify some of the men marching in the rally" in order to expose them "for the racists they are" and to see to it that they face, what she called, "the appropriate consequences."⁴ Noting that a petition to have a University of Arkansas professor fired had been abandoned after it was discovered that he had been misidentified as one of the rally-goers, Helm urged anyone with "actual RECEIPTS" to do their "part and expose the racists today."⁵ Helm's call for social media users to come together in an effort to dole out their version of justice is not novel, and neither are the assumptions that undergird it.

The call to identify rally participants and to notify their employers relies on the notion that employers will find the views and actions of their employees to be sufficiently reprehensible and out of step with the goals and objectives of their companies so as to warrant their dismissal. It assumes, also, that the firing of these employees, and the subsequent destabilization of their places within the market, will hurt their cause rather than embolden it.

What we have come to is an antiracist war of attrition waged through pink slips that pivots on the idea that bigotry is bad for business. It is a war that tacitly accepts the logic governing what scholar Jodi Melamed has described as the "formally antiracist, liberal-capitalist modernity" of the postwar United States—a logic, she argues, that is better equipped to promote "U.S. global ascendancy and leadership of transnational capitalism" than it is to bring about the end to "Western domination and capitalist exploitation" that "antiracist and anticolonial social movements had envisioned."[6] If bigotry is bad for business now, there is no reason to believe that it will always be.

Just as social media and appeals to corporate bottom lines can serve antiracist objectives, they can also achieve other, less tolerant ones. The National Football League's treatment of football player Colin Kaepernick is a case in point.[7] In August 2016, instead of standing for the national anthem, Kaepernick, citing police shootings, chose to kneel in silent protest of a system that, as he put it, "oppresses black people and people of color."[8] A Rasmussen poll taken in October of that same year revealed that "nearly one-third (32%) of American Adults [said] they [were] less likely to watch an NFL game because of the growing number of Black Lives Matter protests by players on the field."[9] As journalist Mike Ozanian has reported, this drop in viewership, accompanied by calls on social media to #BoycottNFL, caused the NFL to lose significant revenue. In September 2016, Ozanian wrote that Kaepernick's protest was accomplishing what "the concussions, domestic violence and Deflategate could not do—drive down television ratings for the National Football League."[10] It is unsurprising, then, that despite his talents on the field, Kaepernick has not yet found new employment in the league.[11]

Kaepernick's fate, it appears, has been determined by the same forces now being called upon to punish those who participated in the Charlottesville rally, revealing the Janus-faced nature of social media and the market vis-à-vis the struggle against racial injustice.[12]

Are the men who gathered at Charlottesville victims? Yes. But they are not victims in the sense that they claim. They are victims, instead, of their own expectations—expectations born of their belief that white racial domination would last forever. There is no reason to believe that it will. That some in the Alt-Right have resorted to acts of terrorism is, perhaps, evidence of its decline.[13] It is becoming more difficult, it seems, to hold the wolf by its ears.

What might be most unsettling, however, is that the end of white racial domination will not necessarily provide a remedy for the inequities produced by it.[14] It could deepen them. One of the major challenges of our time, then, in the face of so much uncertainty, is to be unafraid and to refuse to surrender our sense of right and wrong to the cold calculus and machinery of the market. More often than not, the market has proven to be a poor and unreliable moral arbiter.

Notes

1. https://www.aaihs.org/measuring-racial-progress-past-and-present/ [https://perma.cc/HB7H-A3WJ]
2. https://www.washingtonpost.com/news/made-by-history/wp/2017/08/13/what-would-jefferson-say-about-white-supremacists-descending-upon-his-university/?utm_term=.48cfbd7be2e0 [https://perma.cc/862W-HBD7]
3. https://www.whitehouse.gov/the-press-office/2017/07/06/remarks-president-trump-people-poland-july-6-2017 [https://perma.cc/CY25-EKJB]

4. http://www.theroot.com/maskoff-social-media-exposes-racists-from-charlottesv-1797791599 [https://perma.cc/5WRP-W4H8]
5. https://web.archive.org/web/20170814162111/http://5newsonline.com/2017/08/12/university-of-arkansas-responds-to-rally-photo//
6. https://www.worldcat.org/title/represent-and-destroy-rationalizing-violence-in-the-new-racial-capitalism/oclc/794714022 [https://perma.cc/2BQD-MHVX]
7. https://www.aaihs.org/black-protest-white-backlash-and-the-history-of-scientific-racism/ [https://perma.cc/E7C9-WZ9U]
8. http://www.nfl.com/news/story/0ap3000000691077/article/colin-kaepernick-explains-why-he-sat-during-national-anthem [https://perma.cc/AFU5-MYXE]
9. http://www.rasmussenreports.com/public_content/politics/current_events/social_issues/are_americans_tuning_out_the_nfl_over_protests [https://perma.cc/AQK5-CZFH]; https://www.aaihs.org/new-age-activism-maria-w-stewart-and-black-lives-matter/ [https://perma.cc/H8B9-EBGR]
10. https://www.forbes.com/sites/mikeozanian/2016/10/05/confirmed-nfl-losing-millions-of-tv-viewers-because-of-national-anthem-protests/#6b75f2b8226c [https://perma.cc/66AS-XEVP]
11. https://www.sbnation.com/2017/8/14/16058454/colin-kaepernick-film-breakdown-free-agency [https://perma.cc/7QLH-VUSD]
12. https://www.aaihs.org/whats-going-on-race-brutality-and-injustice-since-rodney-king/ [https://perma.cc/F7EZ-LR84]
13. http://www.npr.org/2017/08/13/543176250/charlottesville-attack-james-alex-fields-jr [https://perma.cc/DF8N-DS33]
14. https://www.aaihs.org/this-is-a-country-for-white-men-white-supremacy-and-u-s-politics/ [https://perma.cc/7529-4ZCK]

Endgames

Mark Stephen Jendrysik

"What are you rebelling against? What have you got?"[1]

Protesters are often asked: What is your final goal? What is your endgame? What do you want? The answer quite often and quite properly is: we don't know because we don't yet fully understand the extent of the repression we are suffering under. We are still learning. As we learn more about the conditions of our oppression, we discover that more changes must be made.

So many things in our culture work against protest. Protest and protesters are devalued and made to seem ungrateful or irrational. After all, "We passed those laws, so now those people should be satisfied." Reactions to any civil rights movement in the United States show a desire on the part of the privileged and powerful to establish an endpoint beyond which demands are illegitimate.

When you entertain the idea of an "endgame," a final stopping point to political protest, you are buying into an idea which has a lot of currency and power—that is, the idea that we can find a final resting place for political dispute, that we will eventually come to a final and universally acceptable conclusion that will appeal to everyone. This idea goes back a long time. A desire for "still time," a "Nunc stans,"[2] an endpoint, is part and parcel of human political interaction. This mindset reflects a deep-seated desire to end political dispute once and for all. Of course, this is impossible. But the Aristotelian idea of a telos, or the Christian idea of an end to all things, or the simple desire to pretend that problems lie the past ("Why you gotta keep bringing up old shit?") all combine to make challenges to any existing order, especially one as self-congratulatory as that of the United States, that much more difficult.

We protect ourselves against the fluidity of modernity (the fact that everything changes, the center cannot hold, etc.) with a set of comforting myths. We hold tight to the idea that we can reach a final agreement on contentious issues, that critical questions of rights, of citizenship, of recognition, of respect, can be answered once and for all to the (apparent) satisfaction of all concerned. This belief is foundational to modern conservatism, which often claims those final agreements were made fifty, two hundred, or two thousand years ago. Whether there ever was a time of universal agreement on such questions is a matter of philosophical debate. But in our times, there can be no doubt that a politics based on the idea of rights is open ended. If the history of politics of modern times and questions of individual liberty central to our politics teaches us anything, it is that there is no final stance, there is no final resting point, and there is no last position. In our times, all agreements and decisions are conditional, temporary, and contingent. In the end, all positions are subject to renegotiation.

Victories in the fight for human rights are not necessarily forever. Nor are defeats. Nor can the powerful console themselves with the idea that if we simply give the subordinate groups some recognition, some scraps from the table, they will shut up. This is impossible, and yet this demand happens all the time. The question of Colin Kaepernick is a perfect example. The powerful ask, "Didn't we do enough for these people?" As though the recognition of human rights and equality was a gift from some powerful entity and not something people possess based on common humanity and citizenship.

Accepting conflict doesn't mean agreeing with protestors or accepting their goals. It means recognizing their right to protest. We would be wise to recognize that protest and the fight for recognition and respect can have no end. If we accept the idea that people are equal and "endowed by their Creator with certain unalienable rights," we will never reach a final moment of total agreement. If we are truly committed to human liberty, we will accept the uncertainty and conflict that comes with freedom. To do any less is to betray the very principles of our nation.

Notes

1. Marlon Brando as Johnny in *The Wild One* (1953).
2. Eternity or eternal existence, especially as an attribute of God, conceived not as infinite temporal duration but as a form of existence not subject to the limitations of time, and hence involving neither change nor succession. Also, occasionally in extended use, especially with reference to mystical experience. Attributed to Thomas Hobbes.

Reparations as Fantasy: Remembering the Black-Fisted Silent Protest at the 1968 Mexico City Games

Jamal Ratchford

This essay originally appeared in *Process* on October 16, 2017 and an extended version of this essay will appear as a chapter in his book, *Kneeling for Freedom: Selected Essays on the 20th and 21st Century Revolt of the Black Athlete*. http://www.processhistory.org/reparation-as-fantasy/ [https://perma.cc/AZP3-EJLX]

On October 17, 2005, San Jose State University unveiled a twenty-foot fiberglass statue of Tommie Smith and John Carlos, in commemoration of their black-fisted protest at the 1968 Mexico City Olympic Games. Eleven years later, on August 1, 2016, SJSU commemorated the event once again. On that day, President Mary Papazian and Athletics Director Gene Bleymaier announced that SJSU would resurrect the intercollegiate men's track and field program on October 16, 2018, exactly fifty years after Smith and Carlos's demonstration at the medal ceremony for the 200 meter dash. Their audience, which included San Jose Mayor Sam Liccardo and former U.S. Secretary of Transportation Norman Mineta, as well as hundreds of SJSU track and field alumni, learned that the program would compete at Bud Winter Track, a new, five-million dollar facility named after their deceased coach, a USA Track and Field Hall of Fame member. Three decades after cutting track and field for budgetary reasons, SJSU reignited it. In this way, and by symbolic commemoration and monuments, SJSU endeavored to redress the racial oppression faced by Smith and Carlos.[1]

The integration of American sports is often imagined to have advanced race relations in the United States. By allowing for meritocratic, rules-based competition among persons of varying racial backgrounds, Americans have supposedly overcome a long history of racial oppression. This defining achievement has affirmed an exceptionalist notion of America as the land of the free. My research program builds on recent scholarship that challenges this assumptive myth, particularly as it applies to sports and memory. As historians have carefully demonstrated, the commemoration of sports and sports activism serves multiple purposes and produces multiple meanings. Sociologist Douglas Hartmann has charted shifts in public perceptions of Smith and Carlos's silent protest from the 1980s through their receipt of the Arthur Ashe Courage Award at the 2008 ESPYs. He suggests that the appropriation of protest for mass consumption dilutes or subverts original meaning and intention. By extension, the radical impulses of a sporting past can be made impotent.[2]

Smith and Carlos's now iconic silent protest in Mexico City was rooted in direct critiques of racial inhumanity and marginalization. However, it has become misinterpreted as a post-racial symbol of inclusivity and appropriated as a trendy fad. Monuments and celebrations in honor of Smith and Carlos have not fulfilled their purpose as reparation. Rather, these faux honors have stifled the intent of the black freedom movement and of black athletic revolt more specifically. Remembrance too often waters down the original purpose of demonstrations such as Smith and Carlos's. It silences the urgency to redress economic, political, and social injustices faced by persons of color.

Smith and Carlos's protest was more radical and more purposeful than is often remembered. At San Jose State in 1967, Smith and a future Olympic teammate, Lee Evans, who later won gold in the 400 meters, joined former SJSU athletes Harry Edwards and Ken Noel in a campus initiative known as United Black Students for Action (UBSA). The UBSA and its forty members immediately pressured the SJSU administration to address racism in housing, Greek organizations, athletics, and more broadly across campus in the recruitment of black students, faculty, and staff. The UBSA and SJSU held campus-wide forums on each of these concerns in September 1967. UBSA members threatened to disrupt the home-opening football game against the University of Texas at El Paso if the university did not work to rectify racial inequality on campus. As a result, President Robert Clark cancelled the football game, drawing the ire of then Governor Ronald Reagan for his decision.[3]

Edwards, a sociology instructor, rallied Smith, Evans, and numerous others to use their celebrity for activism on a national and global stage. On October 7, 1967, the trio met with four other UBSA members—George Washington Ware, Ken Noel, Jimmy Garrett, and Bob Hoover—to discuss boycott strategies learned from the cancelled SJSU football game. Together, these men formed the Olympic Committee for Human Rights (OCHR). Edwards persuaded them that the best way to mobilize black athletes was to invite them to a workshop to discuss an Olympic boycott of the 1968 Mexico City Games. The segment of the OCHR that originally dealt with the proposed boycott was designated the Olympic Project for Human Rights (OPHR). The OPHR articulated five objectives: that the New York Athletic Club (NYAC) desegregate; that the all-white teams from South Africa and Southern Rhodesia be barred from the Olympics; that an additional black coach be added to the Olympic coaching staff; that at least one black staff member, not Jesse Owens, be included on the United States Olympic Commission; and that Muhammad Ali be reinstated as world heavyweight champion.[4]

Collectively, black athletes refused to boycott the Mexico City Olympic Games, but some, including Smith and Carlos, decided to protest injustice on individual terms. For Smith, who participated in ROTC at SJSU, the demonstration was a rallying call for freedom in a nation that treated him "like just another nigger off the track?"[5] His black glove represented the lack of empowerment for black people. His black scarf symbolized black pride and his lack of shoes stood for the poverty and neglect experienced by black communities in a racist nation.

Journalists virulently criticized Smith and Carlos for their demonstration. Brent Musburger, then a sports writer for the *Chicago Daily News*, wrote, "Smith and Carlos looked like a couple of black-skinned storm troopers, holding aloft their black-gloved hands during the playing of the National Anthem. It's destined to go down as the most unsubtle demonstration in the history of protest . . . and it insured maximum embarrassment for the country that picked up their room and board bill in Mexico." How dare these black athletes rebel?

Forty years later, ESPN honored Smith and Carlos with the Arthur Ashe Courage Award at its ESPY award ceremony. How was it that Smith and Carlos, banned by the International Olympic Committee (IOC) in 1968, came to be appreciated by 2008? Had Americans become more tolerant of black athletes? Or does the explanation lie elsewhere? Urla Hill has suggested that "Smith and Carlos have transcended their place as villainous traitors to become a sort of brand for gallantry and pluck in the face of inestimable odds." In the face of sanction and criticism, Smith, Carlos, and a host of other black athletes in the late 1960s expressed a will for self-determination. In so doing, they tested the limits of American participatory democracy. But since that time, American popular culture has de-radicalized their protest. In ways similar to the cooption of Martin Luther King Jr., Smith and Carlos's protest has been repackaged and removed from its original context and intentions.

Smith and Carlos's 2008 ESPY award perhaps encouraged American spectators to reflect on the history of race in the United States. But evidence suggests that most Americans are not yet willing to accept displays of black political self-determination at sporting events, or elsewhere. Roughly 60 percent of Americans disapproved of the interracial 1961 Freedom Rides and the 1963 March on Washington. Eighty-five percent of Americans felt civil rights demonstrations in 1966 hurt avancement of black rights.[6] In 2015, PBS found that 30 percent of white citizens ages 17-34 felt no admiration for black people, believed blacks to be lazy and unintelligent, and believed blacks face little or no discrimination. In 2017, an estimated 72 percent of Americans interpret the silent, kneeling protest of San Francisco 49ers quarterback Colin Kaepernick as unpatriotic.[7]

By commemorating Smith and Carlos, SJSU attempted to correct past wrongs, but not even that campus was immune to racial violence. In 2014, four white students locked their black roommate Donald Williams Jr. in a room laden with Confederate flags, called him "three-fifths," wrote the dreaded N-word in his room, wrestled him to the ground, and put a U-shaped lock around his neck. In 2016, Williams's assailants were found not guilty of a hate crime.[8] That same year SJSU continued its commemoration of Smith and Carlos. Those men deserve recognition for their heroism and patriotism. Much in the spirit of James Baldwin, they sought to improve the nation by critiquing it. But they did not protest for a statue or the renewal of a track program. Rather, their central aim was black freedom and the insurance of citizenship and human rights. SJSU and the nation more broadly would be wise to institute policies that guarantee participatory democracy, equity, and equality for the United States' black and brown citizens.

Notes

1. Maureen Margaret Smith, "Frozen Fists in Speed City: The Statue as Twenty-First-Century Reparations," *Journal of Sport History* 36 (Fall 2009): 393-414.
2. Smith, "Frozen Fists in Speed City"; Murray G. Phillips, Mark E. O'Neill, and Gary Osmond, "Broadening Horizons in Sport History: Films, Photographs and Monuments," *Journal of Sport History* 34 (2007): 284-85; Douglas Hartmann, *Race, Culture, and the Revolt of the Black Athlete: The 1968 Olympic Protests and Their Aftermath* (Chicago: University of Chicago Press, 2004).
3. Jamal Ratchford, "Black Fists and Fool's Gold: The 1968 Black Athletic Revolt Reconsidered," (PhD diss., Purdue University, 2011).
4. Harry Edwards, *The Revolt of the Black Athlete* (New York: The Free Press, 1970): 50-51; Frank Murphy, *The Last Protest: Lee Evans in Mexico City* (Kansas City: Windsprint Press, 2006): 140; Tommie Smith with David Steele, *Silent Gesture: The Autobiography of Tommie Smith* (Philadelphia: Temple University Press, 2007): 22, 161-63; Kevin B. Witherspoon, *Before the Eyes of the World: Mexico and the 1968 Olympic Games* (DeKalb, IL: Northern Illinois Press, 2008); Hartmann, *Race, Culture, and the Revolt of the Black Athlete*; Amy Bass, *Not the Triumph but the Struggle: The 1968 Olympics and the Making of the Black Athlete*, (Minneapolis: University of Minnesota Press, 2002).
5. Jamal Ratchford, "The LeBron James Decision and Self-Determination in Post-Racial America," *The Black Scholar* 42 (Spring 2012): 49-59.
6. Elahe Izadi, "Black Lives Matter and America's long history of resisting civil rights protesters," *Washington Post*, April 19, 2016.
7. Sean McElwee, "The Hidden Racism of Young White Americans," http://www.pbs.org/newshour/updates/americas-racism-problem-far-complicated-think/ [https://perma.cc/633H-36EC]; Matt Vespa, "Poll: 72 Percent See Kaepernick's National Anthem Antics As 'Unpatriotic,'" *Townhall*, September 24, 2017.
8. Jason Song, "White students who bullied black classmate at SJSU escape hate crime convictions," *Los Angeles Times*, February 23, 2016.

Section Six

Others in the Arena

Why Sports Journalists Shouldn't Just "Stick to Sports"

Brad Elliott Schlossman

"Stick to sports" is a phrase so commonly heard by sports journalists and athletes these days.

The phrase generally comes after a story is written—or thoughts are shared—with political implications.

Yes, sportswriting is about covering the games. But it's also about covering the people involved in the games. It's about telling their stories. The most compelling stories are always about people—and the most compelling topics aren't always about the sports they play.

Off-the-field stories are frequently covered by journalists: an athlete's charity work, his or her upbringing, the meaning of new tattoos, his or her obsession with animals, etc. But those types of stories don't produce the same visceral reactions as ones that become political.

That doesn't mean politically charged stories should be avoided. They are important stories to cover, too. That's especially the case when there are public displays.

When the NBA's San Antonio Spurs' coach Gregg Popovich walks into his press conference, makes a political statement, and walks out, it's the journalists' job to relay what happened and what was said, regardless of whether the journalist personally agrees with the statement.

When J.T. Brown of the NHL's Tampa Bay Lightning raises his fist during the national anthem, it is the journalists' job to report it and ask Brown why he decided to do it.

And when NFL players kneel for the national anthem, it is the journalists' job to report and find out why.

It is a news reporter's job to hold up a mirror to a situation and report, for the record, what happened. A good journalist will observe, ask, listen, and report.

That's what football writer Steve Wyche did in August 2016.

Wyche was covering the San Francisco 49ers vs. Green Bay Packers preseason game when he noticed that quarterback Colin Kaepernick was not standing for the anthem. Having already recognized Kaepernick's social media posting trends, Wyche suspected something was behind his actions.

After the game, Wyche was the only journalist who asked Kaepernick about it. Kaepernick told him, in detail, why he wasn't going to stand for the anthem. "I am not going to stand up to show pride in a flag for a country that oppresses black people and people of color," Kaepernick told Wyche.

Wyche reported the story and it became major national news, just as the anthem demonstrations by Tommy Smith and John Carlos during the 1968 Olympics captured the country's attention almost fifty years earlier. Back then, it was the job of journalists to explain their protests, just as it was Wyche's to tell Kaepernick's story.

In the following months, journalists across the country began doing the same thing: watching, asking, listening, and reporting similar anthem protests. Those reporters were—and still are—often met with emails and tweets telling the reporters to "stick to sports." However, if they did, they wouldn't be doing their job.

Coaches, Athletes, and Colin Kaepernick

Gelaine Orvik

The autumnal protest by Colin Kaepernick cannot be summed up easily. As a coach, I need to address the constitutional side of the issue before I tackle the professional side.

Since I live in our great nation, the United States, I must address the freedoms that we have and love. I must and do completely support every American's duty, responsibility, and freedom to dissent, dispute, and disagree with matters and issues that are contrary to my principles and ideologies. For this reason, I support Colin's freedom and his opposition.

However, long ago I learned that to make a difference and to implement change, I need to move to the source of the issue. Therefore, I need to shift my attention to the people and causes on the opposing side. Colin and others' kneeling and disrespecting longtime traditions only drives the spike further between his principles and the issues he is trying to address.

I venture to say that J.J. Watt has emerged and accomplished much more by his leadership in reassuring the city of Houston that he will be the Man to step forward with an initial contribution to help with Hurricane Harvey relief and emphatically provide assistance to those in need. His actions have proven to be much more effective than someone who takes a negative stand.

Consider what Colin Kaepernick could accomplish by taking a positive move to make an initial contribution and challenge others—first the NFLPA and its members—to help those who have been suppressed and quelled. Ponder on the positive atmosphere that could be created by NFL game attendees. Maybe something as simple as contribution tubs, placed where NFL fans enter and depart a stadium, could raise millions of dollars in the league's twelve to sixteen stadiums each Sunday. Now that is a positive approach to registering dissent.

From the coaching profession's side, the entire issue basically centers on one tenet: follow the rules. Some are simply the rules of the game; some are rules of the organization sponsoring the contest (High School Associations, NCAA, NFL, NFLPA, MLB, NBA, etc.). These are rules that all participants know they must follow to participate.

Normally, owners, general managers, and coaches have guidelines and procedures for their teams. Coaches generally have lists of dos and do nots. Usually those lists are far too detailed and specific, and they always leave something out. There often seems to be a sense of trying to find a way to circumvent specific rules. As a result, I propose that only two general rules are necessary.

Rule #1 of these two general rules would eliminate occurrences like the Colin Kaepernick display: never do anything that will cause embarrassment, complication, conflict, or need for apology for yourself, your teammates, your family, your coaches, your school, your community, or the integrity of the game. Rule #2: if you have any apprehension or question about any action, refer to Rule #1.

Therefore, if Colin Kaepernick or any other NFL, college, or university football player kneeled or did not honor the American flag, there would repercussions because I, as the head coach, would implement Rule #1. And my decision would not be open for discussion with the general manager or owner.

Some fifteen to twenty years ago, I became involved in an advisory committee to an organization called Coaching Boys Into Men. Sometime after that group was formed, a parallel enterprise called Athletes as Leaders, which focuses on female athletes, was created. In athletics and in life, we as citizens of this great nation need to focus on building, being positive, and taking the "high road." To become men, boys need to always exhibit respect to others. That is not just going through the motions or actions once in a while; our lives must constantly reflect respect.

When the Fargo Gateway Lions Club checks in the athletes for the All-Star Basketball practices and games, the coaching leaders inform them of the program's guidelines. The first one is to *always* remove one's hat/cap when entering a room or in the presence of ladies or anyone older, as well as to show respect for those around; that includes being punctual, respectful, and thankful by sharing appreciation and words of gratitude for all food and services. Think of the Golden Rule: "Do onto others as you would like them to do onto you!"

We, as coaches, are leaders, and we need to have everyone (athletes, assistant coaches, managers, and owners) on the same page. We need to take the "high road" and do and say what is right and appropriate. We need to expect and demand the same from all athletes at all times.

Learning Extends Beyond the Practice Field

Mike Berg

I view the issues surrounding the Colin Kaepernick protests from the perspective of a high school teacher and football coach who spent thirty-eight years as a public school educator. Although a decade into retirement, I find myself asking, "How would I approach the subject with our team? What would I do?" One thing is certain: it absolutely must be approached. It can't be ignored or set aside as something that doesn't concern young athletes, and specifically in my case, high school football players.

Consider the influences in a young athlete's life. Ideally, parents and relatives provide a positive foundation. However, next up is often a coach. I can make a strong argument that good or bad, a coach is often one of the greatest influences on the way that a young athlete sees a sometimes narrowly focused life. Regarding issues like the Colin Kaepernick debate, players are at least superficially aware of what's going on around the country, and they're waiting to hear from their coach. They need to hear from the person who has such a dominant impact on their lives. A coach has the responsibility of bringing perspective to events that, even if they seem distant, are relevant to the world the players live in.

Sadly, too many coaches consider, or are pressured into believing, that their only responsibility is related to favorable numbers on a scoreboard. If all that athletes learn from a coach are sports skills, how to compete and win games, and how to follow team rules (so they're eligible to play), the coach has failed them. The purpose of school athletic programs and other co-curricular activities is to serve as an extension of the classroom. Granted, a coach's area of expertise may not extend much beyond his or her particular sport, but why not call on others to help fill in the blanks? In years past, coaches were fully trained and certified as educators. Their experience and hopefully proficiency in communicating with young people in classroom settings took them beyond the practice field or gymnasium, something that is all too uncommon these days.

So, *how* and *who* are the issues. How do we educate our players beyond the playing field, and who do we bring in to lead the discussions? Some thoughts:

- A program standard must include regular short sessions for programs such as Coaching Boys Into Men and others that address relevant social issues (like the Colin Kaepernick debate).

- Sessions should be scheduled immediately before or after practice, even if it requires that practice be shortened. This will serve to emphasize their importance.

- Specifically related to the Colin Kaepernick protests, it's hard to imagine that a community of any size would not have history teachers, Veterans of Foreign Wars or American Legion members, clergy, or local citizens who could present cogent, discussion-worthy viewpoints. Obviously, the coach must pre-screen all outside presenters for relevant and appropriate content.

- Any team member or coach with strong feelings or opinions should be given an opportunity to address the team as well.

- Sessions should be scheduled and take place whether players seem to have an interest or not. I would consider it as part of the "big picture" educational process that co-curricular activities should offer.

This all looks good on paper. A nice, neat package of how to foster social awareness and responsibility within the context of a high school athletic program. But what about reality? What about that Friday night, when players, coaches, and fans are focused on "the big game" and out of the blue one or more players on the team decides to take a knee during the playing of the national anthem? Do these players have the historical context of what Colin Kaepernick's protest was all about, or are they perhaps simply mimicking what they've observed high-profile athletes doing on the national stage?

As the head coach of the program, how would I handle it? If the program followed the ideas I outlined above, one or more players taking a knee shouldn't have caught us by surprise. We'd have gone to great lengths to consider, discuss, and debate the issue. We'd have taken time away from practice to bring in presenters. We'd have allowed and encouraged players and coaches to express their thoughts in a non-judgmental setting. We'd have been "educated" to the extent that the issue was viewed from several perspectives. Still, how would I handle it? The bottom line is this: participation in a high school athletic program is voluntary; it is not required for graduation. If a player chooses to participate, they agree to meet program standards, and one of the standards for this program is that all members of the team respectfully stand for the national anthem. If a player is comfortable and confident in making an informed decision not to stand, they will be welcomed back if they choose to follow the team's standards. My conversation with the player would go something like this: "It looks like we have more to talk about, and we can sure do that. But until you can meet our expectations, we'll miss you around here."

If You're Explaining, You're Losing: Questioning Kaepernick's Tactics, Not Cause

Mac Schneider and David Butler

Before every home game during our long-since-over college football careers at the University of North Dakota (UND), the last stanza of the national anthem spoke to the duality of Americans' passion for their team and our common identity as citizens of the United States.

There was no misunderstanding the intensity of the fans who loudly replaced "brave" with a collective guttural annunciation of UND's former nickname. While we appreciated their enthusiasm, to us the national anthem was never a school fight song. More than anything, it served as a 122-second reminder ahead of hours of tense competition that the players and fans on the opposing sideline were Americans like us. That we were all on the same team. The national anthem has served as a moment of unity for fans and players who spend an enormous amount of effort attempting to subjugate each other.

Neither of us were NFL material, but like virtually everyone in our country we have seen and considered the protests led by Colin Kaepernick and other professional football players during the national anthem. While we disagree with their decision to take a knee during this pre-game ritual, our disagreement is a matter of tactics, not the underlying cause.

As best as we can as fellow human beings, we empathize with the NFL protesters' desire to address inequality and make the criminal justice system fairer. We are also appalled at racial profiling and the killing of unarmed African Americans.

It's an understatement to say these racial scars run deep. From the abhorrent sin of slavery, to the brutality during the struggle for civil rights, America's history is shaded by unequal treatment and oppression of African Americans.

Our concern during this polarized time is that taking a knee during the national anthem will push away as many—or more—Americans as it draws to the important cause of equality and fairness under the law. There are many who see the players' rejection of injustice as a rejection of our country. Blame the players or blame those taking in their message, but if you're explaining why it's patriotic to take a knee during the national anthem, in many ways you've already lost. That's not to say Kaepernick and like-minded professional athletes should stay quiet. Far from it. Our country's sports stars have frequently influenced social change for the better. In this instance, we're just not convinced that professional football players couldn't better use their status and celebrity to convey their message in a way that brings more Americans along and together. Our suspicion and fear is that the anthem protests have divided Americans further. Contrast this protest with the march across the Edmund Pettus Bridge in 1965, where civil rights leaders and ordinary citizens stood tall in the face of racist violence with American flags unfurled all the while. It's hard to imagine a more persuasive act than this simultaneous embrace of America and an unequivocal demand that our country live up to its ideals.

An issue this complex probably defies sports metaphors, but there are only two situations in the game of football when players are supposed to take a knee: before the half, when you've given up on advancing the ball, and at the end of the game to run out the clock before a victory. We shouldn't give up on being a nation where equality is the norm, and our country certainly can't declare victory when it comes to the treatment of African-American citizens.

Despite our doubts, we hope the anthem protests will lead to greater understanding and progress. We also hope for a future where Americans stand up alongside each other as we drive towards a more perfect union.

How Social Activism Can Clash with Military Core Values

Randy Nedegaard

In August 2016, Colin Kaepernick sat during the national anthem during a preseason National Football League (NFL) game. When asked about it in a post-game interview, he responded: "I am not going to stand up to show pride in a flag for a country that oppresses black people and people of color."[1] He appeared to understand that this may be offensive to many Americans, especially veterans, so he consulted with a military veteran. Together they decided that it would be less offensive if he knelt during the anthem to show greater respect to U.S. military members and veterans. This act of expressing his disapproval of the racism found in our country created a maelstrom, causing many football players to follow his lead, and resulting in some strong reactions by fans to his tactics and message. Some consider him a courageous hero, while others suggest he should consider taking up residence in another country.

Reactions by military members and veterans have also been mixed. Some veterans believe that when they served in the military, they were doing so to defend the rights of every

American to express their displeasure openly—consistent with the First Amendment to the U.S. Constitution that allows all Americans the right to freedom of speech. These veterans believe that professional football players have the same rights to express their message as the white supremacists who were able to return to Charlottesville, Virginia, to protest the possible removal of a General Robert E. Lee statue less than a month after a counter-protester was intentionally hit by a car and killed. Veterans may not be in favor of the tactics being used by these groups of people or even the message that is being conveyed. In fact, they may abhor these groups and the messages they are sending. Others interpret kneeling during the national anthem as disrespectful to the country and to those brave men and women who sacrificed and died in service to their country. This group desires to see this practice stopped, claiming that the team owners should discipline and/or fire their employees for engaging in activities that are construed by some of their fans as disrespectful. Debates within the military and veteran population have been just as fierce and divided as those found outside of military circles.

Compounding this issue from a veteran's point of view is the fact that the military is an organization that highly regards custom, tradition, and honor. Each military branch has a set of core values, emphasizing concepts such as integrity, selfless service, and excellence. Military customs and courtesies are one of the main methods that members use to show respect to others. This respect is thought to be reflective of self-discipline. Discipline is the backbone of military structure and is a necessary component for enforcing core values. Without discipline, how could we trust that military members would stay true to their oaths of enlistment/oaths of office, wherein they promise to defend the Constitution of the United States and swear to obey the orders of the officers appointed over them?

Many military ceremonies and customs revolve around the U.S. flag and the national anthem. These are to be revered and respected. Failure to engage in the conduct the military expects with the flag and anthem can result in significant consequences. In the civilian world, customs have been created around the U.S. flag and national anthem as well. The U.S. Code defines the etiquette that "should" be followed during a rendition of the national anthem and while the flag is displayed.[2] However, there are no real consequences for those who do not adhere to these standards. Therefore, it is up to the larger group to reinforce social norms and "appropriate" conduct in these circumstances. The military trains and encourages members to enforce appropriate conduct among the ranks and to courageously stand up for what is "right." It should be no surprise to find veterans at the forefront of this issue, assertively voicing their opinions about proper conduct regarding customs and etiquette.

It also stands to reason that many citizens (veterans or not) might be offended by actions that are interpreted as disrespectful to our flag, anthem, and country. The U.S. is a country that promotes a strong sense of nationalism, and those who appear to criticize and belittle something valued by the "majority" are likely to elicit a strong emotional reaction. Yet, there is another strong emotional reaction that may be elicited: discomfort. This discomfort comes from the overwhelming evidence indicating that racism continues to exist in our country. Public demonstrations such as football players taking a knee during the national anthem are largely aimed at the majority group. They are targeting the status quo, creating discomfort, and attempting to motivate change. Since majority group members hold the most power in a country, any lasting reductions of racist behavior in the U.S. will likely require supportive white action. It is also important to note that white viewers make up the majority of NFL TV viewership and appear to represent the largest segment of NFL fandom.[3]

Colin Kaepernick may be a courageous, brilliant strategist or he might be an egotistical, entitled professional athlete. It is clear that he was savvy enough to understand that his actions would reach a large audience. Through the first three weeks of the 2017 regular NFL season, the average NFL telecast was estimated to be watched by nearly sixteen million viewers.[4] Colin Kaepernick certainly isn't the first person to use the NFL to further his agenda, either. The NFL has masterfully expanded its presence in the U.S. over the past 50+ years. It supports various charities and has even spent the past several years creating awareness for breast cancer through Pink October initiatives.[5] Kaepernick would also have known that his actions would cause discomfort. After all, protests are often designed to create this. The discomfort caused by increased awareness is then expected to reinforce behavior that reduces this discomfort (and ultimately reduces racist behavior).

Our country has a long history of protest. We celebrate the Boston Tea Party as our first significant act of defiance against the British Empire. This event was motivated by a strong desire for the colonial voice to be heard. It was a defining moment in our history. Our country recognizes and values past leaders, such as Martin Luther King, Jr., who became agents of change through protest. These leaders created discomfort, agitating people in order to move our country from the status quo. The military, however, does not use protest as a tactic for change. Protesting is not allowed while wearing a military uniform and protest is not a tool that is valued by an organization that demands conformity and obedience. While it may not be surprising that many military and veterans do not favor the methods of protest currently being used in the NFL, it is important that they (and the rest of country) do not confuse the intended message—that significant and devastating racism continues to thrive in our country—with frustration over strategies and tactics.

Notes

1. Bryan Flaherty, "From Kaepernick sitting to Trump's fiery comments: NFL's anthem protests have spurred discussion," *Washington Post*, September 24, 2017, https://www.washingtonpost.com/graphics/2017/sports/colin-kaepernick-national-anthem-protests-and-NFL-activism-in-quotes/?utm_term=.aaa29866fbe4 [https://perma.cc/B4Q3-QDFV]
2. "4 U.S. Code Title 4, Chapter 1, § 9 - Conduct during hoisting, lowering or passing of flag," U.S. Government Publishing Office, https://www.gpo.gov/fdsys/pkg/USCODE-2011-title4/html/USCODE-2011-title4-chap1.htm [https://perma.cc/9WBD-YYLX]
3. "The NFL's 2017 ratings slide was mainly fueled by white viewers and younger viewers" as cited in http://awfulannouncing.com/cbs/nfls-2017-ratings-slide-mainly-fueled-white-viewers-younger-viewers.html [https://perma.cc/KXQ9-PFK7]
4. Mike Snider, "Are NFL player protests 'massively, massively' hurting TV ratings?" *USA Today*, September 26, 2017, https://www.usatoday.com/story/money/business/2017/09/26/nfl-player-protests-hurting-ratings/703619001/ [https://perma.cc/ES8L-ZWSG]
5. "NFL Helps American Cancer Society Fight Breast Cancer," American Cancer Society, October 4, 2016, https://www.cancer.org/latest-news/nfl-helps-american-cancer-society-fight-breast-cancer.html [https://perma.cc/R5P9-57GN]

The Veteran View of Colin Kaepernick

Matt Eidson

I'm not writing to share my thoughts on whether Colin Kaepernick was right or wrong for taking a knee during the national anthem. I have an opinion about the matter, of course. But nowadays, the political climate is so contentious that I've come to believe in the importance of breaking down every issue to the smallest detail. I believe in this approach because broad, blanket statements leave too many aspects of a topic open to interpretation. I want to contribute to the conversation from a position that provides clarity, not one that instigates and causes further hostility. In an attempt to accomplish this goal, I intend to give my thoughts concerning Colin Kaepernick's decision to kneel during the national anthem from the perspective of a United States veteran.

I served in the Marine Corps from February 2008 until August 2015. In that time, I deployed to Iraq and Afghanistan, where I lost a few close friends. The names of those friends are etched on two small black bands that I wear on my wrists every day. While I certainly won't speak for my buddies, I will speak for myself: if the roles were reversed, and my name was the one etched on a small black band, I would not have been concerned with whether Colin Kaepernick was respecting my sacrifice in an appropriate manner. During my deployments, I was willing to die for my country, and I'd have gladly died for the rights of any American back home regardless of whether I agreed with them politically or not.

As luck would have it, I made it home. I'm grateful for every day I'm alive, and I'm grateful for the man I am today. When I look at my fellow Americans protesting and speaking out against injustice, I smile. I smile because that's why I served in the military: to make the country a better place. Over my time in the military, I learned the pain of payment, and I developed a strong sense of nationalism. But this love of country doesn't mean I think America is perfect the way it is currently. I love my country not because I think it's perfect, but because it's always striving for perfection.

Kaepernick's decision to take a knee should in no way, shape, or form be viewed as disrespectful toward American troops. Besides the fact that Kaepernick literally said he meant no disrespect toward American troops, the truth of the matter remains: his right to protest is one of the rights many troops died to protect. While Americans may or may not agree with Kaepernick's approach, the assertion that his actions are disrespectful to American troops is ultimately just a distraction from the issues he is trying to bring to light. Personally, I would much rather hear Americans debating the issues Kaepernick was trying to raise, not measuring his patriotism and critiquing his form of protest.

Now that my time in the military is over, I'm pursuing a career in journalism. As a journalist, I'm often critical of my country. I'm critical of America because I know it can be better. I believe in the American experiment so much that I'm not afraid to point out its faults. If I suggest that my country has an issue that needs to be discussed, it shouldn't insinuate that I'm not patriotic or that I don't love America. The same can be said for Kaepernick.

No, he did not serve in the military. But this fact is irrelevant because Kaepernick is an American. As an American, he has every right to stand—or kneel—for whatever he believes is right, so long as it does not endanger the lives of others. Personally, I'm proud to have fought for a country that affords Kaepernick the opportunity to use his highly visible platform as an NFL quarterback to bring light to issues of police brutality against men and women of color. If Americans would debate the issues Kaepernick brought to light with the same fire and passion they brought to his decision to kneel, perhaps we would be closer to fixing the problem.

While I would not kneel during the national anthem personally, I would never presume to tell another person how they should or should not protest an issue they feel needs discussing. Instead of calling Kaepernick's patriotism into question, I believe we would be better off as a country if we would listen to what he has to say. Just as I would hope my fellow Americans would listen to me if I pointed out an issue with our country, I would hope we would do the same for Kaepernick.

I sometimes wonder how the nation would have reacted if a white NFL player had taken a knee during the national anthem to protest violence against police officers. I'm inclined to believe that the white NFL player would have been praised for his courage to kneel for what he believed in, and I'm inclined to believe his voice would have been heard. I'm also inclined to believe that no one would have questioned his respect for American troops, or brought the color of his parents' skin into question, or dissected his NFL career and asserted that his protest was just a ploy to keep his job.

Perhaps the issue so many Americans have with Kaepernick taking a knee has nothing to do with the color of his skin.

I have my opinion about the matter, of course. But setting that argument aside for another day, I believe with all of my heart that Colin Kaepernick has every right as an American to sit, stand, or kneel whenever he sees fit, especially if he does so as a means of protest.

As a veteran of the United States Marine Corps, I support Kaepernick's actions, and I hope the country starts listening to him. Because at the end of the day, America is a country founded on the belief that we can and should continue to be better than we were the day before, and if Colin Kaepernick is willing to risk his livelihood just for the chance to enact social change, then the least I can do is risk a negative reception to this article when I say I support him.

The Difference Between Black Football Fans and White Football Fans

Tamir Sorek and Robert G. White

This essay originally appeared in *The Conversation* on September 29, 2017. https://theconversation.com/the-difference-between-black-football-fans-and-white-football-fans-84810 [https://perma.cc/EJ9T-T6XS]

A significant portion of the NFL's fan base has reacted negatively to the national anthem protests of the past year.[1] The responses tend to follow a pattern:

> The stadium is no place for political protest. The game is a color-blind meritocracy. To protest football is to protest America.

But according to a study we published last year, white football fans and black football fans hold very different views about the relationship between football and national pride.[2] And it might explain why there have been such divergent, emotional responses to the protests.

Black Americans love football, but...

Social scientists who study sports have long argued that sports are a powerful political stage.[3] Popular wisdom, on the other hand, tends to maintain that sports are inherently apolitical, and should remain that way.[4]

It's true that until recently, visible black protests in American sports were rare. Yes, Muhammad Ali was outspoken about politics and became a symbol of black protest in the 1960s.[5] And there's the famous instance of Tommie Smith and John Carlos raising their fists in the 1968 Olympic Games.[6] But generally, athletes have not waded into politics, no doubt in part because of the influence of corporate interests and sponsors. (Michael Jordan, when asked why he wouldn't endorse a black Democratic candidate for Senate in 1990, famously said, "Republicans buy shoes too."[7])

So for many white fans, the racial issues addressed by the protests upend what they see as the innocent, colorless patriotism of football.

But for black fans, feelings of alienation toward the imposed patriotism in NFL games have been stewing for a while. And it may be that black athletes finally decided to respond to the attitudes of their black fans.

In our study, we aggregated 75 opinion polls between 1981 and 2014, and compared the relationship between national pride and football fandom among white and black Americans.

We found that since the early 1980s, national pride has been in decline among American men and women of all races. But among black men, this decline has been especially sharp. At the same time, it's also been accompanied by a marked increase in their interest in the NFL.

We suspect that this inverse relationship isn't coincidental.

Which Americans do patriotic displays speak to?

For decades, the league and broadcasting networks have conflated football with patriotism.[8] Massive American flags get spread across the field before the game, celebrities sing highly produced renditions of the national anthem, military jets streak across the skies and teams routinely honor veterans and active service members.

Networks air segments about the players' lives and team histories that emphasize racial integration and national unity. They also promote the narrative that hard work and following the rules lead to success on the field—the crux of the American Dream.

Many football fans might embrace these displays, which reinforce their beliefs and reflect their view of the country as a colorblind meritocracy.[9]

Indeed, our study did show that enthusiasm for football and national pride are interrelated.

But the nature of this relationship depends on your race.

Only among white Americans did we find a positive association between football fandom and national pride: football fans were much more likely to express high levels of national pride than white Americans who weren't football fans. Among African Americans, on the other hand, there was a negative association. This suggests that when black fans watch their favorite team play, it's a very different type of experience.

And this was happening long before Colin Kaepernick decided to take a knee.

Black identity and American identity

W.E.B. Du Bois once observed that for black Americans, a fundamental tension exists between their American identities and their black identities.[10] We now know from other studies that African Americans tend to see themselves as less "typically American" than other races.[11] Meanwhile, among white Americans there's a common tendency to link American national identity with whiteness.[12]

It could be that the symbols of American national pride—so visible during football games—give white fans the chance to unite their national pride with their fandom. To them, the fact that African Americans make up between 65 and 69 percent of all NFL players is simply part of the country's ethos of "inclusion."[13]

But for black fans, the overrepresentation of African-American athletes might mean something else. Football broadcasts can create highly visible opportunities to express black prowess, pride and resistance. At the same time, watching wildly successful black players on the football field might sharpen the contrast of racial injustice off the field.[14]

Meanwhile, studies have shown that the more black Americans emphasize their blackness, the less likely they are to have patriotic feelings.[15]

Together, this could create a situation where black fans are prone to reject the popular national narrative that links football to a wider, ethnically blind meritocratic order. To many of them, football isn't connected to any sort of national identity in a positive way, so it's easier for black fans to press successful black athletes to protest the status quo and use their platforms to address issues of discrimination and inequality.

In other words, even before black athletes started taking an explicit stand, their presence and success on the field created the conditions to question the dominant ideology of a meritocratic, colorblind society. National debates about inequality, police brutality and incarceration clearly resonate with many players, and they've been pushed to respond.

Looking at it this way, these protests were only a matter a time.

Notes

1. https://www.cbssports.com/nfl/news/poll-majority-of-americans-disagree-with-colin-kaepernicks-protest/ [https://perma.cc/AAM5-K49E]
2. http://plaza.ufl.edu/tsorek/articles/Americanfootball.pdf [https://perma.cc/Y45W-Q6L7]
3. https://books.google.com/books?id=9icbi39vm8AC&dq=-george+sage+sport&hl=en&sa=X&ved=0ahUKEwiqwKin1MjWAhXFPi-YKHb5jAGkQ6AEINDAC [https://perma.cc/ZP89-L3K7]
4. https://www.theodysseyonline.com/sports-politics-should-never-mix [https://perma.cc/8SQM-66KJ]
5. http://www.edgeofsports.com/product/Whats-My-Name-Fool/ [https://perma.cc/PBT3-TYGN]
6. https://books.google.com/books?id=zpYxyEMDJjsC&printsec=frontcover&dq=dave+zirin+john+carls&hl=en&sa=X&ved=0ahUKEwivm5_JzMrWAhVF-lQKHQeLBjEQ6AEIJjAA#v=onepage&q&f=false [https://perma.cc/YXS8-45AQ]
7. https://books.google.com/books/about/Second_Coming.html?id=B-A5mPwAACAAJ [https://perma.cc/C2VV-T76M]
8. https://doi.org/10.1177/0193723508319715
9. https://www.mediaite.com/online/poll-majority-of-whites-see-america-as-colorblind-nearly-80-of-african-americans-do-not/ [https://perma.cc/3YXE-DZW2]; http://www.huffingtonpost.com/howard-steven-friedman/americas-incomplete-thoug_b_1696282.html [https://perma.cc/A4DK-SR3E]
10. https://books.google.com/books/about/The_Souls_of_Black_Folk.html?id=lTXYAAAAMAAJ&printsec=frontcover&source=kp_read_button#v=onepage&q&f=false [https://perma.cc/T93Q-BTB2]
11. https://books.google.com/books?id=A2SXphY-DvIC&printsec=frontcover&source=gbs_ge_summary_r&cad=0#v=onepage&q&f=false [https://perma.cc/26VZ-4NQV]
12. https://www.researchgate.net/publication/7994359_America_White [https://perma.cc/4F5D-GGCH]
13. http://www.celticcreek.org/images/nflreport.pdf [https://perma.cc/KE8J-JEJD]
14. https://books.google.com/books?id=QQglDwAAQBAJ&lpg=PP1&dq=racial%20discrimination%20in%20America&pg=PP1#v=onepage&q&f=false [https://perma.cc/9J8W-2DZJ]
15. http://www.jstor.org/stable/2749514

About the Authors

Eric Burin is Professor of History at the University of North Dakota. He is the author of *Slavery and the Peculiar Solution: A History of the American Colonization Society* (2005) and editor of *Picking the President: Understanding the Electoral College* (2017).

Mike Berg, a native of Pasadena, California, spent thirty-eight years teaching and coaching in Montana and North Dakota. A member of the National High School Athletic Coaches Association Hall of Fame, he was named NFL High School Coach of the Year in 2007. Since retiring from coaching, he has served as the radio color analyst for the University of North Dakota football team and has facilitated the Coaching Boys Into Men program with the Community Violence Intervention Center. A regular presenter at coaching clinics and seminars, he is also an active speaker for both domestic violence prevention and faith-based events.

David Butler works for the Department of Defense Education Activity in Alexandria, Virginia as a projects specialist and is a graduate of the University of North Dakota. He was a starter on the 2001 national championship football team and graduated with degrees in history and secondary education in 2001 and 2002. After college he and Mac Schneider moved to Washington D.C. and roomed together. Although they have some divergent political views, they share a commitment to the respect and dignity of all people, and to living civilly and well with their neighbors.

Sharon Carson is a Chester Fritz Distinguished Professor of English and Religious Studies at the University of North Dakota. Her research interests include American literature and social philosophy, the literature of the American left, comparative religions and literatures, Black literatures and interdisciplinary Black studies, public humanities, narrative journalism, and cross-national and comparative studies.

Sarah Cavanah is Assistant Professor of Mass Media, focused on public relations, at Southeast Missouri State University. Her research examines news, media, and information use, especially in rural communities. She is a former educational writer, reporter, and editor, as well as public relations professional. She earned bachelor's degrees in anthropology and journalism, as well as master's degrees in professional writing and journalism/mass communication, from the University of Oklahoma, and a doctorate in mass communication from the University of Minnesota.

Matt Connolly joined the Aspen Institute as senior digital editor and producer in January 2017. He oversees the Institute's digital channels and editorial content. Before joining the Aspen Institute, Matt was digital managing editor of the *Washington Monthly*, where he helped lead a complete redesign of the magazine's online presence. He has also worked for *Mother Jones*, *Mic.com*, and the local section of the *Washington Examiner*. He graduated from Northwestern University in 2012 with a degree in journalism and political science.

Amira Rose Davis is an Assistant Professor of History and Women's, Gender, and Sexuality Studies at Penn State University. She received her doctorate in history from Johns Hopkins University. Davis specializes in 20th-century American history with an emphasis on race, gender, sports, and politics. She is currently working on her book, *"Can't Eat a Medal": The Lives and Labors of Black Women Athletes in the Age of Jim Crow*. Her work as been featured in various academic journals including *Radical History Review* and in public venues such as NPR and *The Nation*. Davis is also the co-host of the feminist sports podcast, Burn It All Down.

Matt Eidson is a Marine Corps veteran with tours to Iraq, Afghanistan, Japan, and South Korea; a student at the University of North Dakota who will begin his graduate work at UND in spring 2019; an online student at Johns Hopkins University seeking a Master of Arts in Government; and a candidate for the state House of Representatives in District 43 in Grand Forks, North Dakota.

Ashley D. Farmer is a historian of black women's history, intellectual history, and radical politics, and an Assistant Professor of History and African and African Diaspora Studies at the University of Texas at Austin. She is the author of *Remaking Black Power: How Black Women Transformed an Era* (2017), a co-editor of the anthology *New Perspectives on the Black Intel-*

lectual Tradition (2018), and a co-editor and curator of the Black Power Series published with New York University Press. Farmer earned a B.A. from Spelman College and an M.A. and Ph.D. from Harvard University.

Jon Foreman began his music career in 1996 heading an unassuming San Diego-based band, now known all over the world as the multi-platinum, Grammy-winning alt-rock group Switchfoot. Always feeling that there was more music in him than hours in the day, Jon began releasing solo EPs in 2007. Beginning with the Seasons collection, Jon released four EPs over the course of a year; then he released The Wonderlands, a collection of twenty-four songs each representing an hour of the day. 25 IN 24, a documentary that follows Jon playing twenty-five shows in twenty-four hours, is available to stream worldwide.

Mark Stephen Jendrysik is a Professor in the Department of Political Science and Public Administration at the University of North Dakota, where he has been a faculty member since 1999. He received his M.A. and Ph.D. from the University of North Carolina at Chapel Hill. His B.A. is from Providence College. Jendrysik has published and presented papers on early modern political thought, utopian political theory, and contemporary American political thought and culture. He is the author of *Explaining the English Revolution: Hobbes and His Contemporaries* (2002) and *Modern Jeremiahs: Contemporary Visions of American Decline* (2008). His book *Utopia* will be published as part of the Key Concepts in Political Theory series by Polity in 2020.

Clay S. Jenkinson is a North Dakotan. He holds degrees in literature from the University of Minnesota and Oxford University, where he was a Rhodes Scholar. He leads cultural tours throughout the United States and Europe, lectures widely, and writes extensively about the northern Great Plains. He is the creator of the weekly public radio program and podcast, the Thomas Jefferson Hour. He is the author of ten books and is now writing a novel about White-Indian relations in North Dakota. He is the editor of the Lewis and Clark quarterly journal, *We Proceeded On*.

Shontavia Johnson serves as Associate Vice President of Academic Partnerships and Innovation at Clemson University, where she holds a tenured post in the Department of Sociology, Anthropology, and Criminal Justice. She also serves as a consultant to companies, inventors, and creators. Her academic interests include law, innovation, entrepreneurship, and culture. Shontavia's work is widely published, and she received the 2014 Ladas Memorial Award for authoring the best trademark article in the world that year. The American Bar Association named her one of the Top 40 Young Lawyers in America, and she was recently placed on the prestigious Fulbright Specialist roster.

Joseph Kalka is a Master of Arts student in the Department of History at the University of North Dakota. His research primarily focuses on 19th-century America and includes discussions of race relations, abolition, emancipation, and colonization. He is increasingly interested in the role sports plays in shaping social history.

D. M. Kingsford is a Denver-based poet and author whose works have been featured around the globe. For more of his poetry find him on Instagram @roamingpoet.

Chris Kluwe played in the NFL for eight seasons. As a punter for the Minnesota Vikings, he set eight team records. Kluwe has also created a tabletop card game and co-authored two science-fiction books, *Prime: A Genesis Series Event* (2015) and *The Falconers: Fort Eden* (2017). In addition, he is the author of *Beautifully Unique Sparkleponies: On Myths, Morons, Free Speech, Football, and Assorted Absurdities* (2013). During his playing days, Kluwe was an outspoken advocate for sex-same marriage, and he continues to champion human rights.

David Krugler graduated from Creighton University, where he studied creative writing. He earned a M.A. and Ph.D. in history from the University of Illinois at Urbana-Champaign and is now a Professor of History at the University of Wisconsin—Platteville. His nonfiction books include *This Is Only a Test: How Washington, D.C., Prepared for Nuclear War* (2006) and *1919, The Year of Racial Violence: How African Americans Fought Back* (2014). In addition, Krugler is the author of two novels, both spy thrillers: *The Dead Don't Bleed* (2016) and *Rip the Angels from Heaven* (2018).

David J. Leonard is a writer, teacher, and scholar. He is the author of several books, including *Playing While White: Privilege and Power on and off the Field* (2017) and *After Artest: The NBA and the Assault on Blackness* (2012). Follow him on Twitter @drdavidjleonard.

Ameer Hasan Loggins is a Ph.D. candidate in African Diaspora Studies at the University of California, Berkeley. His research explores Reality Television as a social phenomenonand its effects on the perception of African Americans outside of a televisual space. Follow him on Twitter @LeftSentThis.

Emma Long is a Senior Lecturer in American Studies at the University of East Anglia. She has published in the *Journal of Church and State* and the *European Journal of American Studies* and has written for *The Conversation* and *HNN*. She is the author of *The Church-State Debate: Religion, Education, and the Establishment Clause in Post War America* (2012).

Randy Nedegaard is an Associate Professor in the Department of Social Work Education at California State University, Fresno. He spent the previous ten years teaching at the University of North Dakota. He is a retired United States Air Force Lieutenant Colonel. He entered the USAF as a medical officer in 1990 and worked in various outpatient mental health settings and at the Fort Leavenworth prison. He also worked as a behavioral health consultant for a Command Surgeon General and has deployment experience in Afghanistan. Dr. Nedegaard currently teaches and conducts research relating to veterans' issues and trauma-related violence.

Richard Newman is Professor of History at the Rochester Institute of Technology and the author of several books on American abolitionism and American reform, including *Freedom's Prophet: Bishop Richard Allen, the AME Church, and the Black Founding Fathers* (2009) and *Abolitionism: A Very Short Introduction* (2018). His next book, *American Emancipations: The Making and Unmaking of Black Freedom*, will be published with Cambridge University Press.

Gelaine Orvik retired from teaching in 2001 after completing his thirty-sixth year as an educator and coach in North Dakota, thirty-three of which were spent at Fargo South High School. During that time, he taught English and coached track and field, cross-country, football, and basketball. He was inducted into the North Dakota High School Coaches Association Hall of Fame in 1993 and the National High School Athletic Coaches Association Hall of Fame in 1997.

Shawn Peters, an internationally recognized expert on religious liberty issues, has been featured by CNN, PBS, Court TV, *Time* magazine, and *The New York Times*. He is the author of five books, including *The Catonsville Nine: A Story of Faith and Resistance in the Vietnam Era* (2012). Peters holds an undergraduate degree from Rutgers University and graduate degrees from the University of New Hampshire, the University of Iowa, and the University of Wisconsin-Madison. He currently teaches in the Integrated Liberal Studies Program at UW-Madison.

Jamal Ratchford is an Assistant Professor of History and Race, Ethnicity, and Migration Studies at Colorado College. He earned a B.A. (2004) from Morehouse College in African-American Studies, and an M.A. (2006) and Ph.D. (2011) in history from Purdue University. He is revising a book manuscript titled, "Raise Your Black Fists: Race, Track and Field, and Protest in the 20th Century." Ratchford specializes in African-American history, sport history, 20th-century U.S. history, and Africana Studies. His teaching and research interests also include popular culture, race and racism, Ethnic Studies, gender and United States Black Freedom Movements.

Mark Rerick, the Director of Athletics for the Grand Forks (North Dakota) Public Schools, has been a high school athletic director since 2006. He is also a member of the National Interscholastic Athletic Administrator Association's publications committee. His blog can be found at www.youthsportsstuff.com.

Mac Schneider is an attorney, former state senator, and in 2018 was nominated by the Democratic-NPL party as a candidate for Congress in his home state of North Dakota. He is a 2002 graduate of the University of North Dakota, where he was a member of the school's 2001 national championship football team. He and David Butler roomed together during away football games and were roommates in Washington D.C. despite the fact that his co-author's political views are dramatically outside of the mainstream.

Brad Elliott Schlossman, a native of Fargo, North Dakota, has covered sports for the *Grand Forks Herald* since 2003. He has twice won first place in the Associated Press Sports Editors national beat writing competition (2016, 2018). He has a B.A. in communications with a minor in history from the University of North Dakota.

Tamir Sorek is Professor of Sociology at the University of Florida. His research focuses on the intersection of power and culture, particularly in fields of nationalism, political memory, and sport. He is the author of *Arab Soccer in a Jewish State* (2007) and *Palestinian Commemoration in Israel* (2015), and co-editor of *Sport, Politics and Society in the Middle East* (2019).

Elizabeth C. Tippett is an Associate Professor at the University of Oregon School of Law, as well as the Faculty Co-Director of its Conflict and Dispute Resolution Master's Program. She researches harassment, discrimination, and wage and hour law. Her research has been cited by a number of state and federal courts, including two opinions by the United States Court of Appeals. She is a co-author of the fifth edition of the West Academic textbook, *Cases and Materials for Employment Discrimination & Employment Law: The Field as Practiced* (2016).

Andrew N. Wegmann is Assistant Professor of History at Delta State University. He has authored and edited three books and a number of essays on race in the Atlantic World and the early American republic. His current scholarship focuses on the founding of the Republic of Liberia and its North American roots. He supports Fulham FC as well as the French and United States national teams. A native of New Orleans, he lives in Cleveland, Mississippi.

Jack Russell Weinstein is Chester Fritz Distinguished Professor of Philosophy and Director of the Institute for Philosophy at Public Life at the University of North Dakota. He is the host of public radio's *Why? Philosophical Discussion About Everyday Life* (www.whyradioshow.org). He is the author of three books, most recently *Adam Smith's Pluralism: Rationality, Education, and the Moral Sentiments* (2013), published by Yale University Press. He maintains a philosophy blog aimed at general audiences (www.pqed.org) and can be found on Twitter @jackrweinstein.

Robert G. White is an Assistant Professor of Sociology at the University of Florida. He received his Ph.D. in sociology from the University of Wisconsin, Madison in 2009. His current research concerns the relationship between health, schooling, and adult socioeconomic attainment and the consequences for social inequalities. He uses data from the United States and England in a series of studies assessing the lasting effects of child health for educational achievement and adult earnings. His work links approaches for studying individual attainment to population level phenomena to characterize changes over time in social inequalities.

Azmar K. Williams is currently a Ph.D. candidate at Harvard University in Cambridge, Massachusetts studying post-emancipation U.S. intellectual and African American history. He received his Master of Arts in history from Harvard and is at work on a dissertation that examines the interrelated histories of race, empire, and the rise of the modern university in the Anglo-Atlantic world. Williams graduated from Yale University in New Haven, Connecticut *cum laude* with a Bachelor of Arts in history and African American studies.

J. Corey Williams, M.D., received a B.S. in Kinesiological Sciences from the University of Maryland, College Park with a focus on physical culture. He completed a Master of Arts in Teaching at American University while teaching middle school science in Washington D.C. public schools. He went to medical school at Johns Hopkins University and completed his residency training in Psychiatry and Behavioral Sciences at Yale-New Haven Hospital. He is currently a physician in Child and Adolescent Psychiatry at The Children's Hospital of Philadelphia. His research and scholarly writing are focused on the intersections of race and medicine and critical race theory in popular culture.

Made in the USA
Middletown, DE
16 October 2018